Phil Lyn

The Rocker

Phil Lynott
The Rocker

By Mark Putterford

OMNIBUS PRESS
LONDON · NEW YORK · PARIS · SYDNEY

Exclusive Distributors:
Music Sales Limited,
8/9 Frith Street,
London W1D 3JB, UK.

Music Sales Corporation,
257 Park Avenue South,
New York, NY 10010, USA.

Macmillan Distribution Services,
53 Park West Drive,
Derrimut, Vic 3030,
Australia.

To the Music Trade only:
Music Sales Limited,
8/9 Frith Street,
London W1D 3JB, UK.

Every effort has been made to trace the copyright holders of the
photographs in this book but one or two were unreachable. We would
be grateful if the photographers concerned would contact us.

Typesetting by Galleon Typesetting, Ipswich.
Printed and bound in Great Britain by Cox & Wyman Ltd, Reading,
Berkshire.

A catalogue record for this book is available from the British Library.

Visit Omnibus Press on the web at www.omnibuspress.com

Contents

Introduction

Philip Lynott was one of the most colourful and charismatic characters in the history of rock'n'roll. As leader of Thin Lizzy he was responsible for some of the best rock music of the Seventies and Eighties, including a string of smash hit singles such as 'Whiskey In The Jar', 'The Boys Are Back In Town', 'Dancing In The Moonlight', 'Rosalie', 'Waiting For An Alibi' and 'Sarah'. But as the consummate Rocker he couldn't resist burning the candle at both ends, and he died a slow and painful death in 1986.

This is the only major biography of Lynott ever published[1] and it has been researched through a wealth of interviews with his family, close friends, band members and associates, roadies, management, former record company employees and most other people who knew or worked with him.

It tells the amazing story of an illegitimate half-caste kid born into a strict Catholic family from Dublin in the late Forties. It shows how with a mixture of talent and determination Lynott overcame prejudice to make Thin Lizzy the first internationally successful Irish rock band, and become the biggest black rock star since Jimi Hendrix.

Furthermore, it illustrates how Lynott shrewdly managed to avoid rock's backlash by aligning himself with new trends – punk, the New Romantics and synth pop. He was always keen to discover and nurture new talent, and he had a hand in the early careers of Bob Geldof, Midge Ure (with whom he wrote a *Top Of The Pops* theme tune), Huey Lewis, Mark Knopfler and

---

[1] Since this book was first published *Hot Press* in Dublin have published *My Boy: The Philip Lynott Story* by Philomena Lynott, Philip's mother.

more, not to mention the dazzling array of guitarists who passed through Thin Lizzy.

The book also takes a close look at Lynott's outrageous lifestyle; his romantic gypsy spirit, his legendary eye for the ladies and his astonishing capacity for drink and drugs. Many friends speak for the first time about his seemingly unstoppable demise after Lizzy split in 1983.

It also reveals a softer side of this celebrated hellraiser; the family man who doted on his two young daughters, wrote sensitive poetry and cared deeply about his supporters (he always refused to call them fans).

The Rocker is a remarkable story which will surprise and shock most people. It is an honest and moving tribute to one of rock's greatest stars, a warts'n'all requiem for a tragic genius.

Preface

Dublin, August 1993

Peacefully ensconced within the rich emerald countryside of Howth, just north of Dublin's fair city, Glen Corr dozes in the mid-summer sun like any other quaint family home. The pungent aroma of ma's cooking wafts across the lawn on the breeze that squeezes past Ireland's Eye out in the bay, a tiny white terrier yaps playfully at passers-by in the leafy lane out front, and the sound of garden shears snipping unruly hedges into shape completes the picture of sleepy suburbia.

Only this is no ordinary rustic retreat. To step across the threshold of this sprawling Victorian chalet is to plunge into the private world of one of rock's most celebrated sons, to actually touch the existence of a man whose unbearably tragic death nearly eight years ago threatened to consign him to the mercy of mere statisticians.

Glen Corr is the house where Philip Lynott lives.

In the hall shine the trophies of his endeavour, presentation discs for albums such as *Jailbreak*, *Johnny The Fox*, *Live And Dangerous*, *Black Rose* and *Chinatown*. A Manchester United mirror takes pride of place just outside the dining room. In between, framed photographs preserve special moments from an irresistibly energetic life: on stage before a packed stadium in America, on the beach with his dog Gnasher, in the arms of his mother as a babe, and between the shy smiles of his two daughters as a proud father.

In the study paintings adorn the walls, some professionally commissioned, others sent by fans. A favourite old jukebox stands in the corner, opposite a teak dresser which creaks under the strain of books and gifts and a cornucopia of

9

personal knick-knacks. Everywhere you look, Thin Lizzy hits you in the face.

Upstairs in the bedrooms there are poignant mementoes of a colourful youth. Downstairs are boxes upon boxes of letters sent by admirers and friends from all over the world, and baskets of flowers which arrive daily. Fans peer nervously over the garden wall to catch a glimpse of the house, bolder ones knock on the door to pay homage, and all are warmly welcomed by Philip's mother, Mrs. Philomena Lynott, and her companion of 35 years, Dennis Keeley.

Meanwhile across the old town Philip Lynott's presence remains as tangible as the images in his lyrics. Walking around its vibrant streets inspires resounding echoes of lines from many early songs, as the sights and sounds of O'Connell Street, the Liffey and St. Stephen's Green engulf you like a favourite memory. A lunchtime pint in The Bailey pub in Duke Street is the closest you'll get to tasting the atmosphere of days when Philip would drink and philosophise with friends about politics, music, literature and life, upholding a grand Irish tradition which since the Eighteenth Century has served to nourish the creativity of many other literary talents either born or educated in Dublin: James Joyce, Oscar Wilde, George Bernard Shaw, W.B. Yeats, Sir Thomas Moore, Brendan Behan, Oliver Goldsmith, Jonathan Swift and more.

Philip Lynott's literary achievements might not be as celebrated in the highest academic circles as many of these former Dubliners, but down on the streets where he once belonged his profile is significantly higher. A plaque on the wall at Merchant's Arch near the famous Ha'Penny Bridge commemorates his achievements on behalf of the Irish tourist board. A six-foot painting of Lynott graces the façade of the Barnstormers pub on the corner of Parnell Street. And on the other side of town waif-like street artists peddle their pencil caricatures and pastel likenesses of 'Philo' to the busy shoppers on Grafton Street.

The Baggott Inn in Baggott Street houses a large *Thunder And Lightning* era painting of Philip. The Backstage Bar in Essex Street has another large painting which features Philip as one of the Twelve Apostles in a Last Supper scene. A whole wall of the Fox & Pheasant pub in Great Strand Street is plastered with photos of Thin Lizzy in action, while further down Capel Street at Slattery's bar, ex-Lizzy drummer Brian Downey is urging his new band, The Swamp, through reverent recollections of Thin Lizzy classics from 'Dancing In The Moonlight' to 'Whiskey In The Jar', all lapped up by the regulars like free pints of Guinness.

Talk in the rock pubs is of little else other than Thin Lizzy, and the bands who continue to clone them some ten years after their demise. There's local boys The Elite, who pack them in all over Ireland playing the legendary *Live And Dangerous* set note for note. There's another band called Ain't Lizzy doing the rounds, another called Roisin Dubh having a go, one from England called Limehouse Lizzy, one from Sweden called Fat Lizzy, one from Norway called Bad Habitz, plus Phil Lizzy, Jailbreak and a host of others. If the radio stations and pub jukeboxes don't play Thin Lizzy enough, just about any stage in Dublin is fair game for those who still cling to every note of Lynott's precious legacy.

After all, Lynott was more than just Dublin's favourite son, he was the first real Irish rock star. A musician, a poet, a performer, a leader, a Lothario, a Casanova, a fighter, a charmer, a gambler, a gypsy, a rogue, a cowboy, a renegade, a hellraiser, a hero . . . he was unique in every way.

Dark-skinned, Dublin-voiced, his thick afro hair pulled down over one eye, a pencil thin moustache like all the best Hollywood Romeos and impossibly long leather-clad legs stretching from one side of the stage to the other, he had the style and charisma that the boys craved, and a cheeky grin that could seduce any girl from the far corner of a crowded dressing room. He was at once a man's man and a woman's man, and he knew it only too well. He was equally at home boozing and brawling with the boys as he was playing with children and animals or flirting with the girls armed with bunches of fresh flowers.

He was an immensely proud man, too. Proud of his mother, proud of his daughters, proud of his colour and proud of his country. It is, therefore, only right that Dublin remains fiercely proud of him.

There's talk of a statue being erected in the city at some point in the future, as well as the possibility of having a street named after him. Some folk are even spreading the idea of a Thin Lizzy museum in Dublin. There's a special Philip Lynott Trust being set up to help a new generation of Irish musicians aspire to the heights that he once knew. And every January 4, the anniversary of his death, there's the bitter-sweet celebration of a tribute concert, the pilgrimage being made by fans and musicians from far and wide.

Lynott himself rests in the soothing tranquillity of St. Fintan's cemetery in Sutton, a mile or so from Glen Corr. His mother decorates his gravestone daily with the flowers that arrive at the house, and a constant stream of fans leave rings, watches, bracelets, pendants and all manner of personal belongings by the plot, as if making offerings to their God.

It is not the way it should have ended. But then there's more to life than simply being alive. In the summer of '93, in a quiet corner of old Dublin town, the memories of one particular life are stronger than ever.

Perhaps the Philip Lynott story has only just begun.

Chapter I

A Little Black Boy

After preserving a precarious neutrality during the Second World War, the 26-county state that was Southern Ireland awoke in 1945 to find itself gripped by the after-effects of the great conflict. The industrial depression of the Thirties had been alleviated to some extent during the war, as people of all faiths joined the armed forces or played their part in the production of arms and other vital machinery, but peace brought widespread unemployment. And while the country's overseas trade began a slow revival after the war, the trade deficit was still around £125 million by 1950, a predicament which invoked special legislation to restrict imports and boost home industry.

For the young in Ireland during the Forties and Fifties the easiest way to find employment was to move abroad, most commonly to mainland Britain. Indeed, during the Fifties over 90,000 people emigrated from the Republic (14 per cent of the population), and the trend would continue for several decades, marking Ireland as the only country in the world with a declining population over the last century.

One of the thousands of young Irish people who was unable to resist the lure of employment in Britain, advertised every day in the Irish papers, was Philomena Lynott. Born into a respectable Catholic family in Dublin on October 22, 1930, she was the fourth of nine children born to Frank and Sarah Lynott who were raised in the working-class district of Crumlin, on the south side of the city. However, by the time she was 17 necessity took her across the Irish Sea where, like many of her compatriots, the choice of destination was between the two closest cities, Liverpool and Manchester. She chose the latter and set about earning her first wages.

Back in Ireland, Philomena's parents had barely reconciled themselves with her emigration when their daughter returned to Dublin with the news that she was pregnant. At first the shock was considerable, as it would've been for any God-fearing Catholic family faced with the shame of an unmarried, 18-year-old mother. But instead of conscripting their daughter to the notorious Magdelane laundries, where nuns confined unmarried teenage mothers for years on end, the family rallied round to support the wayward Philomena.

Another, even greater, shock was in store for the Lynotts. The man Philomena had fallen for was a black South American who lived in England, and the chances were that such a genetic combination, extremely rare for its time and strictly taboo for whites of lofty religious morality, would be difficult to disguise.

Sure enough, when the baby boy was born on August 20, 1949, he arrived with a coffee-coloured complexion which would set scores of loose tongues wagging all over Dublin. His Christian name was to be Philip. "When my mother was having me my father got ill," recalls Philomena, "so my mother prayed to St. Philomena and pledged that if he recovered and the baby was a girl, she'd call her Philomena, and if he was a boy she'd call him Philip. I remembered that when I was having Philip." His middle name would be Parris, his father's surname. Other than that Philomena guarded the identity of the father jealously, and that of course simply added fuel to the fire for the idle gossipmongers around town.

Indeed, to this day little is known of the tall dark stranger who courted the teenage Irish virgin on her arrival in England. Philomena remembers him as "a fine, fine man, who did the decent thing and proposed marriage to me when I told him I was pregnant", but insists that as her erstwhile suitor has long since married his anonymity should be protected for the sake of his new family.

Philomena, or Phyllis as she became popularly known, stayed in contact with Philip's father for about four years after their baby was born, but when it became clear that marriage was not an agreeable option, the two drifted apart. For a while she considered staying in Dublin and seeking work there, but unmarried mothers had to pay for childminders and they were expensive. Not only that, but when potential employees discovered the child they would be looking after was black, their rates miraculously doubled.

Inevitably, Phyllis experienced varying degrees of racial taunts during her first years with Philip in Dublin, some due to naïveté, some to blatant prejudice. Young mothers would peer into his pram on the street and remark, "Ah what a lovely baby . . . let's hope they send him back to Africa soon." Others would fix Phyllis with disgusted glares and brand her a "nigger-lover", or even worse.

It is almost impossible today to imagine the hardships that Phyllis endured during the early years of her son's life. Today's permissive, multicultural society is a very different world from the repressed, deeply religious Southern Ireland in the early Fifties. Ultimately, it was decided that Phyllis should return to England to work and that Philip's grandparents would raise the boy in the Leighlin Road family home in Crumlin, funded by the wages which their daughter would send over each month. Phyllis herself would visit home about four times a year, armed with presents and intent on making as big a fuss of her son as possible in the time she had available, but for most of the year the family Philip knew was his grandfather Frank, his grandmother Sarah, Phyllis's younger sister 'aunt' Irene and Phyllis's two younger brothers, 'uncles' Timothy and Peter, who in reality became surrogate siblings.

Timothy was ten years old when Philip came on the scene, Irene seven and Peter just 16 months. Many local people assumed Philip had been adopted; few guessed that he was in fact the nephew of the Lynott kids. The confusion lasted for years.

"When he was a baby," Phyllis recalls, "I'd be pushing him around in a pram and I'd get the strangest looks because he was black. Then when he got older and we'd go out together people would give us funny looks because they thought I was his floosie. It would be like, 'Who's that old dear with that young lad? It's disgusting!' You couldn't win."

"We didn't care too much about what the neighbours thought," says Timothy. "Philip was like a kid brother to us and that was that. He was family and we looked after him as best we could. Obviously being the colour he was he stood out like a sore thumb, but the colour thing wasn't such a big issue in those days, not like it is now. He was a very popular kid in our area."

"When he was old enough to go to school, I had to take him in and keep my eye on him," adds Peter, "but there really wasn't too much to worry about. I'd say for the first month or so he got called a few names, but after that he became accepted by most people, and admired as well.

"He was a really talented kid, too. I remember once at home he did this cartoon strip about Superman, making up a storyline and doing all the drawings in pen and ink to go with it. I suppose it was an example of the kind of creativity that was within him, even at an early age. Although having said that I never thought for one minute he'd end up as famous as he did. He had the determination alright, but I never dreamt he'd go so far."

Much of Philip's early inspiration came from Timothy's record collection. He'd tag along every Saturday afternoon when his uncle went shopping for new records in Dublin and nag him to buy the sounds he wanted to hear.

"I was the only one working at the time, so I was the only one with money," says Timothy, "and I used to spend it all on music. I'd buy one or two LPs a week, but when I'd get them home Philip and his friends would spend all day listening to them.

"One of my favourites was The Mamas & The Papas, and Philip loved them too. He was also very keen on the black American groups, the Tamla Motown stuff. And then he was into the heavier groups from England, like The Who and Cream. The only trouble was, when he eventually moved to London the cheeky bastard took all my records with him, and I never saw them again!"

Although Timothy was the prime source of music in the Lynott household at the time, he was never inclined towards performing himself. Peter, on the other hand, began learning to sing and play the guitar, and as a teenager started dabbling with a local group called The Sundowners.

"It was nothing serious," he insists today, "just a bit of fun. I couldn't really play the guitar that well, but I used to have a go at singing."

Around this time a neighbour called Joe Smith was putting together a band around his two sons, Danny and Frankie, and he had his eye on Peter Lynott as the singer for the group. Eventually Smith tried to poach him from The Sundowners, but the attempt proved unsuccessful. By way of compensation, Philip took the job instead.

"They offered me the gig in the hope that I would go back (to Peter) raving about the group," Philip told Smiley Bolger years later, "and they would then throw me out and get Peter in. It didn't work out like that though."

In fact the gangly half-caste kid soon made such an impression on those who were turning up to see them play at places like St. Anthony's Hall, the John of Gods and the local youth clubs, that Joe Smith soon gave up the idea of trying to coax Peter Lynott into the group, which was now going under the name of The Black Eagles. The younger Lynott may have been asthmatic, but his voice was strong and distinctive.

"The Black Eagles was a really good band," Peter admits. "They became really popular really quickly and got lots of gigs. They played the popular chart songs of the day, dressed in Lurex jackets and all the latest fashions. To a lot of the local kids, Philip was a star even then, and he used to like getting recognised on the street, or at dances."

"I was so proud of him," says Phyllis, "and I used to make such a fuss of him every time I came home. I used to miss him terribly, particularly when my father passed away [Frank Lynott died from a heart attack while asleep in his bed on May 20, 1964, when Philip was 14], because he took it so badly. I flew home and found him standing in the corner with tears in his eyes. He was devastated."

Also in 1964 Philip had to contend with the news that his mother had met a new boyfriend. Dennis Keeley was from Manchester, and the two set up home in a flat in Didsbury. At first Phyllis didn't know how her son would take to the idea of his mother living with a man, so the first time Philip visited the flat in Didsbury she made Dennis sleep in the spare room, to avoid any embarrassment.

"In the morning," Dennis laughs, "Philip looked at me with a grin as if to say, 'Oh, she made you sleep in the spare room because of me, did she?' It was very funny, he wasn't fooled at all."

"Philip used to come and visit us in Manchester quite a lot after that," Phyllis continues, "and I could see him getting more and more into his singing. One time when he was about 16 I took him, Peter and three of their friends from Dublin to the Cabaret Club in Manchester, and secretly told the compere to announce Philip as being the guest singer that night. I didn't tell Philip what I'd done, so when this guy introduced him out of the blue poor Philip nearly fainted. He was very embarrassed, but he eventually got up and sang 'I Left My Heart In San Francisco'! He actually sang it beautifully, but he never appreciated me reminding him of it years later when he was a macho rocker."

In 1966 Phyllis and Dennis took over the management of a hotel in the Whalley Range area of Manchester, initially on a six month trial basis. The hotel, Clifton Grange, a detached and slightly ramshackle Victorian residence on the corner of Wellington Road, was a showbusiness refuge which had fallen on hard times. Neither Phyllis nor Dennis had any previous experience of running a hostelry of any type, but by the end of the six months she'd begun to enjoy it enough to make a purchase offer to the original owner. They bought the place outright and stayed there for 14 years.

"We ran the hotel to suit showbusiness people," Phyllis states proudly, "not normal people. Breakfast wasn't at 8.00am, it was at noon. If you missed noon, then you just got in the kitchen and cooked it yourself. You pleased yourself at that hotel, because I knew that the happier my patrons were the more likely it was that they'd come back.

"Actually," she announces with a flourish, "it wasn't really a hotel, it was showbiz digs. That was the way we liked it."

The Clifton Grange soon became infamous in the North West, and even those who hadn't experienced its legendary hospitality referred to it by its nickname, The Showbiz (or simply The Biz). Any lost soul wandering through its charming portals was likely to be confronted by a troupe of Maori dancers in grass skirts, a magician pulling white balls out of his mouth, a transvestite comedian or the odd female contortionist. Slip into the bar for a livener and you'd be rubbing shoulders with conjurers, singers, jugglers, pop stars, ventriloquists and a vast assortment of struggling entertainers. Life at The Biz was, as Liza Minelli might have commented, a cabaret.

Whenever school holidays would allow, Philip used to revel in this slightly unreal atmosphere. He'd travel to Manchester with other members of his family – usually accompanied by his grandmother – and spend the summer happily mingling with his mother's colourful clientele. He couldn't fail to be influenced by the bohemian attitudes of this eccentric and exotic collection of artistes.

Philip's closest friends amongst the Biz regulars were the members of a Canadian cabaret trio called The Other Brothers, who'd moved to England in 1964. He became particularly close to one of its members, Percy Gibbons, and Phyllis attributes much of her son's development to the genial adopted Mancunian. Modesty prevents Gibbons from accepting such an accolade comfortably, but his assessment of the Clifton Grange years in general is unhindered by understatement.

"For me they were 12 years of madness, the like of which the world will never see again," he laughs easily. "The Biz was a special place in the insane world of entertainment. No matter who you thought you were, when you got there you became who you should've been all along.

"Anybody who was anybody stayed there, and anybody who was anybody became human again while they stayed there. That was the influence of 'Aunty' Phyllis. It was a totally unique place and a totally unique time; it would be almost impossible to recreate the scene with mere words.

"Philip came over for the summer holidays and we'd go up to my room in the attic and mess around. I had this room in the attic for 12 years, and Phyllis would lock the door when we went on the road and only allow special people like Philip to use it. It was a special place.

"Philip was ten years younger than us, so he was a kid brother to us all. We'd sit in the attic and strum around on acoustic guitars, or I'd play the congas and we'd sing and jam and do a lot of rhyming together. Philip would love to get words to rhyme, it was a lot of fun. A lot of the ideas that ended up on Lizzy albums – especially the first two – came from those days. In fact, on later albums like *Johnny The Fox* I'd hear stuff that came from conversations we had way back when, and I felt privileged to know I could trace those songs back to their roots, and that I knew what he was thinking about when he wrote some of those words.

"I used to criticise him a lot, too," Gibbons eagerly admits. "In the early days I used to tell him that he was trying to write 15 songs in one . . . and he was! We'd argue a lot about music . . . and politics, and life, and him being black. We told him that he should forget about the black thing, because we'd toured around the world for 20 years and it hadn't affected us as we hadn't let it. I think he understood that.

"I honestly don't know if he learnt anything from us, but if he did he took his influences from us without us knowing. In fact, I think we took as much from him. We got the 'go for it' attitude from Philip, because he was so determined to make it, even though he was so shy and sensitive.

"He just picked up an acoustic guitar and went for it. He used to play the guitar backwards, but it didn't matter. He used to get all his words wrong, but it didn't matter. He used to say things like 'gigolo' (pronounced as gig-olo) instead of 'gigolo' (pronounced as with a soft 'j'), but it didn't matter. He was having a go at it all, and you could see the genius in him coming through."

Percy went to Ireland with Phyllis to see Philip play with The Black Eagles, and he was much impressed. But it was when he returned to see the earliest incarnation of Thin Lizzy that the reality of his talent hit him. In response to what he'd seen, The Other Brothers "went electric from that day on".

"We were just amazed," Gibbons exclaims. "It was like anybody discovering their kid brother was a star."

"That was actually the first time that I thought Philip was destined to be something in showbusiness," adds Phyllis. "Percy was over in Dublin for my brother Timothy's wedding, and we went to see Philip in this tiny nightclub. At one point

Percy turned to me and said, 'Your kid is brilliant!' and I replied, 'Well, I was just thinking that myself, but I didn't want to say anything!' "

"Philip and Phyllis had a unique relationship," Gibbons emphasises, "maybe because they didn't see each other that often, and so when they did they made up for the time they'd lost. If someone had done a psychoanalysis job on Philip they might have got to the bottom of their relationship. But then everything was there in his lyrics, and I know that Phyllis found the answers to a lot of questions when she could finally bring herself to listen to his music again, five years after he died."

"With me running the hotel in Manchester and him at school in Dublin I couldn't be a normal mother to him," Phyllis admits, "so I was more like a big sister. I was his mother, his sister, his best friend . . . we'd tell each other everything. We only ever had one row – that was over a suitcase which I'd bought him and which he lent to a roadie – but apart from that we were extremely close in a . . . different sort of way."

The young Philip also developed a special relationship with Dennis, who never imposed himself as a 'stepfather' figure, preferring to subscribe to Percy's theory that they "were all equals".

"We were the greatest of buddies," Dennis declares, "solid gold pals. The only time he ever got on my nerves was when I'd take him shopping and he'd spend three hours in every shop, chatting up the girls who were serving."

Back in Dublin Philip had acquired quite a taste for girls and clubs, and would go to as many dances as he could afford. He'd dress in his sharpest clothes, lay on his thickest charm for the "chicks", and try out all his new dance steps while the DJs pumped American soul into the night.

"Philip was a bugger for staying out late at the clubs," says Peter. "I used to lay awake with my mother all night long, waiting for him to come home. He was a real swine at times, he really used to get up my nose. We used to go to dances together quite a lot and we'd be told to get home by 11 o'clock. I used to say to him, 'Come on, we'll be killed if we're late,' but he'd say, 'Oh, just one more dance,' and he'd stay until the bitter end!"

"One night," Timothy recalls, "I'd told them to be home by

11 o'clock but they never showed up. In the end I locked the door and went to bed, and when they eventually did show up and started banging on the door, I refused to let them in. I made them stand out in the cold for ages before I unlocked the door. Then I grabbed hold of Philip and gave him a real mouthful. I told him never, ever, ever to be late again, or else I'd throw him out the house. But of course it didn't do any good."

Or perhaps the only good it did do was provide the inspiration for a certain lyric in the hit single 'Dancing In The Moonlight': 'It's three o'clock in the morning and I'm on the streets again/I disobeyed another warning, I should've been in by ten/Now I won't get out 'til Sunday, I'll have to say I stayed with friends . . .'

"Actually," Timothy concedes, "his friends weren't a bad bunch, he never got in with the really rough kids. Apart from the staying out late Philip was a really likeable chap and rarely got into trouble as far as I can remember. I think his music kept him on the rails, especially when he started playing with people like Brian Downey and they really began to go places."

Brian Downey, a fellow pupil at the Christian Brothers School in Crumlin, was a couple of years younger than Philip, but was fired up with the same passion for music. He remembers his first encounter with Lynott with a vividness untainted by the years.

"In those days, we had what they called a 'Low Babies' school, then you progressed to 'High Babies', and then you went on to the CBS. One was a nursery school, the other like a primary school, and then the CBS was like a secondary school, I guess. Anyway, I was about seven, maybe eight, when one day this black kid came to the school. He was the only black kid in the school so he really stood out, everyone knew his name immediately.

"The first thing I remember about him was that he was given this assignment: he had to go around collecting what was called 'Black Baby Money', for the missionaries in Africa. So every day he'd come around with this collection box, with pictures of black babies on the side. You'd see him coming out of the corner of your eye and you had to get your penny ready – it happened every day, and this went on for years. All I knew him as was the kid with the collection box. I thought he was doing a marvellous job, until years later when I found out that he'd sometimes stick a knife in the side of the box and nick a few pennies when he was skint!

"Anyway, I was always interested in music, mainly because my dad was the drummer in an Irish pipe band and he'd turned me on to Irish dance music. Then I heard The Shadows and completely freaked. My cousin who lived with us had all their records and I'd listen to instrumentals like 'Apache' time after time. On one of their records there was a drum solo by a guy called Tony Meehan, and I couldn't believe my ears when I heard it. I used to play it so much I ended up scratching it to hell.

"Then I started to hear stuff by The Kinks, The Stones and The Beatles, and around this time the London club scene started to hit Dublin in a big way. My dad started giving me more pocket money and I'd spend it all on records – stuff like The Yardbirds, which totally blew my mind.

"I knew I had to start playing in a band, so I persuaded my dad to buy me a drum kit from this old furniture store called Cavendish's, which also sold musical instruments on the side. It cost about ten bob. All it consisted of was a bass drum, snare drum, a hi-hat and one cymbal, but I thought it was fantastic, and I'd bash around on it all day.

"Anyway, as soon as the guys in the street heard I had a drum kit they suggested we all put a band together. There was a kid called Tom Cullen who played lead guitar, another called 'Bomber' Fagan on rhythm guitar and this lad called Robbie Welsh who sang. I don't even think we had a bass player! None of us could play properly, but it seemed like a good idea at the time – as did our eventual name, The Liffey Beats, after The Mersey Beats!

"We did a few gigs and then split up, something that always seemed to happen to the bands I played with. I ended up forming another group called The Mod Con Cave Dwellers with some of the guys from The Liffey Beats, but again we didn't do too well because the Mod thing wasn't that popular in Dublin, it was more of a Rockers town.

"However, one gig we managed to get was supporting The Black Eagles at St. Paul's Hall in Dublin, where they had a residency. We were keen to do well as we thought it might mean some regular work, but on the first night our guitar player broke a string and had to ask The Black Eagles' guitarist if he could borrow his guitar. Unfortunately, he ended up breaking a string on that too, and Joe Smith, the manager of The Black Eagles, went absolutely spare. We got kicked off the bill after that.

"So I saw Phil in school a couple of days later and said to him, 'Look, I'm really sorry about that guitar string, but it wasn't my fault. Will you give us another chance?' Phil just said, 'Speak to Joe.' So I approached Joe Smith, but he didn't want to know, he hated us, probably because we were too good – which we were.

"Shortly after this Phil came up to me in school again and told me that The Black Eagles' drummer was going into the army. He asked me if I'd like to join if and when the vacancy came up, and I told him yes, I would. The next thing I know there's an ad in the local paper asking for a drummer for The Black Eagles!

"So I answered the ad, phoned Phil and said, 'Hey, it's me! I thought you were going to give me the gig!' He made some excuse and invited me over to Joe Smith's house, where all the gear was set up in his bedroom, and as soon as I walked in he asked me if I could play 'You Really Got Me'. I told him I could and we blasted straight through it – me, Phil, this bass player called Danny Smith and a guitar player called Frankie Smith – Joe Smith's two sons. At one particular point in the song there's a drum pattern which I managed to play perfectly, and as I did it Phil immediately looked around and said, 'Jesus man, Nick Higgins (The Eagles' old drummer) could never get that bit right!' I knew I'd got the gig there and then, even though we were only halfway through the first number. We ended up going straight into a rehearsal, and spent the rest of the afternoon working through all these Stones and Beatles numbers."

Downey in fact learnt around thirty songs over the next two

days, in preparation for his début with The Black Eagles at St. Paul's Hall, where they were still engaged as the resident band. Those with the sharpest of memories recall it as a big success – 400 or so people in, and most agreeing that Downey was indeed 'better than Nick Higgins'.

Things started to look promising for The Black Eagles. As word got around town they started to acquire bookings in many of the Beat clubs which were springing up around the centre of Dublin – the Club A-Go-Go, the Flamingo Club, the Scene, the Five Club, Sound City and the Green Lounge, a slightly more upmarket version of the Five Club.

"These clubs didn't have a license to sell alcohol," says Downey, "so you'd get wasted before you went in. You'd then try to smuggle a half bottle of vodka in under your jacket, take a few 'downers' or whatever was around, and then stay there until six in the morning. It was great fun. We were only 16, or something."

Another breakthrough came when the Eagles managed to secure a Monday night residency at the Flamingo Club. Over a period of a couple of months they began to attract a healthy regular crowd, and as their reputation grew they began to break into the tennis club circuit, a quite prestigious network of venues at the time.

"We ended up doing about four gigs a week in Dublin," Downey recalls, "which was quite an achievement in such a small town."

One character with more reason to remember these early Black Eagles gigs than most is Ted Carroll, who booked the band to play at a venue called The Bastille Club, in a hotel in Dalky, County Dublin, and later went on to co-manage Thin Lizzy.

"We'd booked this band from Belfast called The Mad Lads, but although it was expected of bands to do a three hour set in those days, they said they could only do an hour. So we needed another band, but we didn't have much money to spend because we'd paid The Mad Lads quite a bit to travel down from the north.

"Then this van driver we knew said he could get us a band for a fiver, or something, and a week later The Black Eagles turned up for the gig. It was so funny: the back doors of their van opened and they all trotted out, already dressed in their stage clothes – these pale blue flared trousers with little bells down the side of the legs!

"Actually, they were quite good. They did all these Yardbirds and Small Faces numbers and I thought they showed potential."

Before long, however, cracks started to appear. For reasons lost to the passage of time, Danny Smith decided he'd had enough and abruptly left the band. Downey suggested a fleeting acquaintance from a year or two earlier called Alan Sinclair as his replacement, but right from the outset there seemed to be some kind animosity between Sinclair and manager Joe Smith, who clearly felt the new kid wasn't a patch on his son.

Nevertheless, the bookings were still flooding in and The Black Eagles found themselves opening for the highly popular Irish 'showbands' of the time, mostly in huge ballrooms up and down the country.

"There were about six hundred showbands in Ireland in those days," says Downey, "big eight or nine-piece groups, most of which just played Irish country music. So if you could get yourself into that scene there would always be plenty of work available. We loved playing the big places, it made us feel very important. I think the highlight of that whole time for us was when we opened for Joe Dolan and The Drifters at the Mayfair Ballroom. We thought we were the bee's knees."

Another personnel change was just around the corner though, with Frankie Smith being replaced by another local teen, Ronnie Deegan. The Eagles continued to attract engagements, but with both of his sons now out of the group, Joe Smith's interest and commitment seemed to wane, and many rehearsals or band meetings would end in arguments. Eventually, in time-honoured tradition, the band just fell apart.

For Philip's grandmother the demise of The Black Eagles was something she secretly welcomed. She didn't want him to be a pop singer. She wanted him to be a plumber. It was, after all, a proper job.

After leaving the Christian Brothers School Philip had been enrolled at Clogher Road Technical College in Dublin (as had Brian Downey), and religiously encouraged to learn a trade. He became interested in architecture and at one point even considered it as a career ("It seemed to me," he confessed later though, "that architects were trying to cram as many people as possible into square boxes. I was making more money from part-time gigs ..."), but by the time he'd left Clogher Road at the age of 18 his grandmother had got her wish. The Lynott's next door neighbour had got Philip a job as an apprentice fitter and turner at a local iron foundry called Tongue & Taggarts.

"My mother wrote to me in Manchester and told me about Philip's new job," says Phyllis, "and of course I was delighted. A few weeks later I came home to visit and decided to surprise him by turning up at the foundry at lunchtime. I don't think he was too pleased. He stood there all dirty, dressed in these dungarees that were too big for him, and said, 'Oh ma! I can't do this kind of thing, it's not me. Look at my hands, they're ruined!' I looked in his eyes and I knew that all he really wanted to do was play his music, so I told him I wouldn't mind if he wanted to pack the job in. He was worried that his grandma would be furious, but I told him I'd stick by him. I felt sorry for him, and I even promised to send him more pocket money to help him out.

"Of course my mother accused me of being too soft on him, but I didn't care. I knew that Philip was really going to go for it with his music, even at the age of 18, so I decided to go for it too. I took on another job to get more money for him and ended up sacrificing a lot of my own life. But I knew music was going to be Philip's life, and I wanted to support him all the way."

It was his mother's support that Philip relied upon when he finally summoned the courage to tell his grandmother that he wanted to leave home. It was 1967. Sarah had already been writing to her daughter in Manchester, expressing her concern that Philip was getting in with the wrong crowd – long-haired kids who dressed like gypsies in weird clothes and stayed out late. To most of the older generation Flower Power was an alien concept to be treated with extreme suspicion. But Phyllis, still only 37 herself, was far more attuned to the quirks of modern youth culture and wasn't unduly worried about what her son was getting up to. After all, it was she who sent Philip most of his 'weird' clothes, including a satin military-style tunic which had become all the rage in the wake of The Beatles' *Sergeant Pepper* album that summer.

"Mammy never liked Philip's dress sense," says Timothy. "Apart from the stuff he used to get sent over from England, he used to pick up a lot of second-hand clothes from the flea markets around Dublin, and of course he'd choose the wildest and cheapest stuff available. Then he'd let his hair go really wild, and my mother would cringe. He had this huge Afro hair-do, and it made his head look massive. In fact, I'll never forget one of the photographs from my wedding in 1970. Philip stood at the back of the group in his big platform-heeled shoes, and all you could see was all this frizzy hair sticking out from behind everyone. You couldn't see his face, just his Afro."

With his mother's blessing Philip ended up leaving the family home in Crumlin and renting a flat in Clontarf. He continued to sing on the Dublin club circuit, and for a while joined a local outfit called Kama Sutra, a period he later acknowledged as an important stage in his development as a frontman, teaching him as it did how to manipulate an audience.

But Kama Sutra was really just a stepping stone to higher ground. As 1968 dawned and the Beat club scene began churning out groups like Granny's Intentions, The Chosen Few, The Green Beats and The Creatures, one name dominated a readers' poll of rock musicians from clubs conducted by Ireland's *New Spotlight* magazine: Brendan Shiels. The word on the town was that Shiels, nicknamed 'Brush' because of "something to do with the new sweeper system that was becoming popular in football", wanted Philip to join his new band.

Bass player Shiels had learnt his trade during the mid-Sixties with bands like Rose Tynan & The Rangers, Brian Rock & The Boys and The Uptown Band, playing the kind of country and western tinged rock that was very much in vogue in Ireland at the time. His reputation and popularity, as emphasised by the *New Spotlight* poll, in which national hero Rory Gallagher could only come seventh, encouraged him to put his own outfit together, and it was with that objective in mind that he sought Lynott's address and turned up on his doorstep one day.

"I didn't particularly want someone who could sing really well," Shiels says today. "I just wanted someone who looked good. Philip was about the best-looking boy around, and I knew that with him fronting the band we'd gets lots of attention from the girls. He was more fashion-conscious than the rest of us, and he even used to get his clothes specially made by this girl he knew. He used to walk up and down Grafton Street looking at his own reflection in all the shop windows, and of course he'd do anything to get noticed by the girls.

"I knew that if I could get Philip in the band we'd have a big head-start. It was a pretty mercenary move on my part, but then that's the way I had to be. Philip saw the sense in that."

Shiels also wanted Brian Downey in his new band, and sent Philip on a mission to try to persuade the young drummer to join. But Downey was more into the blues than the American West Coast sound that Shiels wanted to aim for, and turned the gig down. His place behind the kit eventually went to Noel Bridgeman, and the line-up was completed by a guitar player called Bernard Cheevers.

After toying with the curious title of My Father's Moustache, the quartet christened themselves Skid Row. Their first rehearsal was in a room in Synnot Place, let out to them by a kindly old dear called Mrs. Quigley, whose son Pat was the bass player in another Dublin group, The Movement, and the very first song they attempted together was 'Hey Joe'.

"I remember thinking that it was just like watching Jimi Hendrix without a guitar," says Shiels.

Skid Row fixed themselves a management deal with Ted Carroll, who had also managed The Uptown Band and who by now was establishing the Rock On oldies record shops, and contrived in a most calculated way to create as big a stir as possible through a combination of exciting visuals and a wall of sound. Taking their lead from psychedelic bands such as Pink Floyd, who placed enormous importance on visual presentation, they got a friend to operate some liquid lights for them, and another to show a film projection behind the stage while they were playing. It was the latter innovation which eventually won them some notoriety, as a local newspaper took exception to the band showing a film of The Pope whilst blasting out their psychedelic variations.

The set would usually open with 'Eight Miles High' by The Byrds, and then run through covers of numbers by Hendrix, The Doors, The Animals and, inevitably, The Beatles – 'Hey Jude' and 'Strawberry Fields Forever' being two favourites. As Philip never had a guitar to concern himself with during the lengthy instrumental sections of some songs, he began experimenting with an echo box, squawking into it at full volume and then fiddling around with its dials and knobs to create an ear-splitting swirl of other-worldly sounds.

"Whether it worked or not is difficult to say," admits Shiels, "but at the time it was supposed to be artistic."

Philip also experimented with other theatrics, such as smearing black boot polish under his eyes to enhance his menacing glare, and 'fighting' with Brush on stage midway through a song, just for the shock effect. The latter gimmick was an idea inspired by the 1958 film *The Defiant Ones*, in which Tony Curtis played a white racist struggling to escape from prison whilst handcuffed to a black inmate, played by Sidney Poitier.

"We played this show at the UCD (University College of Dublin)," recalls Shiels, "and halfway through Philip would be singing and I'd come up behind him and tear his shirt off. Then I'd throw the bass down and we'd roll around on the floor pretending to fight. It was like the black man/white man thing in the film. And it really worked that night, because we had all the bouncers jumping up on stage trying to stop us, thinking it was a real fight. This kind of thing had never been seen before, and word got around town pretty quickly. Within a couple of weeks we were pulling huge crowds."

Skid Row swiftly overtook Granny's Intentions as Ireland's top group, and took another step in the right direction when they managed to finance a recording session at Eamonn Andrews' studios, which produced a Brush Shiels song called 'Photograph Man'.

"I took the tape of 'Photograph Man' to London," says Ted Carroll, "but I couldn't get arrested with it. I tried Apple, Liberty and a whole number of other people, but no one was interested. I got a bit dejected, and as I was also running an agency at the time (Galaxy Productions, which booked Skid Row, The Grass Band, The Few, The Method and The Strangers, and which later brought the likes of John Mayall and Chicken Shack to Ireland) I thought I'd blow Skid Row out."

Back in Dublin there were personnel changes in the Skid Row camp. Drummer Robbie Brennan took over from Noel Bridgeman during the early months of '68, and around the same time guitarist Bernard Cheevers revealed that as he'd won an award as Apprentice Of The Year at the massive Guinness plant in Dublin, he was going to stick with his apprenticeship full-time. Brush Shiels put the word out that he was looking for a new guitar player, and word came back that the hottest property around was a kid from Belfast called Gary Moore.

"I was standing in for a guy called Dave Lewis in this band The Method," explains Moore. "He'd had a car accident and couldn't go on this trip they had planned to Dublin, so they approached me while I was sitting in this park in Belfast one day, and virtually kidnapped me there and then.

"We ended up doing some shows at the Club-A-Go-Go in Abbey Street, Dublin, and I remember that after one of our sets this guy came into our dressing room and was introduced to me as Brush Shiels from Skid Row. I was told he was looking for a guitar player, so I immediately asked him what kind of music he played, hoping he'd say the blues, which I was really into. He said the kind of vibe he was going for was Byrds-type West Coast thing, so I had to tell him that; unfortunately, I wasn't really interested in that sort of stuff.

"However, Brush seemed a nice guy and he persuaded me to check the band out anyway. They were playing across the road at the Seventy Two Club, and in fact he'd come across to check me out while they were taking a break, so while The Method took their break I went to see Skid Row.

"I walked in and the first thing I saw was this big black guy standing on stage singing, making all these incredible sound effects with an echo unit. It was such a tiny stage that he'd be standing there singing, and actually reaching over and twiddling the knobs on this machine at the same time. He was making all these dive-bombing noises, and I'd never heard anything like it.

"I thought they were such a weird band because they sounded like they were coming from a different place altogether, like they were playing in the next room, or something. They had a totally different vibe about them, nothing like the Clapton and Peter Green stuff that I was into. But then when I thought about it, I reckoned it might not be a bad idea to give them a go after all. I was having problems at home with my dad at the time, and I thought that joining a band like Skid Row would be a good way to get out of the house and stay on the road, so I took the job. Plus, they offered me 15 quid a week and a flat of my own, which was nirvana! Needless to say, I never ever got the 15 quid a week . . .

"About a week later," Moore reflects, "I moved to Dublin and got to meet the other guys in the band. I arranged to meet Phil at a shop called Demense Products, which was on the Quays, and he told me he'd show me around town. So there we were, walking around Dublin, and people would be walking past going, 'Hi Skid!' to Phil. I asked him what they were going on about, and it turned out that a lot of people thought Phil's name was actually Skid. He didn't have the heart to tell people they were wrong!

"Anyway, after a quick tour of the town Phil suggested we went to a Chinese restaurant he knew at the top of Grafton Street. Now I hadn't had Chinese food before, but Phil convinced me that the sweet & sour pork was the thing to go for. So I ordered it, absolutely hated it, and sat back and watched Phil happily finishing it off with a big grin on his face. That taught me everything I needed to know about Phil in about five minutes!"

With the precocious talent of the young Gary Moore in the band, Skid Row leapt into a new dimension. Although still essentially a covers band, they decided to start introducing some original material into their repertoire, and by the spring of 1969 had been offered the chance to record a single, once again at Eamonn Andrews' studios. 'New Faces, Old Places', another Brush Shiels composition, was released on the independent Song label in May, and became the band's vinyl début. But the following month concern over the condition of Lynott's voice, a pet gripe of Noel Bridgeman's and an increasing worry for Shiels, led to Skid Row being streamlined to a three-piece.

"Philip sometimes had a problem singing in the right key," explains Shiels, "and I could never work out why. Then one day I decided to take a look down his throat and I saw this thing the size of a golf ball, a horrible growth. It was obviously causing him problems. The final straw came when we were doing 'Strawberry Fields' for a television show on RTE. He was singing so far off-key it was embarrassing. After that he decided he'd have to go over to Manchester to have his tonsils out, but while he was away we continued to play without him, and we thought we sounded easily as good as Cream. When he came back to Dublin I had to tell him that we didn't need him back in the band.

"The decision to let Philip go was a real hard one to make," Shiels confesses, "because he was my best pal. I got married to Margaret in 1969 and he was my best man. We even went to his mother's hotel in Manchester for our honeymoon. So we were close, but . . . y'know, you have to make decisions that you feel are best for the band, and at the time I honestly felt we were better off without him.

"He was very keen to get himself together though, and I told him I'd teach him to play the bass, and how to learn to breathe properly for his singing. He'd stick his head in a bucket of water so he could practise holding his breath, but it didn't really work. However, he did pick up the bass quite quickly, and would come round every day for lessons, regular as clockwork."

Brush Shiels lived in the Cabra West district of Dublin at the time, a long bus ride from Clontarf, but Philip would still manage to be on his doorstep at 10 o'clock every morning, after spending most of the night practising at home. Shiels convinced him that learning bass would be better than learning guitar because "with only four strings to worry about he could have a band together in three months, but with six strings to contend with it would take much longer". He didn't want to wait around.

Shiels also furnished Philip with his first bass guitar, a Fender Jazz, which he'd bought off a friend for £40 and agreed to let Philip have for £36. "Of course, Philo being Philo, I never got paid for it," he smiles wryly. "But in a way I was just glad to help him out, especially after I had to ask him to leave the band."

"When Phil told me he'd been kicked out of Skid Row I was delighted!" laughs Brian Downey. "I was out of a job at the time too, so I thought it was a perfect time for us to start thinking about putting a band together again. After The Black Eagles I really gave up the whole music scene for a while, until out of sheer financial necessity I ended up doing a two or three month stint in this country and western group called The Burma Boys Showband. It was pretty depressing stuff, but I was skint!

"I eventually got an offer to audition for a band called Sugar Shack, and I did really well. The two songs I had to play I knew quite well – 'Key To Love' from John Mayall's album, and 'Hide Away', which Clapton used to do – and fortunately I got the gig. This was around the time that Phil and Brush asked me to join Skid Row, but I wasn't really into the music they were doing, and besides, Sugar Shack had been offered the chance to go into the studio and record a single. We did a version of Tim Rose's 'Morning Dew', and it got to No.16 in the Irish charts. This amazed everybody, because we were an unknown band. We couldn't believe our luck, but suddenly we had tons of bookings all over the country.

"A conflict soon arose in the band, though. Half the guys wanted to move more into the mainstream pop thing, the other half wanted to get more into the blues. We started rowing. I remember at the reception for the 'Morning Dew' single, our guitarist Brian Twomey, who was completed pissed, went up to the microphone and said, 'Here's our new single, it's called "Morning Sickness". This guy Pat Fortune who we had singing for us just completely freaked, and nearly hit

Brian with a guitar – and this on stage, in front of the press and all the record company people! There was a huge fisticuffs situation backstage afterwards, and needless to say we didn't stick together too long after that.

"Some of us did continue playing though, and we got right into the blues in a heavy way. John Mayall, Peter Green, that sort of stuff. We got a couple of residencies – one at the Five Club and one at Ma's Bar, which went down quite well – and we got a couple of gigs in Belfast with Aynsley Dunbar's Retaliation. But in general the bookings began to disappear slowly, and promoters stopped ringing us. The situation deteriorated over about two years, and in the end Brian Twomey got married and the band split up.

"When that happened I didn't know what to do. I was thinking of emigrating to England to try my luck there. But then one day I bumped into Phil and he told me he wasn't doing anything either and . . . 'Hey, let's start a band!' "

Brian suggested they contacted Pat Quigley to see if he wanted to play bass, and when it transpired that he did, he in turn suggested bringing along a guitar player called Joe Staunton. Philip was happy to experiment with different musicians in the band, and in fact advocated a flexible line-up right from the conception of what became known as Orphanage.

"His idea," explains Downey, "was that there should be a nucleus of me, him and Joe, being augmented on stage by whoever was around at the time. Terry Woods came into the picture some nights, I think Gary Moore was around too, and sometimes I'd look around and see about seven or eight people on stage with us, jamming. I thought it was a good idea.

"At this time Phil wanted to get into playing his own tunes. He saw Brush Shiels throw a few original songs into Skid Row's set and get away with it, and he wanted to do the same. So Phil started slipping some new songs into the set – 'Chatting Today' was one of those early tunes, and 'Saga Of The Ageing Orphan' was another. Quite a few of the melodies that ended up on that first Lizzy album were being thrown around in the Orphanage. We also did a lot of Bob Dylan stuff, a lot of soul stuff, 'Knock On Wood', Sam & Dave, early Free, Jeff Beck . . .

and we were getting into the hippy thing, doing a bit of acid, hash and stuff like that. It didn't improve matters, but it was fun!"

One of the characters on the Dublin beat scene who got to know Lynott well around this time was Seamus 'Smiley' Bolger, a north-side kid with aspirations to just about every music biz-related role, from DJ to journalist, from roadie to promoter, and general Mr. Fixit. He'd tagged on to his elder brother during the mid-Sixties and had got to know all the local bands. But he claims he never knew anyone with the same determination to succeed as the kid from Crumlin.

"I first saw him play with The Black Eagles at the Club A-Go-Go on a Sunday afternoon," he recalls. "I went into the dressing room after the show and they were all arguing with each other. I remember Philip rationalising it by saying that The Who argued with each other all the time – so maybe it was a good thing!

"There didn't seem to be any stopping Philip. When he hooked up with Brian Downey again after leaving Skid Row, I remember talking to him in a club just off Grafton Street and him telling me that he was convinced he was going to make it. He knew he had the right drummer in Brian, and there was no doubt in his mind that he was going places, whether it was with Orphanage or not.

"The only two other people to come out of Ireland with that attitude were Geldof and Bono. We used to laugh at Geldof when he said he was going to make it, and I used to have many chats with Bono about whether U2 were going to do anything. It was only after the second U2 album that we started to take U2 seriously. But with Philip you had a gut feeling that he was definitely destined for greatness. Philip believed it, and we believed it."

Orphanage didn't turn out to be Philip's passport to immortality, however. The band continued to work around Ireland throughout 1969, but then a chance meeting with another highly reputed Irish (albeit Northern) musician sowed the seeds for what was to become Lynott's ultimate vehicle.

"Orphanage were together for about eight or ten months," says Brian Downey, "and then one night we were playing at the

Countdown Club when we were spotted by Eric Bell. He was working with John Farrell and The Dreams at the time, but wanted to get into doing something else. That was how Thin Lizzy started."

In fact, Eric Bell's voyage through the parched dance halls of the Sixties to the creative oasis of Thin Lizzy was almost as long as the road from his native Belfast to his adopted Dublin. Inspired by the Liverpool scene, and particularly impressed by how Belfast's own Them were striving to emulate the feats of those across the water, his emerging talent as a guitar player whisked him through a succession of pro and semi-pro bands, from The Bluebeats and The Earth Dwellers to The Atlantics and The Jaguars, while in between he made ends meet by picking up wages as a street gas-lamp-lighter (one of the last in Belfast), working in a pickle factory and, later, in a shirt factory.

By 1965 he'd joined The Deltones (it was while playing with this group at a club in Holywood, a few miles north east of Belfast, that Bell met 'Little' Gary Moore; Moore's father ran the club and his 14-year-old son's band, The Beat Boys, had a residency there), but two years later had moved on to enjoy a brief spell alongside Van Morrison in Them, before eventually putting together a band called Shades Of Blue. Work was regular for a while, but then interest slackened, leaving Bell with no choice when he was approached one night at the Maritime Hotel by singer John Farrell (then with The Movement) with an offer to audition for his new outfit, The Dreams.

Bell got the job and moved to Dublin, not entirely at home in a besuited seven-piece with all the inevitable Beatles overtones, but nonetheless glad to be earning relatively decent money. Not only that, but when The Dreams' manager, Jim Hand, managed to persuade The Tremeloes to write a song for his band, and the result, 'I Will See You There', was a big hit in Ireland, Bell found himself in one of the most talked-about bands in the country.

Nevertheless, by the end of 1969 he'd tired of the chart hits/country and western standards/instrumentals carousel that The Dreams continued to ride on, and wanted to expand his horizons. "I'd made a bit of money working with The Dreams," he explains, "and I'd stashed it all in a building society, so I felt I could afford to take some time out and look around for some musicians to form a new group with. Unfortunately I didn't know much about the group scene in Ireland because I'd always worked on the showband scene, and the two were completely separate. In fact, the group scene used to look down on the showband scene, because although the group scene had all the best musicians, the showbands got paid the best money, so there was a certain amount of animosity there.

"Anyway, for about two months I went round all the pubs and clubs in Dublin looking for the right people, but I had no luck. I guess I looked like the typical showband musician at the time, because I had short hair and wore a suit, so when I went into a pub and said, 'My name's Eric Bell, I used to be with the Dreams, and I'm looking for a bass player and a drummer', the guys with their long hair and wild hippy clothes would just go, 'Good luck!' and carry on drinking their Guinness.

"After two months my money started to run out. Then one night I was in The Bailey bar and I bumped into a keyboard player I knew from Belfast called Eric Wrixen. He'd played in the original Them with Van Morrison, way back in 1963, but more recently he'd been playing with Terry and The Trixons, another showband. So we got chatting and it turned out Eric was sick of the showband scene as well, and wanted to join a group. Although I have to say that the group I visualised was a three-piece like Hendrix and Cream – I didn't really want a keyboard player.

"Anyway, after a beer or two we decided to go to the Countdown Club, because we knew the guy there and we could get in for nothing. Also, they used to sell this cheap sherry in paper cups, and as we didn't have much money that's what we had to drink.

"Then Eric said to me, 'Have you ever tried LSD?' I told him I hadn't, but being one to give anything a go I told him I'd love to try some, so he broke this tiny tablet in half and we shared it. About an hour later I still couldn't feel the effects of it, but Eric kept saying, 'Give it time, give it time.' By this time we were sitting on the floor watching Orphanage play, when all of a sudden the acid hit me. I didn't know what was going on. It was like waking up on Jupiter, or something.

"So I'm sitting there watching the band, and I was blown away by Brian Downey. I thought he played with great feel, really mature for his age. I remember thinking, 'I've got to have him in my band!' I wasn't even watching Philip – he was dancing around doing all these weird moves, but I was only interested in Brian.

"After half an hour they took a break, and I followed Philip and Brian into their changing room. By now the acid had worn off a bit and I thought I was straight. Anyway, I introduced myself and as usual as soon as I mentioned The Dreams I got the inevitable funny looks. I told them I was looking for a drummer and bass player, but they said they didn't know of anyone suitable.

"Then the acid hit me again and I was tripping like a zombie. Brian got a bit worried and said, 'Are you alright, mate?' So I had to own up. I told them I was having my first trip . . . and their attitude towards me changed instantly! I wasn't Mr. Straight any more, I was cool! That was how it was in those days."

"So we had a chat about the possibility of doing something together," Downey takes up the story, "but I wasn't sure about all this, I thought we were doing okay as Orphanage. Yet Phil was aware of Eric's reputation as a great guitar player – I think Gary Moore had told Phil all about him – and he showed a bit more interest in the idea. He persuaded me to give it a go with Eric, and then announced that same day that he was going to be the bass player in the band! I thought he was crazy, but he was dead serious and told me he'd been having lessons from Brush. I thought the idea was hilarious at the time."

"Philip was totally serious about the whole bass thing," Bell laughs, "and he was also serious about writing his own songs. He told me he'd only join the group if he could play bass and do some of his songs. So I thought, 'Well, let's give it a go.'

"So Philip arranged to come to my flat with a reel of tape on which he'd recorded some demos. I didn't have a reel-to-reel tape machine at the time, so I had to borrow one from this chick. But we got it all fixed up and Philip arrived in this huge overcoat, armed with his tape. It was the first time I'd been alone with him, and I found him a really sincere person, very warm, very softly spoken, a really nice guy.

"His songs were good too – just him with an acoustic guitar – but I heard their potential and I knew I could put my style of guitar playing on them. There were songs like 'Chatting Today' and 'Saga Of The Ageing Orphan' on that tape, and I thought they were really good. Obviously with them having been done on an acoustic guitar there was a strong Irish folk influence coming through, but I thought that a good thing, a bit different.

"All the time Philip was saying to me, 'I'm really getting good on the bass, Brush is teaching me, I'm doing three hours practising a day, it's going great . . .' and I was really impressed with his determination. In the end I couldn't refuse him."

"So we all met up in Dublin – at Pat Quigley's house, strangely enough – and we played together with Eric for the very first time," Downey continues. "We did some Hendrix songs, and a 20-minute blues jam that seemed to go on forever. Phil was amazing on the bass, I couldn't believe how quickly he'd picked it up. All in all it was a very successful session.

"Breaking the news to Joe and Pat was pretty hard. It was left down to me to tell Joe, while Phil told Pat. I felt pretty shitty having to do it, but Phil was keen to work with Eric and I wanted to stick with Phil. I guess it had to be done."

"Our next rehearsals," Bell winces, "were at this tennis pavilion about ten minutes outside Dublin. It was absolutely freezing in there. Philip had to play wearing gloves, and I had this scarf wrapped around my head, right across my eyes and everything. Eric Wrixen came along as well because I just didn't have the nerve to tell him I didn't want a keyboard player. He'd given me the LSD tablet that night after all, and I felt I owed him, I suppose. So we were stuck.

"Nevertheless, word got around Dublin that this new band was getting its act together, and before we'd even played a proper gig there was something of a buzz about us."

'The new Eric Bell/Phil Lynott group will go a bomb or die

a very simple death', predicted journalist Pat Egan in his Beat column for *New Spotlight* magazine, on January 30, 1970. Egan continued to keep an eye on the fledgling outfit for the benefit of his regular readers, but was forced to ask in his column of February 6, 'What's holding up the launch of the Bell-Lynott supergroup?'

The answer was they didn't have a name. Like hundreds of bands before and thousands since, they racked their brains to come up with something which was eye-catching, yet not corny, punchy, or posey. They threw around song titles, book titles, lines from poems, anything that came to mind. The best they could come up with at first was Gulliver's Travels, but that sounded too soft, too wishy-washy.

Eventually, they were rehearsing at the Countdown Club one day when Eric Bell began flicking through old copies of the Beano and Dandy comics. He came across a robot character in the Dandy called Tin Lizzie, billed as 'the Mechanical Maid', who along with her friend Brassribs, 'the brassbound butler', was a regular figure of fun between the years 1955–58. Suggesting it to the others he was, at first, roundly jeered ("I thought it was a fucking ridiculous name," says Brian Downey), but by the end of the rehearsal a slight adjustment to the name had suddenly made it much more intriguing.

Given that the Dublin dialect largely refuses to acknowledge the letter 'h', it was with a certain amount of mischief that Bell hinted at the idea of changing Tin to Thin. And while they were at it, to further distinguish themselves from Professor Puffin's cast-iron creation, they decided to customise the 'ie' ending with just 'y'.

"That's it then," said Philip, standing up with a huge white grin breaking across his face. "From now on we'll be known as Thin Lizzy."

Chapter II

Legend Of The Vagabonds

The new band continued intensive rehearsals throughout January and announced the name 'Thin Lizzy' to the press on February 18. The following evening the quartet are reckoned to have played a warm-up show at a school hall in a tiny town called Swords, situated out near Dublin airport, and then on February 20 they made their official live début at St. Anthony's Hall, on the southside of the quays in Dublin. Or at least that's how the most lucid of those present remember it.

By March 5 Thin Lizzy had made their début at the Countdown Club, whereafter shows at Trinity College (March 9) and Liberty Hall (March 10) in Dublin, and The Astor (March 28) and The Carousel (April 24) in Belfast – slotted in between ventures further afield at towns like Cork, Limerick, Carlow, Tralee, Kilkenny and Athlone – kept them working throughout the spring. Promoters still couldn't get the name of the band right – Tin Lizzie was the legend imprinted on most people's minds, it seems – but the press, and especially Dublin's influential weekly music magazine *New Spotlight*, was ensuring that the new group had every chance to establish its credentials. After all, as all four members of the band had established their names with their former groups, Lizzy could loosely be labelled a 'supergroup', perhaps Ireland's first, and as such everyone on the Irish contemporary music scene wanted them to succeed.

"I think the speed with which we picked up a following surprised us all," Eric Bell confesses, "but then we did have an amazing image, we were a very colourful band, and that helped us to make an impression on people. We also had this 16-year-old whizz kid called Terry O'Neill booking gigs for us, and we started to make some money. It was all going so well that we didn't even mind that Eric Wrixen was still tagging along with us!

"One of the funniest things that happened with Eric was when he 'borrowed' this Hammond organ from a pub. The guy who owned the pub had no idea how much this organ was worth, but as soon as he found out he wanted it back! It had a great sound, but it took eight of us to get it in and out of our mini-bus!

"Then Eric decided he wanted to play piano, so we got this upright piano for him to practise on, and Philip and I hauled it up flights and flights of stairs into the flat we shared in Clontarf. After all that effort Eric promised he'd practise every day, but the thing was totally out of tune and he gave up after two days. We could've killed him."

Wrixen kept his job for the time being, however, and Lizzy went from strength to strength. Indeed, on June 19 *New Spotlight* published a Progressive Poll in which Thin Lizzy came third, behind such forgettable adversaries as Taxi and The Urge. In under six months they'd done enough to confirm their potential, and the following month were rewarded further when it was announced that EMI Ireland were interested in signing them. The crunch, it seemed, would come on July 14 when a huge concert at St. Aidan's Hall in Dublin, featuring Granny's Intentions, The Few, The Urge, Blueshouse and Thin Lizzy among others, would act as a showcase for an assortment of music biz bigwigs from Ireland and Britain.

EMI Ireland secured their prize, however, and Lizzy set to work on a single during July in Trend Studios, just off Baggott Street, near St. Stephen's Green in Dublin. The studio owner, John D'Ardis, had offered the band free studio time if they promised to record one of his songs, 'I Need You', and while Lynott and Lizzy reluctantly agreed (the result included a brass section of session musicians) it was one of Lynott's own compositions, 'The Farmer', which ended up as the A-side.

"We were so naïve," Eric Bell admits, "we turned up at the studio with our own PA, thinking that to record something you just set up your PA in the studio and played. The guy at the studio was like, 'Uh, lads, what on earth are you doing?' We were like, 'Er, we . . . er, we dunno to be honest.' "

Released on the Parlophone label on July 31, 1970, 'The Farmer' became Thin Lizzy's very first record release, and folklore has it that of the 500 copies pressed, 283 were sold, with the rest being melted down and recycled. The band itself was undergoing some cosmetic surgery around this time too, and just as the record hit the shops in Ireland it was announced that Eric Wrixen had decided to leave in order to ease the group's financial burden.

"It meant Eric Bell, Phil and I got more money," explains Brian Downey, "and money was pretty tight at that time. We had to keep gigging. We didn't get an instant following, but we got a loyal following, and you'd see the same faces at every gig – not dancing, just sitting there watching the band. However, we needed to keep playing four or five times a week to keep the money coming in, so any chance to play was grabbed by both hands."

Lynott and Eric Bell even took to playing acoustic sets as a duo in folk clubs to reel in a few extra punts on Lizzy's nights off. Some nights they'd make as much as six quid. Still, it paid for a few pints of Guinness and the bus fare home.

"We'd literally just turn up at these folk pubs with two acoustic guitars – not even in cases, just the guitars themselves – and we'd ask the owner if he'd mind if we played a few songs," says Bell. "If we were lucky he'd agree, and we'd sit on the floor and do half an hour or so of Django Rheinhardt songs, Bob Dylan songs, Simon and Garfunkel songs, and maybe we'd throw in one or two of Philip's. It was a good experience.

"Actually, Philip and I loved getting together and mixing up our influences. Obviously we both loved Hendrix, but our record collections were quite different and we turned each other on to different bands. He turned me on to Spirit, Free and The Stones, and I turned him on to all this weird stuff I had. He'd go through my collection and pull out stuff like the Nat King Cole Trio and 'Marty Robbins Sings Gunfighter Ballads'! Philip actually used to get inspiration from those records, because he'd never heard anything like it before."

Other records which influenced Lynott in these formative

years included Van Morrison's *Astral Weeks, Beck-Ola* by the Jeff
Beck Group (both Van Morrison and Rod Stewart had enor-
mous effect on the development of Lynott's vocal style), *Hang
Me, Dang Me* by Heads, Hands And Feet (Philip always cited
bassist Chas Hodges – now the pianist with Chas & Dave –
as one of his main bass playing influences), 'House Of The
Rising Sun' by The Animals, *There's A Riot Going On* by Sly &
The Family Stone and The Beatles' *White Album.*

"We ended up living together in this big house in Clontarf,
and the record player was on constantly," Eric Bell reminisces.
"There was no such thing as watching TV in those days. We
lived there with Philip's girlfriend, my girlfriend, Eric Wrixen,
this guy called Larry Mooney (former manager of The Uptown
Band) who wanted to manage us, and God knows how many
other people.

"We got this reputation as being the place to go when all the
clubs had shut, and the door bell would still be ringing at two
o'clock in the morning. We didn't even know a lot of the
people who came round, but most of them brought some
dope with them, so as Philip and I couldn't afford our own
we'd go, 'Hello! Of course you can come in! Welcome to our
house!' Some of the parties we had were incredible."

Another fleeting resident at the house in Clontarf was Peter
Eustace – Freaky Pete from the song 'Here I Go Again' –
accredited with being Lizzy's 'first and last' roadie. Eustace had
crossed paths with Lynott several times: once at the Embassy
Club in Derry when he was working for Skaboo and Philip was
in Skid Row, and again at a club in Galway when Philip was with
Orphanage. But in 1970 he was passing through Clontarf when
Lynott asked him to take care of Lizzy's stage lights, and that
was the start of a working relationship which lasted throughout
the band's career, as Eustace swiftly took over as the band's live
sound engineer and proved indispensable.

"My first impression of Philip was that he was a very noble
person," Eustace considers. "He was very aware of right and
wrong. He was also very aware of his own uniqueness. He was
literally a black Irish bastard, and he was never allowed to
forget that. He told me once that a friend who he was very
close to said to him one day, 'Jesus Phil, you're not bad for a

black fella after all.' That freaked him out and completely undermined him. After that Phil thought, 'Well I suppose I really am different if even one of my best friends can make a comment like that.' The fact that Phil managed to rise above all that says a lot for his determination."

Eustace's opinion of Thin Lizzy as a live band in those early days is equally as revealing, exposing a young singer who was almost paralysed on stage by his own inhibitions, very much the antithesis of the swashbuckling lionheart he became.

"Phil was very introverted, he never even spoke between numbers. He was almost embarrassed to be on stage and he seemed to try to hide up there. You could see terrific energy and terrific charisma about him, but he was focused on himself as he hadn't learnt to project to an audience.

"At that time Phil was really just an artist in the making. He'd always been in the shadow of Brush (Shiels) – his mentor and hero – and now he was in Eric Bell's shadow. Thin Lizzy was very much Eric's band at the beginning and Phil barely got a look in. My earliest memory of Thin Lizzy live was that it was just Eric going through his Jeff Beck and Jimi Hendrix routines."

Humble pie was still very much the staple diet, especially for Philip. Yet as Percy Gibbons insists the adversity "simply made him stronger and he refused to look back. There was something inside him pushing him all the way."

All Lynott and Lizzy needed was a bit of the legendary Irish luck, and indeed the band's fortunes did take a turn for the better when one of the characters that used to hang around them suggested he might have cracked it with an important contact in London.

"There were several guys that wanted to manage us at the time," Brian Downey explains, "and to be honest we just went along with whoever was going to get us from A to B. One of these guys was Brian Tuite (who also managed Granny's Intentions), and for a while he sort of loosely co-managed us with Terry O'Neill. Anyway, Brian owned a place called The Band Centre, which used to hire out equipment, but he also said he knew a guy in England called Frank Rodgers who worked for Decca Records, and he said to us, 'Look, I think there's a chance of a record deal here.' He told us that Rodgers (brother of Sixties singer Clodagh) was coming over to Ireland to check out a singer called Ditch Cassidy, and he hatched a plan to get us on the same bill, so that this A&R man could have a look at us as well. It seemed like a good idea to us.

"So we're rehearsing like crazy in Dublin, and some of the stuff Phil was coming up with was amazing. His arrangements were getting really complicated and advanced – almost bordering on jazz, with intricate time changes and very fast bits that were extremely difficult to play on the drums – and we'd have these intense rehearsals at this ballet school near Parnell Square trying to get it as tight as we could.

"Finally, we got this bunch of songs together – effectively the first Lizzy album – and we played with Ditch Cassidy for Frank Rodgers. As it turned out we didn't do any of Phil's songs, we simply backed Ditch on his own songs. But the upshot of it all was Frank Rodgers liked us more than he liked Ditch, and told Brian Tuite that he wanted to sign us. It was quite funny really, we couldn't believe it.

"Rodgers wanted us to go to London as soon as possible, and before we knew it we were on the boat. We went straight into Decca's studios in West Hampstead [situated on the corner of West End Lane and Broadhurst Gardens in NW6] and we were really nervous, because this was where Eric Clapton and John Mayall had recorded, where the Stones had recorded, and all those guys. We set our gear up and we were shaking!

"The next thing I know I'm setting my drums up and I notice that my skins are a bit dodgy. I asked Brian if I could go into town and buy some new ones, and he agreed, so I jumped in a cab, flew into Shaftsbury Avenue, bought a new set of skins, and was back in the studio within an hour. I mean, we didn't have a second to waste.

"I was really sweating trying to fix all the new skins on, and the engineer kept coming over the intercom going ''Urry up, mate!' Then he told me to put my cans on, and I was like, 'What?' He was going, 'Your headphones, you prat!' That was how naïve we were then.

"We eventually got around to checking the drum sound and

the engineer told me the drums weren't in tune. He ended up telling me to stick all this tape and bits of paper over the skins, and after that he told me not to hit the rims of the drums, because it was making a ringing sound. So I had to play the whole album just by hitting the top of the skins, and with all this tape stuck all over the skins. I didn't know what I was doing.

"We did two numbers on that first nightmare day, and then we trudged off to our hotel in Sussex Gardens, near Paddington, where we all slept in the same room. Then it was up at 8.30 the next morning and on the tube back to West Hampstead to start work again. Not a minute was wasted. Fortunately, we were so well rehearsed that things went quite smoothly, and we finished the whole record in five days, with two days to mix it."

"We were totally bombed for the duration of that record," adds Eric Bell wistfully, "completely out of our tree. We all smoked a lot of dope, and then on the first day our producer, an American called Scott English [who'd written 'Hi Ho Silver Lining' for Jeff Beck, and who'd also had a hit with a song called 'Brandy'], turned up with this enormous bag of grass. We ended up on the moon. Our eyes were out on stalks, like in the cartoons. There was so much smoke in the studio it was like standing in the middle of Bangkok. I mean, I couldn't even see Philip standing on the other side of the studio, there was so much smoke in the room!

"And Scott English was in an even worse state than us! We were tuning up at one point and Scott said, 'OK guys, let's tape that.' Philip looked around in shock and said, 'Er, Scott, we're only tuning up.' God knows how we got anything done. We were all an inch and a half off the floor for two weeks."

"Despite the distractions, I think we actually made a good job of that album," says Downey. "There's a couple of mistakes on the drums that I can hear on the record even today, but overall there was nothing major wrong with it . . . or so we believed at the time."

Decca had other thoughts. When the tapes were played to Frank Rodgers he was disappointed with the work of Scott English and insisted that the record would have to be remixed.

Without consulting either English or the band, Decca called on the services of their young house engineer Nick Tauber, and hastily remodelled the sound of the album.

"A little while later," says Downey, "we were sitting in a club in Dublin and Brian Tuite came in and said, 'OK lads, the album's mixed, and I've got a copy in the car if you want to hear it.' So we rushed off and listened to the finished record, and all of a sudden Eric said, 'Oh fucking hell! They've used the wrong guitar tracks!' He was furious. Somehow the tapes had got mixed up, and the stuff that Eric preferred had been lost, or whatever.

"I guess we came to realise later that those kind of mishaps were typical of Thin Lizzy."

Thin Lizzy, the album, was released on the Decca label in April 1971, and despite its technical shortcomings managed to capture the essence of the band's firey Celtic spirit and progressive intentions. Indeed, much of Lizzy's early material had ambitious arrangements which tended to make some tracks (like 'Remembering') sound disjointed, like a collection of riffs looking for a song. But beneath the creative puppy fat Lynott's talent was solid muscle.

Many of Lynott's lyrical references were intensely and intriguingly personal. 'Look What The Wind Blew In' was about his girlfriend Gail ('Then somewhere from the north/ This Gale I knew just blew in . . .'), while 'Eire' paid a poignant tribute to his adopted homeland and 'Clifton Grange Hotel' extolled the virtues of his mother's Mancunian retreat. There was even a faint echo of his own family confusion in the concept behind 'Didi Levine'. And in 'Saga Of The Ageing Orphan', an admission of his fear of growing old, he gives a mention to his Uncle Peter and his grandmother.

Other ideas were more obscure, and tracks such as 'The Friendly Ranger At Clontarf Castle' undoubtedly suffered from Lynott's enigmatic lyrical introspection. Eric Bell's 'Ray Gun', meanwhile, was a wholly simpler effort, far more in line with the band's raw live sound and awash with wah-wah effects which evoked comparisons with the guitarist's hero, Jimi Hendrix.

"I was sent a copy of the album at Radio Luxembourg and I

was immediately struck by it," says veteran DJ David Jensen, "there was something effortlessly accessible about it. I loved the songwriting. I was intrigued by the name. I thought the band had a spark. So I contacted Frank Rodgers at Decca to see if I could find out more about them.

"At the time there was a club in Luxembourg called the Blow Up Club, and I used to suggest bands for them to book. I would then play the bands on my show, and sometimes I'd get a live link to the club going and interview the bands on air. That was the case with Thin Lizzy; they came to Luxembourg and went down a storm.

"In those days Luxembourg was a really thriving station, because all the commercial stations we have now didn't exist then. So during the day you listened to Radio One and during the night you listened to Radio Luxembourg – even though the signal would be constantly fading in and out, as it was on what is now the very unfashionable Medium Wave. Of course, television in the UK was only available on three channels then, and even those would shut down before midnight, so I felt I had the ears of the nation when I broadcast my shows. I also had tremendous freedom – three hours on a nightly basis, during which I could pretty much do as I pleased.

"The one thing I tried to do with my show was play as much new material as I could get my hands on. The only opponent I had in terms of radio competition was John Peel, and I was always on the lookout for bands he hadn't already picked up on . . . so I could immediately champion them! When I got the chance to get a hold on Thin Lizzy, I really went for it. They became, in a sense, 'my band'.

"It was a very exciting time for me, seeing Lizzy mature the way they did, and especially seeing Philip grow into a great frontman. He struck me as being a simple, straightforward guy who was honest and earnest at the same time. He cared a great deal for his music, was very softly spoken and had a sensitive nature that was completely at odds with the image he portrayed on stage, where he aspired to the power and presence that Hendrix had.

"Because of my patronage of Lizzy, I guess, Phil and I became great friends. I'd stay at his mother's hotel in

Manchester whenever I was there, and he often used to stay at my flat in Luxembourg. We'd sit up all night listening to records – and I distinctly remember one of his favourite tracks being 'Sweet Thing' from Van Morrison's 1968 album *Astral Weeks*. He'd get up and act out all the lyrics, and we'd fall about laughing. It was always a pleasure to spend time with him, wherever we happened to bump into each other."

Back in Ireland, meanwhile, Lizzy continued to tour the clubs in their white Ford transit van, tuning into Jensen's *Dimensions* show on the way home and cheering whenever he played a track from their album. They also revised their management set-up, as Ted Carroll appeared on the scene once more, fresh from another stint with Skid Row, assisting Fleetwood Mac manager Clifford Davies handle the band's affairs for six months.

"Terry O'Neill had sold his stake in Lizzy to Brian Tuite for £250," Carroll laughs, "and Brian had got into a partnership with a guy called Peter Barden, who managed a lot of showbands. They were interested in me joining the team, but I'd got into the mail order record business by this stage, and I wanted to concentrate on that.

"Then I heard the first Lizzy album and quickly changed my mind. I listened to Phil's songs and there was just something about his melodies, his lyrics and his delivery which convinced me that this was something special. I told them I was in."

The Tuite/Barden/Carroll partnership also managed a twin-guitar band from Ireland called Elmer Fudd and a folky outfit called Mellow Candle. Neither band set the world on fire [although copies of Mellow Candle's début album change hands for exorbitant amounts of money these days], and neither did Peter Barden, who ran into severe financial difficulties when the showband scene started to dwindle and eventually had to abandon ship.

"Brian and I carried on – on a wing and a prayer," admits Carroll. "We didn't really know how we were going to make it until the end of the week, but we did get enormous encouragement from the airplay we were getting from Radio Luxembourg."

"I think it was because of the interest Radio Luxembourg

was generating for us that Brian Tuite suggested we moved to London and tried to break into the London club circuit," Brian Downey suggests. "Ireland was too small for us at that time, we'd explored every nook and cranny and come to a standstill. The only sensible thing to do was head for deeper waters.

"So once again we got on the boat and headed for England. The difference was, this time the first person we saw on the boat was John Peel, who we immediately became friendly with. John really liked Phil and soon after that he began playing us on his show too. [Peel also presided over a number of Lizzy sessions for the Radio One programme *Sounds Of The Seventies*, commencing with a recording at the Beeb's Maida Vale studio in July 1971 and continuing at fairly regular intervals throughout the decade]. So now we had two big allies on the radio.

"Anyway, we got to London and if my memory serves correctly our first gig was at Blaise's Club. There was about 25 people there, and it freaked us out. We were used to playing to packed houses in Ireland, and here we were playing to nobody. It was very disillusioning, but afterwards we agreed that it was right for us to be in London, because the atmosphere was great for rock at the time. All our favourite bands were in London, it was a really happening scene, so we looked for more gigs."

"The first gig I remember Lizzy doing in England was upstairs at Ronnie Scott's Club, for four quid!" says Ted Carroll. "It was March 1971, the Thursday before Easter, and there were very few people in. That night Phil broke a string on his bass, and with the next day being Good Friday we couldn't find a shop open anywhere to buy a new string in time for a gig that night supporting Status Quo at the Marquee. Thankfully Quo lent us their bass guitar, and they also lent Brian some of their drum kit, to save time when changing over. We did the gig and it went really well, although when we went to leave we discovered our van had been broken into and Phil's guitar and Brian's drums had been stolen. That was our introduction to England."

Undeterred, Lizzy continued to gig up and down the country, learning to keep a stiff upper lip at the worst of times. Like the time they arrived at a gig in East Anglia to find themselves supporting a sub-Supremes trio of black girls called The Flirtations . . . in a marquee! (Ted Carroll: "Phil said, 'Jesus, we only left Ireland to get away from playing in marquees, and here we are back in a fucking marquee!' ") And like the time they supported the Edgar Broughton Band at Quaintways in Chester for £20 and their van broke down on the way home, leaving them with no choice but to get a cab all the way from Cannock Chase to London at 5 o'clock in the morning.

"We blew about a week's worth of money on that taxi," Ted Carroll winces. "We almost had to do a quick Irish tour to get the money back!"

For convenience the band located themselves in the West Hampstead area, close to the start of the M1 (for when the van worked). If they were playing within 50 or 60 miles of Manchester they'd crash over at The Biz – "I'd get them out of their sweaty clothes, get them in the bath and then send them to bed," Phyllis insists – but any further and they'd press on back to London. Philip and his girlfriend Gail rented a small flat at Embassy House on the corner of West End Lane and Cleve Road, Brian got a room just around the corner in Greencroft Gardens, while Eric lodged nearby at 31 Belsize Avenue, in the same house that once accommodated Granny's Intentions and which now housed Ted Carroll, Gary Moore, Terry Woods, roadie Frank Murray "and about 20 other struggling musicians, not to mention the odd aspiring actor".

It was a big step for Lizzy, but hardly a pioneering one. As if to underline the seniority they felt over their aspiring rivals, the Skid Row of Shiels, Moore and Bridgeman had already moved to London the previous year, settling in the rougher district of Upton Park, E13, and releasing their eponymous début album through CBS during the October of 1970, some six months before Lizzy's.

"Everything Lizzy did, we'd been there just before them," says Brush Shiels today, "so we felt that they weren't really a serious threat to us. I thought we were in a different league to them, a much more sophisticated band. We saw Lizzy as a bit of a joke band at first, a kind of pop act which was at the other end of the scale to us.

"But to his credit Philip was always determined to prove his point to us after we'd let him go from the band, and he worked hard to achieve that distinctive Lizzy sound. It was no surprise to me when Lizzy began to make some progress of their own."

It was no surprise to the folk back home either. Smiley Bolger remembers seeing Lizzy open for Skid Row at the Countdown Club just as Brush's band were about to hit the big time, and being convinced that it wouldn't be long before the tables were turned.

"It was Skid Row's leaving party, the big boys had signed to CBS and were off to London to find their fame and fortune, and Lizzy were brought in just to make up the numbers really. Thin Lizzy were the new kids, just starting out, but I remember me and the boys thinking that night that Lizzy were the band that were going to make it. We had nothing against Skid Row, but there was just something about Philip that made you feel he was onto a winner."

Gary Moore also recognised the ambition that was burning inside his erstwhile Skid Row colleague in the earliest days of Thin Lizzy. In fact, Moore had remained in regular contact with the Lizzy boys, particularly Philip, and had a better view than most of Lynott's determined gravitation towards the recognition he craved.

"We really became great friends after he got the elbow from Skid Row," Moore recalls. "In fact, I moved into his flat with him, and he'd come up to Belfast with me and stay at my parents' place. We'd hang out a lot together, go to clubs, that kind of thing . . . we were pretty close, even then.

"We shared the flat with a guy called Jimmy Doon, who was the singer in a band from Limerick called Granny's Intentions, and we had some great times there. Phil was different in those days. He'd be up at the crack of dawn, going round the markets buying second-hand clothes, and then he'd come back and cook breakfast for us. Can you imagine that? He'd come in and go, 'C'mon, here's your breakfast – GET UP!' He'd have made these huge platefuls of beans and mushrooms and eggs and bacon . . . he used to eat like a pig in those days. He was always so full of energy then, so lively, so ambitious . . . driven, really.

"Then when we both moved to England, of course we kept running into each other, although Skid Row really were the No.1 band at the time, and Lizzy were a poor second. In fact, I remember going to see them play at a place called the Pheasantry Club in the King's Road and thinking how sad it all was for Lizzy. They were just playing to a handful of posey people sitting there drinking cocktails, and the whole scenario just wasn't right.

"At the end of their first set the DJ took the mike off them and said, 'That was a lesson in how not to use amplification from Thin Lizzy.' I thought it was great, listening to them doing stuff like 'If Six Was Nine' by Jimi Hendrix in this little room – it sounded really heavy. But the DJ thought they were too loud, and told them to piss off. I felt so sorry for them.

"On another occasion we were both playing in Folkestone – Skid Row were at the Leas Cliff Hall and Lizzy were at a little club nearby – but because we were both playing on the same night they didn't sell any tickets because all the fans were down the road watching us. So we invited them to come along to our gig instead, and we ended up having one great big jam.

"In fact, although there was some friendly rivalry between the two of us, we always had a laugh when we got together. Phil and I would just go off and get pissed somewhere. It was easier for us to get along when we weren't working together, because there wouldn't be any pressure on us, we could just get on with being friends. In truth, I was better friends with the guys in Thin Lizzy than I was with the guys in Skid Row!"

With Moore coming unerringly into his own, Skid Row recorded another album, *34 Hours*, for CBS in the summer of '71, but then somehow lost their way the following year. Brush Shiels would keep the name Skid Row alive for some years to come, and even attempt (unsuccessfully) to prevent a popular American band from using the same name during the late Eighties. But for Gary Moore Skid Row had run its natural course, and the opportunity to embark, albeit rather prematurely in retrospect, on a solo career for CBS would produce a rather patchy solo album entitled *Grinding Stone* in May 1973.

Lizzy, meanwhile, had continued their recording career with the surprise release of an EP in the August of '71. *New Day* featured four new tracks – 'Dublin', 'Remembering Part 2', 'Old Moon Madness' and 'Things Ain't Working Out Down On The Farm' – and was largely felt to be something of a watershed release; a fond farewell to their homeland as the band ventured towards new horizons across the Irish Sea.

"At the time Decca weren't sure about doing a second album," Carroll reveals, "so I argued that in that case we should be released from our contract immediately. We reached a compromise and decided to do an EP, although Decca weren't too keen on putting any money into it. We ended up getting a kid who worked for the Plastic Doll agency (which we used) in Bristol to do the artwork for us, and persuading a friend from Dublin called Tony Bradfield to print the sleeve up for us. It was done totally 'on the cheap', but I think Decca were pleased with it because they kept us on."

"*New Day* was a weird venture for us, because in those days EPs were extremely rare," says Downey. "We did it at Decca's studios in Tollington Park, North London, in about two days. It was mixed in about an hour. Or at least it sounds as though it was! I think it was really just a stop-gap between our first and second albums. We didn't really want to stop working in those days."

Indeed, with the kind of continuity which must seem alien to most of today's young rock recording artists, Thin Lizzy were soon whisked back into the studio by Decca to hammer out their second album. They were given the choice of using Decca's West Hampstead studios again, or trying out the new De Lane Lea studios in Wembley, and somewhat against the wishes of Brian Downey, Lynott opted for De Lane Lea.

"I thought it was a mistake," Downey maintains, even today. "The drum sound at De Lane Lea was terrible, and in fact the whole album still sounds flat to me. I spent the whole time wishing we'd gone back to Decca."

"The reason why we chose De Lane Lea was because we wanted Martin Birch to produce the album," explains Carroll, "and he was working out of the new Wembley studios. Birch had done Fleetwood Mac and Deep Purple and Phil was really keen to work with him, but as it turned out he was too busy to do our album, so we ended up with another guy. He was good, but with the studios being so new there were all sorts of teething problems with the equipment, and I think it showed on the final result."

"The other thing about that record was that, unlike the first album, there didn't seem to be too much room for ad-libs or improvisation," complains Downey. "The songs seemed to be shorter, and the direction wasn't quite there. There were a few songs which shouldn't have been on the album at all – like 'I Don't Want To Forget How To Jive', for example. I think it was a dedication to Elvis, but whatever it was it wasn't right for the album. I wasn't too pleased with 'Sarah' either, and the title track was a bit weird as well; it went on too long and sounded a bit morbid to me.

"Having said that, some of the tracks were really good. 'Buffalo Gal' was great, so was 'Chatting Today' and 'Call The Police'. Looking back on it I like most of the album, but I still felt that it wasn't as good as our first album. I was a bit disappointed with it at the time."

"Obviously all our best material went on the first album," explains Eric Bell, "so when someone said, 'OK lads, you've got three weeks to do another album', we were stuck. It was like, 'Oh shit, we'd better write some stuff quick.' It was too much of a rush."

Released in March '72, *Shades Of A Blue Orphanage* took its title from two pre-Lizzy groups, Bell's Shades Of Blue and Lynott and Downey's Orphanage. As with the first album there was a degree of curiosity about some of the themes, such as the title track and 'The Rise And Dear Demise Of The Funky Nomadic Tribes' (Lynott had already developed a penchant for long titles). And, also in the style of the début, there were a number of highly personal references. The delicate ballad of 'Sarah', for example, was written for his grandmother.

Overall though *Shades* . . . lacked the quality of *Thin Lizzy* and few of those questioned about the record today have had their slightly negative feelings about it erased by time. After the excitement of releasing their début, the follow-up smacked of an anti-climax.

Lynott actually nearly left Thin Lizzy during the recording of *Shades Of A Blue Orphanage,* having been flattered by the attentions of Deep Purple's Ritchie Blackmore and lured towards the temperamental guitarist's latest whim. With his interest in Purple on the wane, Blackmore had hatched a plan for a new part-time supergroup, featuring Lynott, Purple drummer Ian Paice and possibly Free singer Paul Rodgers, and while Chris O'Donnell maintains the project was no more than "a few rehearsals which had Phil thinking he could live out his Rod Stewart/Faces fantasy", Brian Downey insists it nearly led to Lizzy's demise.

"Ritchie came up to De Lane Lea while we were recording the *Shades* . . . album, and he just plugged in his guitar and started jamming with us. We were all completely freaked. Then a few days later I was talking to Phil and the whole idea about Ritchie's new band came out. He told me he didn't want to leave Lizzy, but that he really wanted to work with Ritchie, and he was really in two minds. He told me he didn't want to upset me or Eric, but I said, 'Look, you just do what you want to do.'

"I think that was the first time I'd ever seen Phil hesitate about anything. He thought about it for a long time, but in the end I think he felt he could prove himself more by sticking with Lizzy and continuing to build the band up, than simply jumping into another band just because the guitar player was a big name."

Thus, Baby Face (as it was suggested the band be christened) was aborted, and Blackmore returned to Deep Purple. But that wasn't the end of the Lizzy/Purple connection for it was around this time that financial necessity dictated that Lynott, Bell and Downey would surreptitiously record an album of Deep Purple songs under the guise of Funky Junction.

"The management called a meeting at our offices in Dean Street one day and told us that some American guy had offered us some money to go into the studio and do an album of Deep Purple's greatest hits," explains Bell. "We were mortified at the prospect at first, but when it was explained to us that we really did need the money to keep the band going, we had to give it a re-think. The next thing I know I'm back home at my flat listening to all the Deep Purple albums, trying to work out Ritchie Blackmore's licks."

"The saving grace," says Downey, "was that it wasn't going to be 'Thin Lizzy plays Deep Purple'; in fact we were told we didn't have to tell anyone it was us at all. It was going to come out on some small independent label, we were going to get 500 quid or whatever, and that was that. It was a real 'take the money and run' job.

"The only problem was Phil said he couldn't sing like Ian Gillan, so we'd have to get someone else in. The best person for the job was this guy we knew from Dublin called Benny White, who sang with a band called Elmer Fudd and who was really an Ian Gillan clone. He brought along his keyboard player, Dave Lennox (known as Mojo), and we went straight to De Lane Lea and bashed some stuff down.

"Fortunately we knew most of Deep Purple's material anyway, because we used to play it in the Dublin clubs, before we even came to England. I think we rehearsed for about two or three hours and then just went for it. And we also threw in a few weird instrumentals which had nothing to do with Purple, just to fill the time up."

The album, *Funky Junction: A Tribute To Deep Purple*, featured tentative versions of 'Fireball', 'Black Night', 'Strange Kinda Woman', 'Hush' and 'Speed King', not to mention a small collection of other oddities, such as Eric Bell's Hendrix influenced interpretation of 'Danny Boy'. It was eventually released in January 1973 on the Stereo Gold Award label with a live photo of the mysterious Funky Junction on the front cover ("Although it's not us at all!" maintains Downey) and a splash of phoney information about the band on the back. Not surprisingly, it remains something of a collector's item.

Also in danger of being obscured by the mists of time are some of Lizzy's forays into Europe around '72/'73. The one man who remembers every painful kilometre driven in the band's white Ford transit is Frank Murray, who worked as Lizzy's tour manager from 1972–78. "If there was a mountain we could play behind, or a valley we could get lost in, we'd be there," he laughs. "We'd play places in Germany that even the Germans didn't know existed. The management didn't care, they'd send us anywhere if it meant getting paid.

"One of our favourite gigs was the Zoom Club in Frankfurt, which was full of the American GIs who escaped going to Vietnam, and we'd always have a wild time with them. But a lot of the places we played were dreadful, and quite often we'd get into trouble with the locals, because they'd think we were English and start having a go at us. We'd just get drunk and fight.

"One night Philip and I got into a drinking contest with these German guys, and they got the barman to start serving us this foul-smelling liquid which stank like fish. Philip and I kept up with these guys drink for drink, until the barman literally passed out. Unfortunately though, we got so drunk that Philip ended up having a big row with Eric Bell. Eric smashed this souvenir brandy glass he'd been presented with that night against the wall and Philip went mad. The two punched the shit out of each other and I had to pull them apart. It was all because of the drink inside us, but that's how we were then."

One particular gig in Germany worth recalling is the show in the Olympic Stadium, Munich, in the September after the 1972 Olympic Games. Frank Murray again: "Beck, Bogart & Appice were headlining, but Nazareth were also on the bill, and so was this guy called Udo Lindenberg, who always seemed to get on our bills in Germany for some reason. Anyway, I seem to remember that the backstage hospitality was very generous, so of course we took a keen interest in the selection of refreshments that were available. Eric wanted to remain sober because he was desperate to see Jeff Beck play, but as usual the temptation was too much and he finished up asleep in the back of this car. Fortunately, BBA were so loud they sobered Eric up within seconds of going on stage. I hate to think what would've happened if Eric had missed that show."

"Another time in Germany we ended up at this club called The Eros Centre on the Reeperbahn in Hamburg," Ted Carroll recalls. "The band were so naïve they started chatting up the prostitutes, doing the whole, 'Hello darling, do you come here often?' routine!

"That night we got really out of it and wrecked our hotel rooms. I think the owner came up to see what all the noise was about and found Brian pissing down the stairs. Needless to say I couldn't persuade him to let us stay another night.

"The next day we checked into another hotel a few miles away. We spent the afternoon up in the mountains, taking acid and playing football, and then we returned to this hotel to find a strip show going on. There was this band like a Turkish version of The Shadows playing this awful music, while this woman of about 45 was writhing around, pouring hot wax all over herself. She ended up putting the candle out by sticking it up her ... well, you can imagine. We couldn't believe it, especially after the acid."

Back in London Ted Carroll took a step back from the madness and decided there ought to be a change in the management setup. He told Brian Tuite that he felt they were on a treadmill going nowhere, and that the band needed to have someone with more clout in England if they were to progress to the next level. He offered to buy Tuite out, and Tuite accepted.

"Originally I wanted to team up with Colin Johnson who managed Status Quo," says Carroll. "He worked out of Billy Gaff's office at the time, and I thought having those two on my side would be a great bonus. So I asked our agent, Chris Morrison, to get me a gig at the Marquee so that I could bring Johnson and Gaff down to see the band ..."

"... And I said 'Fuck off!'," Morrison takes up the story. "I was horrified. I said to Ted, 'No way! If you're going to approach Billy Gaff, not only will I refuse to get you a showcase date in London, but I'll pull the rest of the dates I've booked for the band as well! If you need a partner, what about me?' "

"I had to admire his cheek," Carroll laughs. "At the time Chris was managing this awful band called Danto, a kind of Afro-rock band, like a poor man's Osibisa, except they had a sword-swallower and a fire-eater. They were going nowhere, but Chris was getting them a lot of work on the college circuit and I was impressed by his enthusiasm. He was totally into Lizzy too, so I thought I'd give him a chance."

"So Ted and I had a beer and agreed to go into partner-ship," Morrison concludes. "I was tremendously excited, but as soon as we'd finished the drink he said, 'Right, I need £40 for the band's wages', and I went 'Uh-oh, maybe this management lark isn't such a good idea after all!' "

Like most bands who hadn't had the luxury of a hit single, Lizzy's financial status was shaky to say the least. Yet such was their popularity back home in Ireland they were able to use frequent home visits as a means of topping up the coffers, a privilege Lynott gratefully exercised throughout his career.

"Philip always used Ireland shrewdly," says Smiley Bolger. "It was hard for the boys living in England, so whenever they came home they'd ask me to set up all these little club gigs around the country, and they'd go off and make a tidy little profit for a few nights work. Cash in hand, straight into the back pocket, thank you very much.

"The money he made from those Irish gigs really subsidised the band's career, and Philip was very philosophical about it. He'd make a few grand in a couple of weeks in Ireland, then go back to London to play the Marquee for £50, or something. He was very smart like that."

"The Irish tours always seemed to come in December," says Peter Eustace, "and we looked upon them as our Christmas bonus. Work all year for next to nothing, then rake in a few bob to pay for Christmas. The crew always looked forward to going back to Ireland."

"It had to be done really," adds Morrison, "because we'd be literally losing money by playing in England. We'd get paid five times as much for a show in Ireland than we would for a show in England, but then if you wanted to break into the big marketplace you had to keep playing England. The band would've disappeared if they'd just stuck to touring Ireland.

"And things really were desperate when I first joined up with Ted. We'd be constantly holding off Peter so that we could pay Paul. We used to call it 'the long finger' – doing anything we could to avoid paying bills until we absolutely had to.

"In fact, the office we had at 52 Dean Street in Soho was really just a squat. I had the lease in my name, but then the landlord wanted everyone out to re-develop the building and wouldn't accept any rent. Then the building got sold to some-one, who sold it on to someone else, who sold it on again, and all the while we got away with not paying any rent. This went on for five or six years. It was a horrible place – no security, hookers and junkies on the stairs and in the lifts, doing their business – but it was free so we couldn't argue.

"That really is how close to the wind we sailed in those days. Every penny was counted. So those trips to Ireland simply became a means to an end, a way of keeping a lot of people off our backs for a little while longer."

Morrison's first real coup as Lizzy's co-manager was the acquisition of a support slot on one of the hottest tours of the year. Capitalising on his friendship with promoter Mel Bush and ex-Animals bass player Chas Chandler, the man who'd launched Jimi Hendrix's career and who was currently enjoying enormous success as manager and producer of Slade, Morrison edged Lizzy into the frame when Slade's November/December tour of the UK was being finalised. Though Chandler was also put under intense pressure by former Animals producer Mickie Most, who insisted his latest protégé Suzi Quatro should get the gig, he compromised and settled on the idea of a three-band bill, with Lizzy opening the show with a 45 minute set.

The tour kicked into action at Newcastle's City Hall on November 3, and then rattled south, taking in Oxford's New Theatre (5), Wolverhampton Civic Hall (6), Bournemouth Winter Gardens (8) and Sheffield City Hall (9), before two storming appearances at London's Rainbow Theatre on the 10th and 11th. Slade were at the height of their popularity having just had a string of hit singles, including 'Mama Weer All Crazee Now' the previous month, and the scenes of teeny hysteria which greeted the tour's arrival in each town was like nothing Lizzy had ever experienced.

"It was a real eye-opener," says Brian Downey. "Girls screaming and throwing their knickers on the stage. Amazing scenes, like Beatlemania. Nobody wanted to know us, we were incidental. In fact, when we played at the Liverpool Stadium we got pelted off after two numbers with Coke cans and bottles.

"It was great fun though. In fact, that night in Liverpool Dave Hill from Slade broke his leg after getting one of his platform heels caught in the stairs on the way up to the stage. For the rest of the tour he had to sit down on stage with his leg in plaster. Only to preserve the band's glam image they covered this chair in tin foil to match his outrageous silver outfits, and draped all this glittery stuff around his broken leg!

"We almost turned glam ourselves on that tour," Downey coyly admits. "We didn't really know what kind of image we wanted, but we ended up with sparkly jackets and high-heeled boots. I had a streak in my hair. Phil had all this gypsy jewellery. Our management kept on at us to go more glam, but we managed to stop short of putting glitter on our faces or any of that crap."

"I do remember that Philip used to wear his girlfriend's mascara on stage," Eric Bell reveals, "and he was quite fanatical about his image. He worked on his looks all the time, and would spend weeks customising a pair of jeans by sewing bits on to them. Brian and I didn't give a shit about how we looked, but Philip thought about every aspect of his appearance. It was the same with money. Philip got more money than us because he wrote most of the songs, but whereas Brian and I would blow our royalties, Philip would plough his money straight back into the group by buying new equipment or whatever. That's how dedicated Philip was to Thin Lizzy, and I noticed that devotion to the cause reach new heights during our time with Slade."

"In retrospect, that Slade tour was really quite an important one in the development of Lizzy as a live band, and particularly in the overall development of Phil as a performer," considers Chris O'Donnell, a young booking agent at the time who knew Chris Morrison from their days together at the famous Rik Gunnell Agency, which was at the thick of the British blues boom in the mid-to-late Sixties. "It made Phil realise what was expected of him. Slade were huge at the time and they would go on stage and absolutely slaughter the audience night after night with incredibly powerful performances. It was far removed from what Lizzy were doing at the time.

"On the opening night in Newcastle Phil was standing there mumbling as usual, looking at the floor and being all introverted, and someone threw a bottle at him. This shocked Phil because he thought he'd done a perfectly adequate set. But then Chas Chandler came in the dressing room afterwards and really ripped into the band. He said: 'Either you wake your ideas up or you're off the tour. You're here to warm the kids up, not to send them to sleep! What the hell do you think you're doing, standing there looking at the floor? You haven't even got your act together. Sort yourselves out!'

"Phil was devastated. He'd never been criticised so directly before, and to hear it from someone as well respected as Chas – the man who'd discovered his hero, Hendrix! – was the worst aspect of all. At the next show the band made a big effort to improve their presentation, and I don't think they ever looked back, performance-wise."

They did run into more problems at Manchester's Free Trade Hall on the 15th, however. Phyllis Lynott remembers the evening well. "All the crowd wanted to see was Slade. I remember seeing Suzi Quatro in floods of tears because the crowd just didn't want to know her, they kept chanting for Slade. So when Philip went on I really felt for him, because he was getting so much flak.

"Then this guy in the crowd shouted, 'Get off yer black arse – get back to Africa!' Philip heard it and grabbed the mike. He wasn't angry, he was just frustrated, and he said to this guy, 'Look pal, just give us a chance, eh?' I think the crowd responded to that.

"The beauty of it though was the next time I saw Lizzy at the Free Trade Hall they were the headliners. I was taken to the show in a limo and sat right at the front of the balcony. When the flashbombs went off I thought they were real bombs, but then when the smoke cleared Philip came to the front of the stage and picked me out in the audience with the beam of light that always reflected off his guitar. It was as if he was saying, 'There y'are ma, I told ya I'd make it!' That night the Slade gig seemed light years away."

The idea of using a mirror on his guitar to shine in people's faces (most commonly attractive young girls) actually stemmed from the Slade tour, on which frontman Noddy Holder went on stage every night with a top hat covered in tiny mirrors. Philip noticed how the mirrors would spray beams of light in all directions as soon as the spotlight caught it, and decided to experiment with the idea himself.

"One day," recalls Eric Bell, "he turned up at the sound-check with a mirror from a budgie's cage dangling from the machine head of his bass (something eagle-eyed viewers of the band's promo for 'The Rocker' single might recall), and he told us that the idea was to pick out the chicks in the audience with the reflection. The management thought it was a great idea, and later when we did *Top Of The Pops* they insisted I wore this jacket which was covered in mirrors as well. I hated the thing, but the management had been totally inspired by watch-ing Slade every night – this hugely successful band with the complete package of hit singles, a great image and all the right moves – and I'm convinced that from then on they tried to mould us in a similar way."

To coincide with Lizzy's catalytic slot on the Slade tour, which ran right into the first week of December with dates at Plymouth Guild Hall (2nd), Cardiff Top Rank (3rd) and Bristol Colston Hall (5th), Decca released a single which would initially flop, but eventually catapult the band into the upper echelons of the UK charts. However, to Lynott's intense annoyance, not to mention the considerable irritation of Downey and Bell as well, the track that did the trick was not one of the many original compositions the highly productive Lynott was spawning at the time, but a traditional Irish folk tune called 'Whiskey In The Jar' which, to rub salt in the wound, had previously been a hit for The Dubliners.

"At this stage Phil was writing intensely on the road," says Downey. "We'd sit in the van going over ideas on the way to gigs. I'd be tapping out the rhythms on my knees and Phil would be humming the melodies and making up lyrics on the spot. We actually came up with some great tunes that way, and we were really chuffed with the new material. In fact, I thought Phil had really started to come into his own with his song-writing when we came to do the third album. Some of his ideas were brilliant, and I could see him begin to blossom before my very eyes.

"Then this 'Whiskey In The Jar' thing reared its ugly head! Even going back to The Black Eagles days, I can remember hearing people play 'Whiskey In The Jar' – but as a folk song, not as a rock song. I actually quite liked the melody of it, and sometimes we'd jam around with the melody, because Eric had come up with a great guitar lick for it. The trouble was, we only ever mucked around with the tune in rehearsals for a laugh, it wasn't supposed to be a serious attempt at turning it into a rock song."

At this time Lizzy were rehearsing upstairs at a pub in York Way, in the King's Cross area of London. They'd meet at half past one, have a pint and a sandwich and then rehearse from 2–6 o'clock, for a fiver. Occasionally Ted Carroll would stop by for a drink, to see how things were going.

"Anyway, one day we were at this pub and everyone was totally bored," says Eric Bell. "We couldn't think of anything to play, there was no inspiration. We'd done our versions of 'The Green Green Grass Of Home' and 'Bridge Over Troubled Water' and some other nonsense, just for a laugh, and then Philip started strumming some Irish folk songs on a Telecaster . . ."

"One of the songs was 'Whiskey In The Jar'," Brian Downey continues, "and just at that moment Ted Carroll was coming up the stairs and he heard us. He said it sounded good and we ought to record it as a single. We fell about laughing. At the time Phil was writing some great songs, and he had one in particular that he was really proud of, called 'Black Boys On The Corner'. He was convinced that that song should be the next single. But Ted Carroll kept on at us to record 'Whiskey . . .', so in the end Phil said he'd record 'Whiskey . . .' for the B-side of 'Black Boys On The Corner', just to keep Ted happy.

"We ended up at Tollington Park and knocked the two songs out in one day. Everything was fine. Then a few weeks later Ted came up to us and said, 'Look boys, Decca don't want to release 'Black Boys On The Corner' as a single, they want 'Whiskey In The Jar'. Of course we immediately said, 'Fuck off! It's a joke song, it's not Thin Lizzy!' But Ted was adamant it was going to be a hit, and said that as Decca were so insistent on releasing it anyway, we didn't really have much of a choice in the matter. We were furious, but we had to go along with it."

As it transpired, Lizzy's version of 'Whiskey In The Jar' was as far removed from the quaint Gaelic original as Eric Bell's piercing electric guitar and Lynott's chesty Rod Stewart delivery could make it. Indeed, one critic declared that a British equivalent might be a reggae version of 'Greensleeves'. But that didn't prevent Lizzy from being lumbered with a folksy image that would take years to flush from their system.

'Whiskey In The Jar' shot to the very top of the Irish charts, and enjoyed a 17-week run in the limelight. While in Britain it finally breached the Top 30 in the week of February 3, 1973, eventually peaking at No.6 during a 12-week run on the chart. The novelty value of the song couldn't be underestimated of course, and the band didn't know whether to laugh or cry at such a perverted stroke of luck. But, undeniably, the song had a hook which caught a lot of people's attention, and it even drew critical acclaim from some quarters.

"I thought it was a great pop song from the moment I heard it," proclaims David Jensen, "even though I might have been a little biased at the time. I played the song night in, night out, and it kind of became an anthem for me. Whenever I played a gig – at colleges, universities, polytechnics, or nightclubs – they used to play 'Whiskey In The Jar' as I came onstage. So in a way it became my theme song. But, vested interests aside, I honestly thought the song was a hit right from the start."

In fact, 'Whiskey . . .' took a good six weeks or so to finally break the ice in Britain, and may not have done so if it hadn't been for the shrewd intervention of Chris O'Donnell.

"I always remember Chris telling me about this group called Thin Lizzy," says O'Donnell, "but I was never sure about them. I'd seen the picture on the back of the first album, which was taken from a weird camera angle, and it turned me off them. I know they say 'Never judge a book by its cover', but I certainly judged the band by that cover.

"Anyway, one day I was coming back from a gig in Cardiff when I stopped at a transport cafe for breakfast and heard 'Whiskey In The Jar' on the radio. It completely blew me away and I immediately phoned Chris and told him I thought he had a hit. But Chris said he wasn't so sure it was going to be a hit, because he was having a lot of problems with Decca and it was all a bit tough going. So I suggested that I helped him work on the single, and when I got back to London we put our heads together.

"I had the idea of sending out miniature bottles of Irish whiskey with 'Whiskey In The Jar' stamped on the label to a few key people, and that idea seemed to go down well. Then I insisted that they got themselves an independent plugger, who would be much better at working the radio stations than the Decca guy. After a few weeks the record began to get some airplay, especially from those DJs who'd received the free whiskey, and then – bingo! – they had themselves a hit."

With a view to exploiting their moment of fame, Chris Morrison contacted a livewire London-based publicity agent and pleaded with him to take Thin Lizzy on his books. Tony Brainsby had made his reputation working for the likes of Paul McCartney, The Strawbs, Cat Stevens, Steeleye Span, Queen and many others, and was deemed the ideal man to help boost the new Irish band's profile.

"It took me ages to get round to listening to the tape Morrison sent me," Brainsby confesses, "probably about two months in all, and during that time Chris hassled the life out of me. Every day he'd be on the phone giving me the hard sell about this Irish rock group with a strange name, and in the end I just gave in to him.

"So I invited Philip, Eric Bell and Brian Downey to my office in Winchester Street, and I was actually quite surprised at how shy, naïve and very young they were. Fresh out of Ireland, literally.

"Phil was particularly striking. What I'll always remember about him was my first impression that day: this gigantic pair of legs and this thick Irish accent. There's only two people about whom I've immediately thought, upon meeting them for the first time, 'This guy's a star'. One was Freddie Mercury, the other was Phil Lynott. When you met either of those two you knew you were in the presence of a special person, a genuine rock star in every sense."

Brainsby secured a string of articles and interviews in the pop papers on the back of the 'Whiskey In The Jar' success, and allied to TV appearances such as their nervously mimed turn on the prestigious *Top Of The Pops* and another spot on the popular kids show *Crackerjack!* (where they were introduced by Philip's future father-in-law, comedian Leslie Crowther), Lizzy's stature appeared to grow overnight.

"It was a very exciting time," Phyllis remembers with immense pride. "The song was on the jukeboxes all over town, and my son was on the telly. We couldn't believe it! I used to love to show off a bit when they were in Manchester. We always looked forward to them coming to stay at The Showbiz, and we always tried to put up whoever was supporting them on the road, because Philip would give me a sob story and say, 'Oh ma, they haven't got any money, could you please just help them out tonight?' We didn't mind really, although sometimes Philip would prefer to stay elsewhere, because he was embarrassed about taking girls back to his room at his ma's hotel!

"Anyway, one day they turned up in Manchester to do a TV show for Granada and Philip was wearing this old woolly hat, covered in holes, because he thought it was macho to go on the telly looking scruffy. But I was furious. I made him go and wash his hair, and while he was in the bath I sewed up the holes in his hat.

"Eventually Philip came downstairs and said, 'Right, if I've got to wash my hair, then so has Brian!' So I made Brian Downey get in the bath as well. He didn't like it and kicked up a real fuss, but I didn't care.

"So we went to Granada for the show, and first of all we saw Lulu, then Joe Dolan, and then out came Thin Lizzy. I was horrified. Philip had picked all my stitching out of the hat, and had pulled clumps of his hair through the holes. He thought it looked great, but I could've strangled him."

Lizzy ended up appearing on TV all over Europe with 'Whiskey . . .', although the strict routine of the promotional merry-go-round wasn't something which Eric Bell particularly enjoyed, and this led to some tension within the camp.

"We'd fly to Paris, mime to the single, then fly back to England, all in an afternoon," Bell complains. "It was a crazy lifestyle and it got to me after a while. We went to Spain for the day, Holland for the day, Germany for the day . . . and in fact in Germany I snapped and ended up having a fight with

Philip. I guess being a pop star just wasn't what I thought it was going to be. I was a kid from the back streets of Belfast, and suddenly I was on *Top Of The Pops* and I was thinking, 'Is this it? Is this what the fuss is all about?' "

In a way Eric Bell bitterly begrudged the success of 'Whiskey . . .', but then ironically when the follow-up single, 'Randolph's Tango', was released during May and failed to make the UK charts (reaching only No.14 in Ireland), problems of a different kind besieged the band. Panic began to set in behind the scenes. Would Thin Lizzy be stuck with the stigma of being 'one hit wonders' forever?

"They just couldn't follow 'Whiskey In The Jar', for whatever reason," explains Tony Brainsby, "and my bills began to mount at a worrying rate. Lizzy just weren't making any money, but fortunately I had confidence in them, I liked Phil a lot, and so I hung in there with them when perhaps a more sensible move may have been to drop them like a hot potato.

"In fact, the press I got them kept them going through the darkest days when they couldn't get a hit record. To the outside world I suppose it looked like they were doing alright, because they were always in the papers. But the reality was they weren't selling many records at all.

"Of course, the secret of good PR is to keep your client's name in the papers, no matter how economical you have to be with the truth at times, and so we'd be forever inventing ideas and ways of getting more coverage. We constantly fed the papers with news stories, tour dates, the odd 'scam'; we used our imagination and exploited every situation for as much as we were worth.

"Someone might have thrown a bottle at Phil onstage and it might have slightly cut his forehead, or something. But that would be turned into a life-threatening situation by the time we fed it to the papers, with Phil being rushed off to hospital, having an operation and nearly losing an eye. It's just a matter of expanding on the facts with the license you're given as a PR.

"One of our best stories was the one about Phil going deaf. We leaked that one out and it caused quite a stir. I mean, for years afterwards people would be shouting in his ear, thinking he couldn't hear properly. It was quite funny really, but it kept the name Thin Lizzy on people's lips for a while, and that was what I was paid to do."

Over fifty volumes of scrapbooks pay testament to the column inches that Tony Brainsby gained Thin Lizzy from 1972 onwards, but rapidly increasing debts was the reality of Lizzy's fragile predicament, and both Carroll and Morrison realised they were going to have to pull some major strokes to keep the band from going under.

"Chris was in a bit of a state at the time," Chris O'Donnell recalls. "The band were working on what became *Vagabonds Of The Western World*, and I assumed that as soon as they'd finished the album they'd be going straight out on tour to promote it. But Chris told me he was finding it difficult to get the band gigs, so once again I offered to help.

"Chris persuaded me to go and see Lizzy at the Leas Cliff Hall in Folkestone, and I actually thought they were really good. My only problem with them was that I felt Phil still didn't project enough. He stood stage right, with Eric Bell taking the centre stage spot, and he really did come across as the bass player who happened to sing as well, rather than the frontman of the group. Eric Bell was having to do all the frontman work, and while a lot of lead guitarists handled that role well in those days, I felt the onus should be more on Phil.

"All the same I knew Phil had it in him to develop that side of his performance, especially after the lessons of the Slade tour, and the show didn't do anything to deter me from going through with my promise to help Chris out.

"I told Chris that he was caught in a silly situation; in order to keep the band alive he was having to get them doing 'pop' gigs for £400 a night. But once the audience had heard 'Whiskey In The Jar' that was it, and unless they had another hit single soon those kind of pop audiences would lose interest in them. When 'Randolph's Tango' was a flop it kind of proved my point.

"Around this time the band delivered another batch of new songs and Chris was having problems choosing a single for radio. He played me a tape of the tracks that were available and I immediately jumped down his throat. I said: 'Are you mad? The track is screaming at you – "The Rocker"! It's huge!'

So Chris suggested 'The Rocker' to Decca, but they said they'd never get it on the radio. I said to Chris, 'Look, stop looking for a hit single – use this track to tell people that the new album is a really good record and get on the road and gig the band into the ground. That's the way to break a band like Thin Lizzy. If you rely on the hit single syndrome all the time you really are putting all your eggs in one basket'.

"I think at this juncture Chris had had enough of me pontificating from the sidelines, so to speak, and in the end he said to me, 'Why don't you come and work with us? You can be your own agent, but why not work with Lizzy and get the whole 10 per cent. If the band get big you'll make more money than the salary you'd earn working for an agency.'

"I was only 22 at the time and I only had £400 in the bank, so I thought 'Why not?' It was the July of '73. I started on a Monday morning and booked 28 shows for the 31 days in August."

O'Donnell convinced the band that they should offer themselves to the right clubs at £100 a night, about a third of the usual price, against a percentage. The goal was to knock on the door of all the fashionable gigs in the country – Mother's in Birmingham, Quaintways in Chester, the Boat Club in Nottingham, the Winning Post in Twickenham, the Farx Club in Southgate and of course the Marquee in Soho – so that anyone opening the *Melody Maker* on the gig page couldn't fail to spot the name Thin Lizzy week after week.

"It was a question of me convincing promoters that Thin Lizzy weren't just about 'Whiskey In The Jar'," adds O'Donnell. "I'd even agree sometimes to just take expenses to do the gig, because although it would mean we wouldn't make any money, it would ensure that people were opening the *Melody Maker* and seeing Thin Lizzy playing Friday, Saturday and Sunday at three of the main clubs in London. It gave the impression that the band were really happening, and gave me the chance to go to other promoters and say, 'Look, Thin Lizzy are everywhere – you'd be a mug not to book the band!' "

Thin Lizzy's next release was the album *Vagabonds Of The Western World* in September 1973, and luckily it was a cracker. Anxious to avoid the predicament which had led to *Shades Of A Blue Orphanage* being rushed, the band allowed themselves more time to prepare their third album, and even insisted on the luxury of a decent amount of mixing time.

"We did the record at Tollington Park," Downey explains, "and I think we were all chuffed with the result. As far as I was concerned some tracks were spoiled by the mix – the cymbals were a bit 'splashy' and so on – but the quality of Philip's songwriting and the aggression in our playing made it a good album for me. I think 'The Rocker' just about sums up what Thin Lizzy was all about at that time."

The title track was another pretty good benchmark for the band at this time too. Once again the Irish influence rose to the surface like the head on a pint of Guinness, and the twin thrust of Bell's guitar and Lynott's bass pointed the band towards a harder-edged and more aggressive future. The double-tracked guitar playing on 'Little Girl In Bloom' was also an early glimpse at the harmony-lead style that the band would adopt upon expanding to a quartet.

'Mama Nature Said', inspired by an article Dennis had read in a newspaper, was a freewheeling r&b romp with an environmentalist message which pre-empted by several years the trend towards 'green' politics in music. 'The Rocker' didn't pull any punches either, but portrayed the author in more of a hellraiser mode, just as he liked it sometimes. And then completing the triad of Lynott's most common poetic styles, 'The Hero And The Madman' reflected the romanticism inherent in his rich imagination.

The latter track also featured a narrative by Kid Jensen, whose escalating euphoria over Lizzy continued to assure the band of precious airplay. He remembers Lynott's invitation to appear on the album well.

"I'll never forget what a tough taskmaster Philip was," he vows. "On the one hand he had this rebellious nature, and he loved to play the part of the rough, leather-clad biker. But on the other hand when it came to studio work he was thoroughly professional and knew exactly what he wanted to achieve. He would insist on take after take after take, until he was 100 per cent satisfied with what he was getting. It was fascinating watching him work, and of course the *Vagabonds* . . . album as a whole was another triumph for Thin Lizzy."

The record also marked the dawn of a new era for Lizzy in that it was the first product to feature the artwork of Jim Fitzpatrick, whose stunning images would adorn the band's record sleeves and merchandise for years to come. Lynott was a big fan of Fitzpatrick's work and always claimed that he was an old schoolfriend of his. But this was not true. In fact, the two met in a pub.

"I was in Neery's one day with the poet Peter Fallon, for whom I'd done a couple of book covers, and Eamonn Carr from Horslips," explains Fitzpatrick, "and we were all having a great time. We were talking about this magazine we had called Capella, which David Bowie, Marc Bolan and John Lennon used to contribute to, and which I used to design the covers for. Then all of a sudden Philip came over and told me how much he liked this surrealistic drawing I'd done for one particular issue. He asked me if I'd like to do something for Lizzy, and there was something about him which made it impossible for me to refuse.

"Of course, I'd seen Philip around Dublin before. I'd always noted his charisma, his presence, and I found him an exciting person to be with. I was always into Celtic mythology, and as one of the five races which make up the Celtic race is a black North African race, the idea of this black Irishman floating around intrigued me immensely.

"So I did this piece for the *Vagabonds* . . . album, and then designed the Thin Lizzy logo for the single 'The Rocker'. I used it in the context of Philip on a motorbike. I was very influenced by Judge Dread and 2000 AD – as was Philip – so that's how that came about. Philip was very pleased with what I'd come up with, and from then on whenever Lizzy were working on a new album he'd give me a call."

'The Rocker', released in November '73, was the first Lizzy single to be culled from an album. Neither 'The Farmer' nor its B-side 'I Need You' made the first album; none of the tracks on the 'New Day' EP were considered for inclusion on the second album; 'Whiskey In The Jar' and its B-side, the excellent and occasionally Zeppelinesque 'Black Boys On The Corner', were strangely omitted from the third LP; and both 'Randolph's Tango' and its flipside 'Broken Dreams' were also overlooked by *Vagabonds.* . . . In keeping with the tradition of using unreleased tracks, the B-side of 'The Rocker' featured a song called 'Here I Go Again', a tale of the long, lonesome road that stretched before the homesick band and their loyal three-man crew (Pete Eustace, Frank Murray and Charlie MacPherson). But it was felt 'The Rocker' had so much potential as a single that the band would have to change their policy of selection.

When 'The Rocker' failed miserably to make the UK charts Lizzy's management began to wobble. Fortunately, however, Chris O'Donnell had lined up a fairly extensive UK tour to take the band through October and keep the wolves from the door, and there was also an Irish tour lined up for December, a guaranteed and much needed money spinner to finish the year on a high note.

The tour didn't quite go to plan for Brian Downey though. The varnish on some new drumsticks irritated the skin on his left hand, and he developed a huge blister on his middle finger, which eventually burst and went septic. He was admitted to a hospital for treatment in Tottenham, North London, but still couldn't play with his left hand for a while, so for several weeks on the tour Lizzy played with two drummers – Downey keeping the beat with his right hand, and Pearse Kelly on loan from Gary Moore's band doing all the fills.

"It was like the fucking Glitter Band," Downey laughs, "really silly."

The tour finally crossed the Irish Sea, and worked its way north to a climax in Belfast on New Year's Eve. It was supposed to be the crowning glory of a hardworking year for Thin Lizzy, but it ended with the band limping along as a duo in the most embarrassing of circumstances. Enter 1974, exit Eric Bell.

"One of the reasons I left the showband scene was that the playing was too disciplined," Bell explains. "I loved playing with Thin Lizzy around the time of the first album because there was so much more freedom in the music; a lot of the stuff we did was free-form jamming, and I could play whatever came off the top of my head, which was how I liked it. It was a healthy group, and lots of fun.

"Then 'Whiskey In The Jar' became a hit and all these

people came out of the woodwork and started being friendly to us; people who wouldn't give us the time of day before were suddenly calling us by our first names. It made me sick.

"Suddenly, the group wasn't ours anymore. There were six or seven groups of people discussing us behind our backs – deciding what we should wear, what we shouldn't wear, what we should say, what we shouldn't say, what we should play, what we shouldn't play – and for me it was like being in a showband again. I just freaked. Plus, my health wasn't what it should've been because I was drinking too much, doing too many drugs, not eating properly and not sleeping properly, and at the end of the day it began to take its toll on me.

"The whole thing came to a head when we reached Belfast. As it was my home town I decided to visit my family on the afternoon of the show, but when I got to my uncle's house there was no one at home. Anyway, our next-door neighbour, this lovely old lady of about 70, heard me knocking and suggested I went in next door to wait for them to come back. She got a bottle of wine out and we both had a little drink, and then before I know it she'd got the whiskey out as well. Then my auntie turned up and more drinks flowed, until I ended up quite pissed.

"I eventually managed to get out of the house and got a taxi to the Queens University where we were playing. But when I got there I found the dressing room empty – except for this massive table laden with food and booze, which had been laid on by the promoter. I just couldn't resist tucking into a few more drinks, could I?

"Finally the others arrived, so I nipped out into the bar for another drink and bumped into all sorts of people I knew. It was like, 'Hey Eric, what ya drinking?' I ended up completely wasted by the time we went on.

"So I staggered on stage and I might just as well have been in Toytown. I remember looking at the front row and seeing all my cousins, Philip's girlfriend's parents, everyone I knew. I realised I'd blown it. It was all I could do to go through the motions.

"Then I started hallucinating. I looked over and saw a crowd of people standing on my side of the stage, about ten feet away from me. I looked away, then looked back, and they were gone. I was losing my mind and I couldn't handle it, so I threw my guitar in the air, kicked my two 4x12 cabinets off the stage and walked off, collapsing just as I got to the side of the stage.

"It all went extremely hazy, but I remember being shaken awake by one of our roadies, who was frantically trying to get me to go back on. I could hear Philip and Brian thumping away in the background, trying to carry the song, and this roadie was going, 'If you don't go back on I'll break your fucking neck!'

"Eventually I told this guy that I'd go back on if he got me three bottles of Guinness, so off he went. While he was gone these two young kids came over to me and said, 'Amazing show, Eric!' They thought it was all part of the act! They had this bottle of lemonade and offered me a swig, and I gulped down about a pint before I realised it was full of whiskey, which they'd smuggled into the gig in a lemonade bottle. I puked up everywhere.

"Finally this roadie returned with the Guinness and I got pushed back on stage, with a guitar which was way out of tune. God knows how we finished the gig, but we must've sounded awful.

"After the show all these people came backstage for a reception, and I made a fool of myself again, swearing at everyone and falling all over the place. I remember my cousin saying to me, 'I don't ever want to speak to you again, you're a disgrace to the family!'

"In the end someone bundled me in a cab and sent me home. Luckily my uncle was in bed, otherwise he would've killed me. All I can remember is sitting in front of this big coal fire for about two hours, just staring at the flames. I'd lost my mind.

"The next day I went into town, to the hotel where Philip and Brian were staying, and I found everyone in the lobby, getting ready to leave for Dublin, where we had a show that night. No-one was speaking to me. I didn't really know what to do, but then one of the roadies came over and said, 'I think you'd better call Chris Morrison.'

"So I called Morrison and got an almighty bollocking. I just said, 'Chris, I'm resigning.' He replied with, 'OK, I'll just phone Gary Moore and get him to finish the tour if that's how you feel.' So I just said, 'Fine, you do that. I'm exhausted. I'm finished. I can't go on.'

"Not surprisingly, Philip was furious with me and we didn't speak for ages. I didn't blame him. But I really couldn't help it. I was ill. I just had to get away from the whole scene, or I might have ended up as another casualty. It was Thin Lizzy or me, and I chose me."

Chapter III

The Rise Of The Emerald

Over in London Gary Moore had heard about the problems Lizzy were having with Eric Bell, so when Chris Morrison knocked on the door of his flat in Cricklewood one morning he knew exactly what was coming.

"I just said, 'OK, what time's the flight?' " Moore laughs at the memory of Morrison's shocked expression. "I had a feeling Eric would do something crazy, and it didn't surprise me that Philip would think of me as a stand-in. He liked to stick with people he knew.

"So I flew over to Dublin the next day, had about four or five hours rehearsal with them, and did the gig that night. They had a few more shows in Ireland after that during the January, and it worked out really well, it was a great laugh.

"For me, joining Thin Lizzy was just like one big holiday after all the shit I'd been through with my solo career. I hadn't had a drink for about two years as I'd had to really pull myself together in order to deal with all the responsibility I had. I was virtually managing myself at the time, and I was only 19 or something, so things were really getting on top of me. But with Lizzy I could go right off the rails, get pissed every night and just go wild. All I had to do was play guitar for two hours or so on stage. Easy."

"Gary was like a Chinese firecracker when he joined Thin Lizzy," Peter Eustace reflects. "You wouldn't want to rely on Gary for anything – he was very gifted, but very mercurial and very unpredictable. In a way that was good for Philip after the almost boring predictability of Eric Bell, but at the same time things began to get a little dangerous with Gary around. Carrying him out of clubs in the early hours of the morning was par for the course."

"Gary really was in a bad way with drink and pills," Frank Murray agrees. "We'd carry him from the dressing room to the car, lay him across the back seat, drive him home and literally dump him on his doorstep. We'd ring the doorbell until the lights went on upstairs, and then leave him there. I don't think he sobered up all the time he was with the band."

With their Irish commitments complete (including a show in Belfast on January 12 which would be the band's last in that city for four years), Lizzy returned to the UK to kick off a new tour at the Central London Polytechnic in New Cavendish Street, on February 1. The next night it was Manchester University, followed on the 5th by an appearance at the Marquee Club in Soho's Wardour Street, which was partly filmed by a Thames TV crew for the current affairs programme *Today*, which was compiling a report on 'Deafness And The Decibel' (remember the 'Lynott Goes Deaf!' scam?).

On February 7 the band travelled to Liverpool to perform at the famous Cavern Club, spiritual home of The Beatles, and then it was a flying visit to the Aberdeen and Glasgow Universities north of the border, before another batch of shows in England and Wales: Barbarella's in Birmingham, Boob's in Merthyr Tydfil, the Northwich Memorial Hall in Cheshire, the Red Lion in Leytonstone, East London, and the Kings Lynn Corn Exchange in Norfolk.

"Our set for those shows was mainly stuff from the first three albums," says Moore. "We'd usually open with 'Things Ain't Working Out Down On The Farm', then go into 'Little Darling', followed by something like 'Showdown' or 'Black Boys On The Corner'. We also did 'Hard Drivin' Man' by the J. Geils Band, and I sang a couple of songs myself – a thing called 'Crawling', and another tune called 'I Love Everything About You'.

"The highlight of my whole time with Lizzy that year was the gig we did at the Roundhouse. It was such an important gig for us, and even though we did it on a Sunday afternoon, I remember thinking that we'd finally made it."

It was on February 17 that Lizzy played the famous Roundhouse in London's Chalk Farm, lining up alongside Kokomo and The Heavy Metal Kids. The idea once again came from Chris O'Donnell.

"They used to have this thing at the Roundhouse called The Implosion," he recalls, "where for ten shillings you could get into the gig and stay from 2–10pm, and see loads of bands playing. It was *the* place to hang out on a Sunday in London. So I suggested we put together the Heavy Metal Kids, Thin Lizzy and Kokomo and charged a pound to get in. It was a good bill, and Lizzy really rose to the occasion. We did the gig on the Sunday and on the Monday morning the phone didn't stop ringing."

Bookings came flooding in, and the band managed to gig regularly throughout March and April. They also took time out to record two new songs at Decca's Tollington Park studios – 'Little Darlin'' (released as a single in April), and 'Sitamoia' (which eventually cropped up on the *Remembering – Part One* compilation album) – and even began work on three tracks for the scheduled fourth album: 'Showdown', 'It's Only Money' and 'Still In Love With You'.

"'Still In Love With You' was originally recorded at Saturn Sound Studios in Worthing, West Sussex, where the engineer Tony Platt used to work," explains Moore. "I actually wrote part of the song too, but I never got credited for it as usual!

"What happened was, Phil and I had the same chord sequence. My song was called 'I'll Help You See It Through' and his was called 'Still In Love With You'. We simply put the two songs together, but then after I left the band Phil decided he'd written all of it. I'm not moaning about it, that's just the way it was. You leave the band, I'll take your song. Sorry mate! It didn't seem to matter though – the stakes weren't so high in those days."

By April Moore had burnt himself out in Thin Lizzy. Four months of hangovers had finally got the better of him. Plus, according to Chris O'Donnell, a bit of jealousy between him and Philip had begun to creep in, with each of them insisting on a greater share of the spotlight. Naturally, Moore saw it differently.

"I was getting all the attention, being the new guy in the band and being the kind of extrovert I was on stage in those days. I was going wild and getting all the good reviews, and that's probably where all the trouble started.

"Ultimately, I left Thin Lizzy because I realised I was killing myself. I remember thinking: 'This is great fun, but there's got to be more to playing music than getting wasted every night.' I was out of control and I needed to install some discipline into my life and my music. That's why I ended up working with Jon Hiseman in Colosseum II."

Lizzy were a duo once again, but with a batch of German dates set to commence on May 15 at Mausefhalle in Stuttgart, they simply couldn't afford to remain so for long. Lynott put the word around at clubs like the Speakeasy that Lizzy needed a new guitarist, and the management crossed all available digits.

"We knew we'd have to postpone the German dates at least," Ted Carroll recalls, "but we didn't want to break the news to this German promoter in case he held on to his deposit. In the end we were so desperate to get the deposit (around £1,000–1,500) that Chris O'Donnell flew to Hamburg, met this guy Klaus at the airport, picked up the money and flew straight back to London. And all the time we knew we didn't even have a band!

"Eventually O'Donnell had to pluck up the courage to ring Klaus and tell him we'd have to put the tour back. He gave him some cock and bull story, and everything was rescheduled. Then fortunately shortly afterwards we picked up two new guitarists – ex-Bullet and Atomic Rooster guitarist John Cann (a.k.a. Johnny Du Cann), and a German player called Andy Gee, who'd been gigging with the Steve Ellis Band – and we made the tour after all."

"We had about two days to rehearse," Downey remembers, "and to give them their due both guys did well to pick up the songs so quickly. But when we got to Germany Phil and John just didn't hit it off. Andy was great, but John changed into a different person on the road, and Phil soon got fed up with him."

"I think he had a bit of a hang-up about being Ritchie Blackmore," opines Frank Murray, "and to make matters worse he looked a little like him as well. He also had an ego to match, and so when he joined Lizzy he expected to be treated like a superstar. At the first gig in Germany he got out of the car and left his case on the pavement, expecting someone else to carry it for him. I said to him, 'Look pal, in this band you carry your own fucking case!' I think it went downhill from there."

"So not only was there a problem with John," Downey continues, "but the clubs we'd been booked into were really strange, and the guest houses we were staying in were dumps. In the end I said to Phil, 'This is mad, we've gone back to square one!' So I jacked it in and went back to England. I was out of the band for about six weeks and even started looking around for a new band."

"That German tour was a classic case of picking up musicians just because they were around," curses O'Donnell. "Really we shouldn't have done that German tour, but we had to pay the rent. It turned out to be the lowest ebb for the group.

"After Brian had left Chris Morrison was very depressed. One day he said to me, 'Come on, let's forget about Lizzy and go and find ourselves another group to manage.' So I thought about it, seriously. Then I looked at the dates I'd booked for Lizzy and wondered if there was anything I could do to salvage the situation before it all collapsed completely. I ended up ringing up Phil and telling him he was a fool to let Thin Lizzy slip through his fingers like that."

Lynott thought about all the work he'd put into getting the band where they were, with three albums under their belts, and confessed that he didn't want to throw it all away just yet. He would continue with Lizzy, he said, but only if Brian Downey came back.

"The next thing I know," says Downey, "Morrison's knocking on my door offering me an extra £50 a week to rejoin the band. That was a lot of money in those days . . ."

"Brian didn't even own his kit at the time," Ted Carroll adds, "so he really did need the money. We'd made an approach to Bob C. Benberg from Supertramp, in case Brian refused to rejoin, but as soon as he got wind of the fact that there might be more money in it, he was back in the band."

The next problem was finding the right guitar player (again). It was a task that neither Lynott or Downey relished, and in fact Philip's moods swung from one extreme to the other during the long search; one day he'd be as keen as mustard, the next day he'd be ready to throw in the towel. But good news filtered back from America, where *Vagabonds* . . . was hovering just outside the Top 100 album chart, a real boost which renewed Lynott's faith in Thin Lizzy. And then, like a spark to the touch paper, along came 'Robbo'.

Brian Robertson was the kind of TNT-tempered nutter you might encounter staggering along Sauchiehall Street on any Saturday night, attempting the second verse of 'Bonnie Scotland' through kidney-crushing slugs of Johnny Walker's. Except this particular teenage tearaway had a talent for the guitar which was to whisk him from the tough streets of Glasgow to seek his fame in London.

Robertson had gravitated towards the guitar after spending eight years learning to play classical piano. His first band was Rue Morgue, which he formed with his brother Glen in 1969 at the age of 13, although over the following four years he was to flit in and out of numerous other bands on the Glasgow scene, including Heidi and Dream Police, the latter of which evolved into The Average White Band.

Fortunately for Robertson, an old friend from Eastwood High School in Glasgow known as Charlie McLennan had moved to London some years previously, and was earning his keep humping gear for Thin Lizzy. When Lizzy started auditioning for a new guitar player 'Big' Charlie had no hesitation in forwarding the name of his friend, and on a brief trip back to Glasgow managed to persuade Robertson to go to London and give it a shot.

"I left Glasgow with £25 quid, my guitar and a pair of drumsticks," he recalls, "because I also fancied myself as a bit of a drummer at the time too, so I thought I'd bring them just in case. When I got to London though I sat around for about three weeks, because at that point I don't think Phil wanted to continue the band. So while I was waiting I auditioned for a band called Slack Alice as a drummer, and I got the gig. They thought I was joking when I told them later that I couldn't join because I was playing guitar for Thin Lizzy."

Robertson's audition was held at African drummer Ginger Johnson's Iroquo Country Club in Hampstead, just behind

Belsize Park tube station on Haverstock Hill. It was June 1974 and 'Robbo' was 17.

"I walked in and the band were playing with Andy Gee and another Irish guy on guitar," says Robertson, "so I had to sit there and watch them for a while. I thought both guitarists were a bit lame, so I didn't see it being a problem for me to impress Phil and Brian.

"Eventually we got together and played some blues stuff, as well as a few things I knew off the *Vagabonds* . . . album, and that was it. I got the job there and then."

"I'm glad we got Robbo in," Brian Downey confesses, "because before he came along we were almost agreed on asking this other Scottish guy called Cosmo Vinyl to join! How we would've got on with someone called Cosmo Vinyl in the band, I don't know.

"Robbo was the right man for the job though. Actually, I'd met him before he came to the audition, although I don't think he'd thank me for reminding him. When we were in Glasgow on the Gary Moore tour he came up to my hotel room with his guitar and his girlfriend, and he started playing all these Thin Lizzy tunes to me. He was only a kid at the time, and I thought it was very funny. When he turned up for the audition in London I couldn't believe it."

Originally the line-up was to remain three-strong, but within a few rehearsals it was decided that a second guitar player might give the band the extra edge it had been missing. Word was leaked that Lizzy were looking for another lead guitarist, and the news reached a Californian called William Scott Gorham who was kicking his heels on the London pub circuit, looking for a way out.

"I originally came to England with the hope of getting an audition with Supertramp," says Gorham, "because my brother-in-law, Bob C. Benberg, was the drummer. Roger Hodgson didn't know if he wanted to play guitar or keyboards in the band, so Bob tipped me off that there might be a vacancy for a guitarist. But by the time I finally got to England Hodgson had decided he was going to play both, so that idea went straight out of the window.

"I was really pissed off because it took me months to work up enough money for my ticket. I was working at a place called ABC Records in Glendale, stacking records in the warehouse, and I would steal as many records as I could and sell them, just to get enough cash to get on that plane.

"So with the Supertramp thing not happening, I ended up putting a band together called Fast Buck, and we managed to get a lot of pub gigs, mainly in the East End of London. One night Bob came along to the show and brought with him a saxophonist called Ruan O'Lochlaun, who he'd played with in a band called Bees Make Honey. This guy told me he liked my playing and he hoped I didn't mind but he'd put my name forward for a group called Thin Lizzy. I said, 'Are you *sure*?' I thought it was the stupidest name I'd ever heard for a rock group.

"I'd never heard anything by Thin Lizzy in those days, not even 'Whiskey In The Jar', which was good because when I did get to hear it later I never liked it. It meant I could go to the audition without any preconceptions."

Lizzy were still at the Country Club at this time, contemplating asking keyboard player Jan Schellhaus (formerly with the Gary Moore Band) to join them. They were also ploughing through the endless procession of half-witted hopefuls in search of a player who could play 'off' Brian Robertson, rather than against him. They'd audition people all day and then return to Philip's flat in West Hampstead in the evening to listen to the recordings they'd made. It was a bit of a grind, and on the surface things didn't look any more promising on the night Scott Gorham walked in.

"It was a real depressing scenario," Gorham winces. "It was pissing down with rain, I spent ages looking for this place, and when I finally found it I stumbled in and it was all dark, with these weird African drawings all around the walls. The first guy I saw was Phil, sitting on this stool. Brian was fiddling with his drums, and Robbo was standing around the edge of the stage. They all looked totally pissed off, because I guess they'd been through 25 guitarists already and they still couldn't find the right guy.

"So I turn up and it was like, 'Oh, here's yet another guy, and oh dear he's American, and he's wearing a big check lumberjack jacket and bad-fitting jeans . . . oh, and he's got a Japanese Les Paul copy . . . great!' I guess I didn't amaze them with my appearance. In fact, they weren't very friendly towards me at all. Before I played a note I thought to myself, 'Jesus, what am I getting myself into here?'

"So Phil put on his bass and said we'd do 'The Rocker'. He told me the basic chords and he'd nod at me during the song to take solos, and it went OK. But at the end no-one said a word. All Phil did was jump off the stage and disappear into this little room. Then five minutes later he'd come out, jump back on stage, run through another song, then jump off stage and disappear into this little room again. This went on for about five or six songs, and I was thinking, 'Is this guy some sort of dick, or what?'

"So at the end of the audition I'm packing my guitar away thinking, 'Well, that was a pile of shit!', when Phil came over and gave me his phone number on this tiny scrap of paper. Then later he called me and said, 'We've just been listening to the tapes and we'd like you to join.' I was like, 'Tapes? What tapes?' Of course, they'd recorded everything, and that's why he kept disappearing into that little room, to check the tapes.

"I must admit I thought the whole vibe about Phil and Lizzy was strange at first, but then all I really knew was that I was making £12 a week at the time and they were offering me £30. It sounded OK to me. Then I got to play with the band properly, away from an audition situation, and I couldn't believe how good they were. I enjoyed it so much the money wasn't my prime interest anymore."

With Robertson and Gorham fully ensconced, Lizzy rehearsed intensively for two weeks – 12 hours a day, no slacking – before heading out on the road to work up some of the material Philip had written for their new album. The dates, which included a short Irish tour beginning on July 18 and including a 'homecoming' at Zero's club in Dublin on July 25, were all very low-key affairs. But both of the new guitarists remember their live début with Thin Lizzy well.

"It was at the Lafayette Club in Wolverhampton," Robbo states with mock pride, "a place so small it made those old red telephone boxes seem spacious."

"If you counted the bouncers there was probably about eight people in that night," says Gorham. "All the same, I was pretty nervous because I didn't really know what was expected of me. Then Brian Downey counted us in – 'One-two-three-four-BOOM!' – and all of a sudden Phil and Robbo were jumping all over the place. I was nonchalantly standing there by my amps going, *'Wha-at?'*

"The next thing I knew Phil grabbed me and pushed me to the front of the stage. I figured, 'Well, I guess I've gotta jump around too, huh?' Phil said to me, 'You're not just a guitar player now, you're a performer,' and from then on I had to learn to 'perform' every night. One of the most important things Phil taught me was not to be embarrassed about performing, otherwise I probably would've always been a cardboard cut-out guitar player."

To complete the picture of this most transitional of periods for Thin Lizzy, Ted Carroll decided to relinquish his involvement in the management of the band (he ended up selling his 15 per cent share in the Pippin The Friendly Ranger publishing company for £500!). He wanted to spend more time developing his Rock On business, and would later achieve success with Chiswick Records (who signed Motorhead in 1977) and Ace Records, who continue to do a roaring trade with re-issues. Into his shoes as co-manager stepped the entrepreneurial Chris O'Donnell, who became the artistic driving force which complimented Chris Morrison's cautious business brain.

"I'd told the two Chrises that as soon as we'd cleared a few debts I wanted to leave," Carroll explains. "I figured there was always going to be problems between Phil and lead guitarists by the simple nature of the personalities involved. It was Phil's band and he was the dominant character, but while his songwriting was great and he was a good singer, he wasn't technically as good a musician as the kind of guitarists the band were using. I felt this was always going to cause friction, and I wished the two Chrises good luck in dealing with it."

By this time the band's deal with Decca was up for renewal, although there wasn't an overwhelming desire from the management to re-sign. As Ted Carroll says: "Decca were OK with Tom Jones and Englebert Humperdinck, but they weren't aggressive enough for a band like Thin Lizzy."

The management started touting around the demos the band had recorded with Gary Moore, but they got turned down by Island, RCA and a host of others. For a while it looked as if they would have to re-sign to Decca, an option they'd been relying on as a last resort, but then came a real body blow.

"One day we received this registered letter from Decca," explains Carroll. "Chris Morrison opened it and turned white. Decca said they were withdrawing their offer of a deal – and bang went our £10,000 advance. I think we had a £7,000 overdraft at the time, so this was a bit of a setback.

"Anyway, Saturday came and I was working on my record stall in the Portobello Road when I bumped into Nigel Grange, who was in charge of re-issues at Phonogram. Now we hadn't approached Phonogram because we'd been turned down by Wayne Bickerton who was head of A&R at PolyGram, and we figured it was the same company. So Nigel and I were chatting when he suddenly said, 'Oh, and I've just been made head of A&R at Phonogram, so if you know of any decent bands let me know.' Of course, I replied, 'Er, well since you mentioned it, Nigel . . .!'

"I told him all about Lizzy, and I stressed that I wasn't simply being biased, because I was going to leave the management very shortly anyway. So he suggested I called him on Monday and I did . . . although I left it until after lunch so as not to appear too keen."

"He invited us to his office," O'Donnell continues, "and we took along our new demos, which seemed to go down well. Nigel just loved Gary's solo on 'Still In Love With You'. He turned to me and Chris and said, 'This is a 17-year-old kid from Glasgow?' I could see Chris's mouth open as he was about to say, 'Oh no, that's Gary Moore on the tape', and I gave him a kick under the table. Just in the nick of time I managed to say, 'Yes, isn't he brilliant? He's only 17 and he can only get better.'

"Chris looked at me in amazement, and we had a furious row when we got outside. But I said, 'Chris, I don't care, I'll do anything to get a deal', and that was it. We signed."

"By the time we left Decca our debt was £20,000," reveals

Morrison, "and it took us a while to secure a deal whereby we could pay off that. The deal with Phonogram was a special one, because we got the money for two albums up front, instead of one. That enabled me to pay off our debt, and leave just about enough to record a cheap album. It may have looked good, being on a major label, but everything was done on a shoestring."

"Phonogram gave us £30,000," adds O'Donnell, "but that was to clear our debts, make a record, buy some equipment, buy a van and get on the road. It soon went."

The first fruit of Lizzy's relationship with Phonogram was the single 'Philomena' (recorded on Lynott's birthday and backed by 'Sha-La-La'), which was released through the new Vertigo subsidiary label in October 1974, preceding the album *Night Life* by a month. The album itself was produced by Ron Nevison, whose work on the first Bad Company album and The Who's *Quadrophenia* had greatly impressed Philip, but few within the Lizzy camp were happy with the way the album turned out.

"We chose Nevison because of the big guitar sounds he got on his records," says O'Donnell, "but I think he just wanted to experiment with Lizzy, and he ended up sweetening the whole record. His mix was horrible."

The problems with Nevison surfaced long before the final mix, however. The band initially returned to Worthing to do some overdubs on Lynott's master ballad 'Still In Love With You' (although Robbo refused to re-record Gary Moore's solo "because it was perfect as it was"), and then they spent some time at Trident Studios in Soho, before moving to Olympic Studios in Barnes. At several junctures along the way the producer came close to sampling the famous Sauchiehall Street handshake.

"*Night Life* was the first album Scott and I had ever played on, and it wasn't the best experience of my life," Robbo sneers. "I had wars with Ron Nevison – he was such a dickhead in those days! I remember setting all my Marshalls up in the studio and he said, 'No, you can't play that loud' – and he had me playing through a Fender twin-reverb and a 'pig nose' (a tiny practise amp about a foot high)!

"We had murders on the track 'Night Life' itself. I ended up marching into the control room, plugging a Strat straight into the desk and doing the solo first take. I told him, 'Fuck off, this is the way I'm doing it', and fortunately most of the boys liked the solo, so we kept it.

"Then we came to do the track 'She Knows' (Gorham's first songwriting venture in Lizzy) and the arguments got even worse. Scott and I went to the pub opposite Olympic Studios for a few beers, and when we came back Nevison claimed we were drunk. We were supposed to be doing some backing vocals that afternoon, but Nevison was so annoyed that we'd gone for a drink that he kept moaning about it. In the end I said to him, 'You do the fucking vocals then!', and just to be awkward he decided he would.

"Anyway, when we came to play back what Nevison had recorded we realised that his singing was well out of tune. He obviously realised it as well, but rather than admit it he simply mixed his vocals down, so nobody could hear them. I thought it was hilarious, so when we came to the final mix I slipped one of the faders back up without him noticing it, and we cut the record with Nevison's out of tune vocal in all its glory. I still laugh when I listen to the record today."

Robbo admits that the overall production on *Night Life* was "pretty naff", although Gorham tends to stretch even further with his criticisms of Nevison's contribution. "I thought the record was so ridiculously tame it was unbelievable," he gasps. "I listened to the finished mixes and said, 'Hey, are we a rock band or a cocktail band?'

"To be honest though, it wasn't totally down to production. We just didn't know what kind of band we wanted to be at that point, so we'd have a hard rock song here, and then right next to it there'd be a real syrupy song. It confused the hell out of everybody."

The album swerved erratically between the oozing balladry of 'Dear Heart' and the harder, heavier 'It's Only Money', one of the few tracks which hinted at the band's future direction. 'Sha-La-La' was another, an explosive showcase for Downey's drumming which wouldn't have sounded out of place on an album like *Bad Reputation* several years down the line. But while other inclusions such as 'She Knows' and 'Night Life' were pleasant enough tunes, they were far too mellow to have a healthy life expectancy in Lizzy's live set.

Indeed, parts of *Night Life* were quite soulful, with string arrangements from Jimmy Horrowitz and keyboards from Jean Roussell softening the sound further. Tracks like 'Frankie Carroll' (a character invention based on Frank Murray and Ted Carroll) and the pretty pointless acoustic instrumental 'Banshee' were certainly wide of the mark, while the strings on the title track sounded almost sarcastic, as if the idea was a send-up of the early Seventies American radio rock sound. The girl backing singers and bongos on 'Showdown', meanwhile, made the band sound more like Santana.

Lyrically, 'Showdown' was an early glimpse at the strutting, streetwise Jack The Lad persona that would soon preoccupy Lynott. Here was Johnny Cool, a backstreet cowboy with an eye for the 'chicks' and a sneering contempt for any rival, nonchalantly prepared to use the gun that was tucked into his belt. The imagery, of leather and studs, of turned-up collars and slicked back hair, of hard liquor and smoke-filled hip joints, of sexy, sleazy women and tough sidewalk soldiers, was a blueprint for many future storylines. It was the Continuing Adventures Of The Rocker.

Yet as ever Lynott wasn't just the flick-knife renegade, he was also the tender lover and the devoted son. 'Still In Love With You', complete with Gary Moore's solo and vocals from Robbo's close friend Frankie Miller, was a heart-rending cry from deep within Lynott's soul, while the heavily Irish-flavoured 'Philomena' found the wild roving author paying a moving tribute to his mother: 'If you see my mother, please give her all my love/For she has a heart of gold there/As good as God above'.

Like Lynott's steadily improving lyricism, Thin Lizzy took a small step forward with *Night Life*, but it was still a cocktail long on glass but short on alcohol. There was a lot more to the band, and particularly to its creative spearhead, than the Robertson/Gorham début album suggested. It was as if Lizzy were in view, but out of focus.

Night Life came in another Jim Fitzpatrick sleeve featuring a sleek black cat prowling through a city at night ("No one seemed to get the reference to Phil," Chris O'Donnell complains) and according to the management sold 10,000 copies. It wasn't the most successful of projects commercially or artistically, but then the sheer amount of road work Lizzy were undertaking suggested that the band could only get better.

Indeed, Lizzy's live schedule hardly ever seemed less than punishing. Differentiating between one tour and the next became increasingly difficult, as an almost constant stream of commitments kept the band on their toes throughout the rest of the year. Financially, the band couldn't afford to stop working.

After a 'loosener' at the Marquee on August 23, Lizzy made their first high profile appearance with Scott and Robbo at the Reading Festival on Saturday 24th, lining up with such luminaries as Georgie Fame, Greenslade, G.T. Moore, Procol Harum, Sutherland Brothers and Trapeze. Then it was more motorway madness, bombing around the country in their beaten up transit throughout September, October and November. The advertised *Night Life* tour officially began at Keele University on November 6 and ran through to the Winning Post in Twickenham on December 1, taking in the delights of Derby Art College, Barking Polytechnic, Skipton Town Hall and a plethora of rock'n'roll Meccas along the way. But the band continued to gig until December 21, when they returned to the National Stadium in Dublin.

The pace barely slackened in 1975. In March Lizzy visited America for the first time, warming up with a few dates of their own before joining up with Bob Seger and Bachman-Turner Overdrive, who'd just had a huge hit with 'You Ain't Seen Nothing Yet'. It was an experience which many people agree left a huge impression on Philip.

"America hit Phil like a ton of shit," says Gorham. "He couldn't believe the place, especially New York, Los Angeles and Texas. He wrote a lot of songs about Texas, like 'Cowboy Song', 'Massacre' and so on. He found it totally inspiring. I think going to America changed his life."

"Phil certainly took to LA like a duck to water," adds O'Donnell. "On that first tour all he kept saying was, 'When do we get to LA? How long have we got in LA?' He'd read about all the legendary goings-on in LA, the famous hotels like the Hyatt and the Sunset Marquis, the landmarks, the whole rock'n'roll history of the place, and he was blown away when we finally got there. He realised then that he was just a little fish in a very big pond. This wasn't Dublin.

"Phil had read so much about LA that he seemed to know instinctively where everything was. We'd be walking down the street and he'd go, 'Oh yeah, and just down here is where Jim Morrison used to hang out' and so on. He got a lot of inspiration from the place too. One day he wanted to check out exactly what was at 77 Sunset Strip (the title of a US detective series from the Sixties), and we found a supper club called Dino's Bar & Grill. He ended up using that line in 'The Boys Are Back In Town' . . . well, it sounded better than 'down at Barney's Beanery . . .' "

Before Lizzy actually sampled the decadent delights of Los Angeles, however, there were a number of less glamorous warm-up dates to negotiate. Scott Gorham remembers them only too well. "I'll never forget our first ever show in America," he shudders. "We did two nights at this small club in Louisville, Kentucky, and the second night happened to be March 17 – which is not only St. Patrick's Day, but my birthday too. Let's just say March 17 was always a lot of fun for Thin Lizzy!

"Anyway, in America everything turns green on St. Patrick's Day. This club had green hamburgers, green hot dogs, green beer, green everything . . . and of course in the parking lot outside there was green spew all over the place!

"On that second night we completely lost our inhibitions. The first night was OK, but the second night was nuts. We suddenly thought, 'We don't know anyone out there, it won't matter if we go wild.' So we shredded the place. I even grabbed the mike and started screaming, and I've never done that in my life!"

Brian Robertson's recollections of Lizzy's first batch of concerts in America also remain fresh in his memory. Later on there were great shows with the likes of Aerosmith, UFO and AC/DC, but in the beginning not all the bills were so attractive. "I'll never forget our agent booking us to play this open-air campus gig, at a place just outside Chicago called Normal, Illinois. When we got there we found out it was a bloody folk festival, with Peter, Paul & Mary headlining! We just blasted the place to bits.

"Then later we were staying at this motel and we ran into these two Playboy Bunnies. One of them was called Star, because she had a star tattooed on her vagina. Nice girl. Anyway, I was trying to get into her knickers – while Brian Downey was watching a Muhammad Ali fight on the TV, incidentally – when all of a sudden she bit into my tongue and wouldn't let go. I ended up having to punch her in the face to stop her. There was blood everywhere. Then she bit a huge chunk of skin out of my forehead, so I threw her out of our room with no clothes on. I was terrified! For the rest of the tour I had to do all the photo sessions with my fringe pulled down to hide the scar.

"The upshot of it all was this chick tried to have me arrested for assault and rape. The sheriff came to the motel and was going to haul me in, but fortunately Chris O'Donnell managed to do some smooth-talking. He kept saying, 'My client was merely trying to get some rest when this woman wouldn't leave him alone! It's absolutely outrageous! The woman's virtually a hooker, and my client is a sensitive artist! Who do you think was in the wrong, officer?' To this day I honestly don't know how we got out of that one."

When Lizzy finally locked into the BTO tour they got something of a shock. No groupies. No wild parties. No nothing. "They were all Mormons," explains Brian Downey, "although we preferred to call them morons. You couldn't smoke or drink near them – not even in the room next door, because they thought the smoke was going to filter through the wall! We had a lot of fun with Bob Seger, and Phil and Bob became great friends, but we never had much communication with the BTO guys. They were weird."

"I just remember them having these huge three-course meals just before going on stage," adds Gorham, "and we couldn't believe it. But then they were a very professional band, and it gave us an indication of what was expected of us on a bigger stage. We went on that tour thinking that if we were supposed to be on at 8.00pm, we'd probably make it about 8.30pm. That attitude ended the first night when their manager had our manager up against the wall by the scruff of the neck threatening to throw us off the tour if we were ever late again. The next night we were on by 7.55pm!"

"I think that tour made a big difference to Philip," states Smiley Bolger. "He used to stand by the side of the stage every night, and what he saw inspired him to kick Robbo's arse, kick Scott's arse and kick the band's arse into shape. He wanted Lizzy to project more. He saw other bands putting more effort into their shows than Lizzy, and that drove him on harder."

Lizzy were certainly a tighter band by the time they returned to the UK for some headlining shows of their own in April (most significantly a sold out Hammersmith Odeon on the 5th), and then switched back to support band for Bachman-Turner Overdrive's short European stint during May. The tour took in Glasgow Apollo on May 1, Manchester Free Trade Hall on 2nd and two Hammersmith Odeons on 3rd and 4th, before heading for the Continent on the 5th.

"I think the BTO lads had mellowed slightly by this time," says Peter Eustace, "because I know that Fred Turner got into some heavy drinking sessions with Phil. But the younger of the Bachman brothers, Robbie, used to get locked in his dressing room each night after the show, so he couldn't stray from the good Mormon path. We thought it was hilarious."

By June 1 Lizzy were back out on their own in England, kicking off yet another stretch of shows at the Croydon Greyhound and then taking in Sunderland (6th), Dagenham (7th), Twickenham (8th), Cambridge (10th) and Coventry (15th) before a heralded return to London's Roundhouse on June 22nd (supported by Good Habit and Moon). Chris Morrison remembers this last show as yet another turning point in Lizzy's career.

"I stood in the Roundhouse that day and realised that whenever Philip's aggression came through the crowd went wild, yet whenever he trailed off into some of his more sentimental moments the audience didn't respond as well. After the show I had a long chat with Philip and I encouraged him to concentrate more on the macho side of his image, because I could see that's what the fans wanted from him. I'd like to think Philip took my advice, as the next album was called *Fighting.*"

"We'd had such a nightmare with Nevison on *Night Life* that we decided we'd produce *Fighting* ourselves," explains Robbo. "We went down to Olympic Studios in Barnes again, but as with the previous record we just somehow didn't get the balance right."

"We were still getting dragged down by the hit single syndrome," adds Downey. "We'd released 'Rosalie' (Philip's favourite Bob Seger song) in May, but it didn't go anywhere. So when we did the album people were going, 'We've gotta have another single.'

"Unfortunately, I think the material on both *Night Life* and *Fighting* simply went above the heads of the mass markets in Europe. There was too much light and shade on those albums, and a lot of the stuff was too subtle. We didn't have a strong identity as a hard rock band at that time, and so we were kind of caught in no man's land."

'Wild One' was the next choice for a 45 (released in October), a call for the return of all the talented and tormented souls, the so-called 'Wild Geese', who'd fled Ireland during the struggles for power in the history books. It never made the charts but it was another interesting example of how Lynott was collecting the threads of Irish history and weaving them through a tapestry of modern dimensions.

Allied to the development of Lynott's mostly moralistic Celtic themes, the twilight tales of desperate people in desperate situations continued to flow. The sordid tragedy of 'Suicide' reeked of dense downtown desolation, while 'Fighting My Way Back' was the hopeful yet unconvincing cry of a sad, sick victim of over-indulgence. An accepted trait of Lynott's lyricism was to always leave a certain amount of the interpretation up to the listener, but patterns and parallels were appearing in his songs.

Death was a frequently recurring theme in Lynott's lyrics. When, in 1979, a book of his poetry entitled *A Collected Works Of Philip Lynott* was published, almost one in five of the 63 songs included dealt with the grimmest of subjects, from the hanging of Jack McDuff in 'Freedom Song' and the underworld murderer in 'Killer Without A Cause', to the mercenary killer in 'Soldier Of Fortune' and the shameful slaughter of 'Massacre'. The trend continued into the Eighties, with 'Genocide' and 'Killer On The Loose' from *Chinatown*, and 'Angel Of Death' and 'Mexican Blood' from the *Renegade* album. It was a morbid fascination which would last right up until Lynott's own death.

Aside from the continuing emergence of Lynott's poetic prowess, *Fighting* made all the right noises yet somehow still failed to hold the right pitch. But it was definitely coming together, as was Lynott's romantic vision of Lizzy as a gang-like unit, a kind of Fantastic Four on the edge of the law. The playing card symbols allotted to each member of the band on *Fighting* were supposed to represent each individual's character, but the innocent fantasy of the idea said more about Lynott than any subtle symbols.

For the cover of *Fighting* someone had the bright idea of photographing the band on a London street armed with offensive and illegal weapons. Everything was going well until someone spotted an unruly gang of thugs fronted by a big black man with a shotgun, and dialled 999. "The next thing we knew we were surrounded by police cars," Robbo laughs. "They were terrified of the gun, and we had some fun trying to convince them that it was only a prop."

Another photo session for the *Fighting* album produced a controversial batch of shots featuring the band with bloody noses, but Vertigo rejected the idea of using them at the last minute. There was, however, a different cover for the American version of the album, an image Robbo describes as "... much prettier. In fact, I even shaved for that shot – something I refused to do for the UK cover. O'Donnell even went out and bought me a razor, but I wouldn't use it and I nearly got sacked over it."

Fighting was released in September and went on to sell around 20,000 copies, by O'Donnell's estimation. It was an improvement on *Night Life* but still not good enough for Phonogram, who began to question the wisdom of retaining the band.

"The Phonogram people never came to our shows," protests

O'Donnell, "so they couldn't see the band was getting better and better, and the audiences were getting bigger. I knew that given time the band would 'click' in the studio and the whole thing would take off. I used to have furious rows with the record company, trying to convince them that if we could only get the third album right, not only would it sell, but it would help sell the back catalogue as well. All it needed was the right song."

"It was frustrating because we'd never worked so hard in our lives," Downey insists, "and yet we weren't in the charts. In the weeks before *Fighting* came out we made a number of high profile appearances in Britain. We did the Cardiff Castle Festival with 10cc, Steeleye Span and Man (July 12) and got great reviews. We also did the Reading Festival (on Saturday August 23, on a bill topped by Yes and also featuring Supertramp, Ozark Mountain Daredevils, Alberto Y Los Trios Paranios, Alan Stivell, Kursaal Flyers, Snafu, String Driven Thing and Zzebra) and also got great reviews. We got some of our first front covers in the music press around that time, and everything was going right for us. Yet the record company just wanted a hit."

"The Cardiff Castle gig was a blast for us, even though it pissed down," says Robbo. "I'd fallen off stage a few days before and had a huge gash across my forehead, and the minute I walked on stage at Cardiff this gash opened up again. I remember playing a solo on my knees in a puddle at the front of the stage, with blood pouring down my face, and thinking, 'If this isn't playing the blues, I don't know what is!'

"Afterwards they had this medieval-style banquet for us, and we got wrecked as usual. The last thing I remember is staggering around the grounds of the castle with Eric Stewart from 10cc, and getting arrested. Just another typical Lizzy gig."

Lizzy's next major undertaking was the 'Rocktober' tour, which actually began on September 27 at Birmingham Town Hall. The bill also featured String Driven Thing and City Boy, and proved an extremely successful exercise, as former Phonogram Artist Relations Manager John Burnham confirms. "In the context of Lizzy's career it was about a minute before they burst through into the big time. They were bubbling just beneath the surface at the time, and it was so exciting to be a part of it. The rock cognoscenti had attached themselves to us, we were fast becoming hip, and there was this feeling in the air that the dam was about to break for us.

"The 'Rocktober' tour was great fun too. Phonogram had given me a new Ford Granada and I was simply told to follow the band around and keep them happy. That could mean anything, of course. But the main bone of contention seemed to be who travelled with me in the new Granada.

"The idea was this: whoever shouted 'Shotgun!' first got to sit in the front seat. Whoever shouted 'Backseat window!' next got the window, and whoever shouted 'Backseat window!' next got the other window. Whoever was last got to ride 'Crackgun' – the uncomfortable bit in the middle.

"Philip always insisted on travelling in the Granada with me, wherever we went. And of course, being the main man, he often got his own way. It meant we spent many hours together driving up and down the motorway, but he was always great company and full of cracking stories."

'Rocktober' continued in Bristol on September 29, visited Cardiff on 30th, and then hit Scotland for shows in Glasgow on October 2 and Edinburgh on the 4th. By the 8th it had encompassed Philip's second home, Manchester, and the occasion was marked by a chance meeting with Marc Bolan in the canteen at Granada TV studios, whereafter the two were taken on a tour of the Coronation Street set.

Newcastle followed on the 10th, Liverpool on the 11th and then London on the 12th, where the band broke with tradition by playing at the New Victoria Theatre. Lizzy then finished the year on an almighty high note, with a storming performance at the Great British Music Festival at Olympia in West London, on December 31. The event, spread over three days during the New Year period, ran from 3 o'clock to half-past midnight, and on Lizzy's day the bill also included Doctors Of Madness, Steve Gibbons, Climax Blues Band, Steve Marriott's All Stars and headliners Status Quo.

"Lizzy were only third on the bill but they really won the day," says Chris Morrison. "That festival went a long way towards showing people how hot Lizzy were, because our labelmates Quo were really happening at the time, and few people expected them to get blown off."

Next stop, new album. As 1976 kicked in Lizzy joined forces with producer John Alcock (noted for his work with John Entwistle), and locked themselves away at The Who's Ramport Studios in Battersea, South London. In between darts competitions with members of The Who's road crew, the new record began to take shape in a way which convinced all those at close quarters that it was going to be The One. It was titled *Jailbreak*.

"We'd matured into each other's way of playing," Robbo explains, "and it just became easier to work together. Personality-wise there was still a lot of friction and we'd all be fighting tooth and nail, especially Phil and I. In fact, I remember a huge row between me and Phil over who was going to play the keyboards on 'Running Back'; I wanted to play the blues on the piano, Phil wanted to get Tim Hinckley, which ended up costing us a fortune. But playing-wise we had begun to click in a big way, basically because of all the road-work we'd done over the previous two years."

"I suppose the most obvious improvement was the twin-guitar thing," adds Gorham, "which we fell into around the time of *Fighting*, but which didn't become a big deal until *Jailbreak*. Wishbone Ash had done that twin-guitar thing before us, but we took the idea and put it into a hard rock context, with more aggression. All of a sudden we were reading reviews which identified the harmony guitars as 'Lizzy's sound'."

"The material Phil was writing at this time was really top notch stuff as well," Robbo continues. "He was really on form, and the album was a huge step forward for us. Phil was an absolute genius at times. I mean, who could argue with a track like 'The Boys Are Back In Town'?"

The original version of the song which would change Lizzy's fortunes forever was actually called 'GI Joe's Back In Town', an idea Philip had got from the *GI Joe* comic strip. Ironically, while the title of the song was changed the track was the most popular song on American FM playlists when US troops returned home after the Gulf War of 1991. Chris O'Donnell considers the origins of arguably Lynott's most famous song: "He was trying to base it on the concept of somebody coming back from the Vietnam War, but he was finding it hard to pin the idea down. The band tried the song all sorts of ways, but it still wasn't working. They even got Brian playing along to a drum track, to try to get that big sound. In the end John Alcock suggested that melodic guitar lick (which was actually modelled on the brass riff from a Bruce Springsteen song called 'Kitty's Back'), and everything fell into place.

"All we needed then was a title, as the GI Joe thing didn't seem right. I was always on at Philip to use his identity as one of the lads – you know, the football crowd thing, the idea of being in a gang with the audience – and he responded to that. It was like a 'Boys Own' club. And that was it: 'The Boys Are Back In Town'."

Philip also explained at the time that some of the inspiration for the song came from a group of people he knew in Manchester called the QSG (Quality Street Gang), a far from 'sweet' bunch of characters if the legend that precedes them is anywhere near accurate. But by the end of the summer of '76 Philip was forced to concede in a radio interview that the song had become an anthem for many of the gangs which ran on the wrong side of the tracks, both in the UK and US.

The track was a godsend. At the time Nigel Grange at Phonogram was under enormous pressure to produce a hit single with Lizzy, and in desperation he'd even begun to consider the option of cover versions. One day he called Chris O'Donnell into his office and played him a song called 'Kicks' by Paul Revere & The Raiders, suggesting that it would make an ideal single for Lizzy.

"I told Nigel that I thought Phil would write better songs than that crap one day, and that's what I was working towards," O'Donnell recalls. "Nigel knew that Phil was going to get better and better, but he was just beginning to get flustered because of the need for a hit.

"Even when I took *Jailbreak* into Phonogram I was told there wasn't a single on it. They said the only song that could be a single was 'Romeo And The Lonely Girl', but only if someone could put a brass track on it and remix it.

"At this point I got on a plane and went to America. I got on to a guy called Mike Bone, who'd been instrumental in turning a lot of people onto *Fighting* in the States. I played *Jailbreak* to Mike and he loved it so much that it gave me a real boost. The upshot of it all was we took the band to America, released 'The Boys Are Back In Town' as a single, and went from earning $500 a night to $5,000 a night within three months, with a Top 20 song under our belts.

"Of course, after we'd had all that success Phonogram in the UK decided, in their infinite wisdom, that maybe they should release 'The Boys Are Back In Town' as a single as well . . ."

The single was released in the UK in April 1976 and went on to reach No.8 in the charts (No.1 in Ireland). The album *Jailbreak* surfaced the previous month and, thanks largely to the success of 'The Boys Are Back In Town', quickly notched up sales of 100,000, far in excess of anything the band had achieved to that date.

Jailbreak was more than just 'The Boys Are Back In Town', though. 'Cowboy Song' was one of Lizzy's most effortlessly seductive rockers to date, a tough Texan tale of ten-gallon gallantry and range-riding romance. And 'Emerald' – the only band composition – was the last word on the author's burning fascination with Irish history, a blood-curdling clash of steel and morality embedded upon a spectacular Gaelic guitar riff.

Indeed Philip's dashing lyrical themes had rarely been so graphic and evocative. Here was the Hollywood hero in all his glory, 'busting out dead or alive' as the fearless fugitive in 'Jailbreak', or 'busting broncs for the rodeo' as the handsome hombre in 'Cowboy Song'. Like a cross between Clint Eastwood and Rudolph Valentino, with a bit of George Best thrown in for good measure, Philip strode into the sunset of his own imagination and always, of course, lived to fight another day.

There was a serious side to *Jailbreak* too. The grisly warnings of 'Warriors' were unspeakably sinister, a chilling, premonitory comment on the fate of those heroes who'd tragically fallen, written specifically with Jimi Hendrix, Duane Allman and Gram Parsons in mind. There was also the Mafia-connected murder conjured up by the images of 'Angel From The Coast'.

And there was even a political message for his 'brothers' to continue their struggle in 'Fight Or Fall'.

Interestingly enough, there was also a subtle reference to Gary Moore in the song 'Romeo And The Lonely Girl' – 'For all his good looks, there were scars that he took' – a reference that confirmed the guitarist's suspicions that the track was about him, especially as Philip had mischievously pointed out to him at the time that Romeo was an anagram of Moore.

Jailbreak was the culmination of all Philip and his band had worked for over the past two years. The fusion of Robertson and Gorham finally came to fruition, particularly on tracks like 'Angel From The Coast' and 'Emerald', and Downey's drumming was an immensely effective foundation. This was Thin Lizzy in focus.

For the *Jailbreak* sleeve Philip insisted that Phonogram once again enlisted the services of Jim Fitzpatrick, especially after the somewhat less than artistic success of *Fighting*. The idea of desperadoes escaping from prison, which referred back to the *Defiant Ones* film from which Philip had stolen ideas in the past, was always going to be the basic theme. But Philip saw the whole concept developing along much more futuristic lines.

"He was heavily into the *War Of The Worlds*, HG Wells and that sort of thing," explains Jim Fitzpatrick, "and he asked me to do something which would fit in with that. I thought, 'Jesus, what on earth am I supposed to do?' But we sat down one day and wrote the sleeve notes which appeared on the back cover, and everything else followed from there. Then Philip decided he wanted me to incorporate the band in the artwork. I wasn't very good at likenesses in those days, so that's why none of the characters look like the band members. But the general idea was that it was supposed to be a Marvel comic-type thing."

The finished article was quite an elaborate affair, the first time many people had seen a fold-out design. The front section featured a TV monitor with a cut-out screen which revealed an image of three of the band members running for cover. In view of the instability of the band's line-up over the coming years it might have been suggested that the omission of what appears to be Robbo's character was deliberate, perhaps the result of uncanny foresight. However, Fitzpatrick flatly denies there was any significance in this *faux pas*, and maintains that it was merely an accident caused by Phonogram insisting at the last minute that he made the figures bigger.

Whatever, the *Jailbreak* package earned Lizzy promotion to rock's First Division, and the band at last started to make money. The British tour in March to promote the new album was also a certified success, complete with the new stage gimmick of a police siren, an idea Philip had nicked from a US comedy group called The Fire Sign Theatre.

Indeed, the tour was only marred by an incident at Liverpool Stadium on March 20, when a girl got raped in the underpass at Exchange station, which abutted the run-down boxing arena. Lizzy were so loud no-one heard her screams for help, and the unfortunate occurrence led to the cancellation of all rock concerts at the venue.

Over in America during May the band reverted to their supporting role. At various points on the tour there were shows with REO Speedwagon (Downey: "They were crap, we couldn't believe how bad they were on stage!"), Styx (Robbo: "Their guitar player used to throw his guitar off stage . . . and they'd have this big mattress in the wings for it to land on!"), Journey (Gorham: "Steve Smith used to set his drum kit up at the side of the stage and play along with us!") and Canadian power trio, Rush (Robbo: "They were brilliant, although they used to have their weird parties where they'd dress up in drag, which we weren't sure about!").

By and large the American press and public took a shine to Thin Lizzy, although references to the similarity between Philip's voice and that of home-grown hero Bruce Springsteen eventually began to grate, despite Philip's insistence that it was "a compliment". Springsteen was even asked to comment on the so-called similarity between the two during a radio interview in New York, and was made to sit and listen to the 'Wild One' single before articulating his judgement. However, he sensibly dismissed the allegations of plagiarism on Lynott's part, and then promptly phoned Lizzy's record company and asked to be sent a copy of *Jailbreak*!

"The common factor in all this was Van Morrison," opines Bob Geldof, "because the Rats got roped into that argument at some stage too. I actually thought the opening to 'Rat Trap' was very Philip, but really I was trying to copy Van Morrison, and Philip copied Van Morrison as well, so that's why it sounded that way. People said I was trying to do a Bruce Springsteen, but I'd never even heard of Bruce fucking Springsteen! Yet it only sounded like Springsteen because, as Springsteen has since admitted, he was steeped in Van Morrison as well! Conjuring up universal imagery from stuff that happened in your own street was very much an integral part of Van Morrison's songwriting style, and both Philip and I borrowed from that. Philip was such a disciple he always made a point of going to visit Van whenever he was in San Francisco."

As the controversy limped on in some sections of the press, Lizzy powered towards a new phase of the US tour – a series of dates supporting Ritchie Blackmore's Rainbow. This, the band felt, was the perfect opportunity to take the bull by the horns and make a big name for themselves. "We were in crushing form at the time," enthuses Gorham, "and we really felt that we could take Rainbow. Our motto was: 'Leave the stage covered in blood and watch the headliners slip all over it.' We loved to give the main band a hard time.

"Anyway, just before the tour Phil and I were at the Rainbow Bar & Grill in Los Angeles with Ritchie Blackmore and John Bonham, and Phil got it into his head that he was going to wind Blackmore up about the tour. He was going, 'Man, when we get on the road we're gonna kick your ass every night! You won't know what's hit you!' John Bonham thought it was hilarious, but Blackmore didn't know quite how to take Phil's boasting. It was a psychological game that Phil was playing, but I guess it kind of backfired on him."

"We were certainly hot at the time," O'Donnell emphasises, "and Rainbow needed us, because they had a very expensive stage production on that tour (based around a 29 ft high electronic rainbow) and tickets weren't going so well. Then on the eve of the tour Phil became quite ill. He went to the hospital and told us that the doctor had told him it was infectious hepatitis, but all he had to do was rest. So I rang the hospital to find out a little more about it and the doctor said, 'Is that guy not back in England yet? Oh my God! We were going to keep him in here, but he told us he was going straight back to England on the next flight, and that's the only reason why we let him go!'

"So I put the phone down and confronted Phil. He'd been playing down the illness because he wanted the tour so badly – especially as we were riding on the back of a hit single in the States – but he'd started turning yellow at that stage and it was getting ridiculous. I put him on the next plane home.

"During all this I was getting messages from our tour manager saying that our crew was getting so much shit from Rainbow's crew that they couldn't take it anymore. So I went down to what was supposed to be the first gig, in Cleveland, Ohio, and told Bruce Payne (Rainbow's manager) that if we didn't get everything we wanted we were coming off the tour. He said, 'Oh yeah?' and I said, *'Oh yeah!'* He still gave us shit after that, so I said to our crew, 'Right, pack up the gear, we're going home!' Of course I didn't mention we'd have to pack up and go home anyway, as Phil was ill.

"The next thing I knew there was pandemonium everywhere. I'd called Bruce Payne's bluff and he was crapping himself. He came over to our hotel later and said, 'OK, you can have anything you want, but you've got to do these dates.' All I could say was, 'Sorry mate, but we're off.' I don't know how I kept a straight face."

"It was a major blow for us to have to cancel that tour," Gorham reflects, "but it couldn't be helped. When Phil came to my room to tell me he was going back to England his eyes were banana-yellow. I said, 'OK, bye!' and slammed the door, because it really looked contagious.

"The doctors told Phil he'd have to quit drinking for good, but he told us that he'd just have to give it a rest for a year. His liver was fried. So he ended up going a year without a drink, and I'd say it was the worst year I had with him, because every morning after the night before he'd take great pleasure in telling you, in great detail, exactly what you did when you were shit-faced. I guess it was Phil's way of making up for the fact that he couldn't get shit-faced."

After the aborted Rainbow shows in June Lizzy returned to London, where a special one-off show at Hammersmith

Odeon was slotted in during July as a 'Thank You' to the fans for an otherwise successful year. Philip just about survived the show, before immediately returning to his sick bed in a Manchester hospital, where over the next few weeks he wrote the band's next album, *Johnny The Fox*.

"It had only seemed like two minutes since we'd done *Jailbreak*," says Robbo, "but I suppose it was good to get the next album done while we were on a roll. Phil had written some fantastic stuff for the album again, but as usual there were one or two bones of contention, and as usual Phil and I ended up at each other's throats.

"One of the problems was 'Don't Believe A Word'. When Phil came in with that idea we were down at this farm rehearsing. The song was really slow originally, and I immediately turned round to him and said, 'That's fucking crap, Phil!' We had a huge bust-up about it, and he disappeared for two days. I began to think that I might have been a wee bit harsh on him, so one day I went into the studio with Brian Downey and suggested that we tried to make something of the poxy song. Brian came up with the idea of giving it a shuffle-type rhythm, and I wrote the guitar riff, and so by the time Phil returned to the studio we'd completely re-worked the idea. He was well chuffed.

"Then when the album came out the song was credited to P. Lynott. There was no mention of me or Brian. That happened quite a lot in Lizzy and it did piss me off at times. I had a lot of input that never got recognised. But I got to understand that's just the way it is in rock'n'roll."

Lizzy were originally going to record *Johnny The Fox* at the famous Musicland Studios, beneath the Arabella Hotel in Munich. In the event they only spent two weeks in Germany before deciding they weren't going to achieve the drum sound they wanted, and they ended up back at Ramport in Battersea by the end of August.

Like most of its predecessors the album was recorded remarkably swiftly, but unlike some of them the haste didn't detract from the quality or consistency of the end product. With Lynott taking a stronger interest in production, the approach was tight and punchy, a crystallisation of the sound they'd long been aiming for. It was the ideal follow-up to *Jailbreak*, a better all-round album according to people like Brian Downey, and confirmation if any was needed that Thin Lizzy were on the crest of a wave.

The record also marked another chapter in the Chronicles Of Johnny, Lynott's fixation with the name having already been challenged by Scott Gorham, who reckoned, "Phil should've been this guy's publicity agent, as he was cropping up everywhere!" In the past we'd heard about the uncompromising Johnny Cool in 'Showdown', the Mickey-taking of Johnny Maguire in 'Chatting Today' and the face-slapping incident at 'Johnny's place' in 'The Boys Are Back In Town'. Now we were witness to the confrontation in 'Johnny The Fox Meets Jimmy The Weed', a further glimpse at gruesome gangland goings on (the Jimmy The Weed in this case was one James Donnolly, a Manchester hotelier, believed to be associated with the Quality Street Gang), while the track simply called 'Johnny' was another desperate tale of drugs and guns, set against the harsh backdrop of modern big city life.

As ever Lynott's lingo was straight from the streets of America: men were 'cats', women were 'chicks', police were 'cops', and there were 'bartenders' instead of barmen, 'highways' instead of roads and 'trash cans' on the 'sidewalk'. There was even a reference to the Low Riders 'hanging out down on First Street and Main', a gang that Lizzy used to watch cruising the streets every night in the Big Bad Apple. Philip had been totally absorbed by American culture and was fascinated by the laws of the jungle, a theme he often referred to in his bleakest commentaries.

Yet for all the New York-at-night imagery, Lynott truly excelled when he returned to the realms of ancient history. 'Massacre' was a shocking account of how 'Six hundred unknown heroes were killed like sleeping buffalo' in a bygone bloodbath over the territory of the southern States. And 'Fool's Gold' was a poignant reflection on how famine and disease had driven many people out of Ireland to look for new hope and prosperity in the Americas. Lynott claimed it went some way to explaining why there were more Irish people spread around the world than there were actually in Ireland.

Of course it could be argued that Philip himself was in search of fool's gold in America, and in 'Sweet Marie' he confessed to the loneliness of being on the road so far from home, so far from his Loved One. Suddenly there appeared a soft-hearted side to Lynott, as in this and in 'Old Flame', while the cocky character of 'Rocky' (written with Robbo in mind, according to Robbo) melted into the wings.

Guesting on 'Johnny The Fox' were Kim Beacon from String Driven Thing ("A great singer but a total idiot," announces Robbo. "We only got him in because Frankie Miller wasn't around"), and Genesis drummer/singer Phil Collins, who is credited as contributing some percussion, even though to this day Brian Downey cannot pin-point exactly what passages he played on.

"Collins was just a mate of Phil's," explains Robbo. "He turned up at a Lizzy gig at the Winning Post in Twickenham once – this was while he was playing part-time with Brand X – and had a jam with us. Then we met in America when he was on tour with Genesis, and I think Phil probably just wanted to get him on the album to name-drop."

The album was released in October, just seven months after *Jailbreak*. With the band in top gear Phonogram's urgency to keep the campaign on the boil was understandable, but the rush to get *Johnny The Fox* out did mean that some aspects of the project were compromised. Artist Jim Fitzpatrick, for example, was required to present a cover before the title of the record was even decided upon.

"Philip simply said to me, 'I want something really good, but totally different; something Celtic, but not the usual kind of Celtic rock thing.' So I did this really strange, neo-gothic Celtic border, with a disc in the centre which surrounded a blank. The blank was for whatever the title of the album was going to be – but as the weeks slipped by there was still no sign of a title from Philip. The record company was screaming at me for the cover, but I was going, 'How can I finish the sleeve when I don't even know what the title is going to be?!'

"In the end I was a little desperate, so I said to Philip, 'Just think of any title, I'll fit anything into the bloody design!' So he replied, 'Ah, call it *Johnny The Fox*, that'll do.' I couldn't believe how cool and casual he was, even at the eleventh hour."

With the album peaking at No.12 in the UK charts, Thin Lizzy hit the road during October and November – 25 shows in 28 days, mostly promoted by newcomer Adrian Hopkins. Nowadays Hopkins owns a merchandising company which has worldwide rights for the likes of Cliff Richard and Dire Straits, and he also still works with Jethro Tull, Van Morrison and Steeleye Span. But he claims he owes it all to Thin Lizzy.

"Philip gave me a break and it became the foundation for my whole career," he attests. "I personally never had a cross word with him, although I know most people did. But that was basically because he was very aware about his career and he wanted control over every aspect of it.

"I was thrilled to be promoting the *Johnny The Fox* tour because the band really were at their peak. They were the best live band anyone could ever work with. But then Philip had doubts about the people who were doing his merchandising, and he suggested I looked after that side of things as well. I remember we were at a gig at Newcastle City Hall and he was unhappy with the way an artist had given him a crew-cut in a band montage. He ordered all the programmes to be taken off sale. That's when I knew how serious he was about even the smallest details, so when I took over doing Lizzy's merchandise I had to make sure everything was cleared by him before I could do anything. Even if it meant flying over to Ireland to get him to approve a photo on a T-shirt, that's what I had to do.

"The only time I think we cocked it up was when we decided to do Thin Lizzy mittens for the fans, the kind that Phil wore on stage. We couldn't do leather gloves because they were too expensive, but we could do fingerless mittens – the Irish burglar's gloves, I called them. The trouble was, they were supposed to be printed with the Thin Lizzy logo pointing downwards, so people could read it when you raised your fist like Phil did at the start of the show. But they were printed upside down and Phil was furious. He ordered them to be taken off sale, and there were bloody thousands of them.

"I got some more printed up properly, but every now and

again I'd slip some of the upside down ones into the boxes
... and of course, the first kid that got backstage after the
show every night would be wearing one of the upside down
pairs!

"But Phil and I got on great," Hopkins continues. "We
must've done because I could joke with him about blacks or
Irish people, whereas I've seen him sort other people out for
saying the same things! If you knew him you were alright, if
you didn't know him you couldn't get away with so much."

One person who did get to know him well on the autumn
'76 UK tour was Huey Lewis, the harmonica player/occasional
singer in support band Clover, who was to enjoy tremendous
success with his own band The News during the Eighties. He
has never forgotten the hospitality shown to him or his group
on either tour, nor the lessons he learnt from working with
Philip at close quarters.

"When we first came to England," says Lewis, "we were told,
'You won't get a soundcheck and you'll probably get treated
like crap, because you're the opening act and it's a kind of
tradition here in Britain.' Well, on the first night of the tour –
in Oxford, I think – we were late setting our gear up because
Lizzy were late soundchecking, so there we were with only five
minutes to go and nothing even plugged in. Meanwhile, on
the other side of the curtain the crowd was chanting football-
style, 'LIZ-ZY! LIZ-ZY!' How does that make you feel?

"So the curtain finally opened, we stumbled through our set
and then retired to the dressing room to console ourselves.
Philip was the first guy through the door, and he had this big
grin on his face. He'd watched the whole miserable set and he
had tons of advice for us. He said, 'Don't worry boys, it's only
the first night, you'll definitely get a soundcheck most nights,
here's a couple of fuzz pedals in case you need them, if there's
anything else you need just let me know . . . oh, and your third
tune is great, you should open up with that.' We were like,
'*Wow!*' Of course, we took his advice and from that night on we
got better all the time.

"I watched Philip all the time on those tours and to me he
was the best live rock'n'roll performer I had ever seen. He had
a suss about the stage which was uncanny. And yet he was

never mean with his knowledge. In fact, he would be forever telling other people how to do certain things, how to handle situations and so on. To the point where he would take me to his room and dress me in his clothes, to show me how a rock star should look!

"Philip was a human course in rock'n'roll. He taught me how to treat the crew, how to handle the band, how to handle the record company, when to listen, when to speak, when to push, when to pull, how to do photo sessions, how to do interviews with the press . . .

"I never realised there was so much to learn, especially with regards to interviews. I just thought you chatted with a journalist and that was it. But Philip used to tell me that if you had two or three things that you wanted to say in an article then you had to think of some snappy quotes to get your points across. He used to say, 'You'll always know when you're tossing them a quote they're gonna use.' But then he also taught me that if you wanted to avoid getting quoted on an awkward subject, you had to give them a boring answer. That way you could direct the interview in whichever way you wanted. He knew about the whole manipulation game."

When the tour reached Manchester, though, Lynott had a bust-up with Brian Robertson which wasn't perhaps the ideal example to set. As Clover's soundcheck time came and went without an appearance from their drummer Micky Shine, Robbo offered his services with the sticks should he still be absent by gig time. When Philip realised his guitarist wasn't joking, he went up the wall.

"He said, 'You ain't going out there, the kids'll recognise you!'" Robbo chuckles. "But tell me I can't do something and I'll want to do it even more. We had a massive row, a real big bust-up. Like, 'I'm doing it!' 'No you're not!' 'Try and stop me!' 'I'll fucking fire you!' 'You wouldn't dare!' and so on and so on. In the end their drummer turned up five minutes before they were due on stage, and I was gutted."

The *Johnny The Fox* tour peaked with three sold out nights at Hammersmith Odeon between November 14 and 16, all three being recorded for a proposed live album. The Odeon's switchboard had in fact been jammed with calls enquiring about ticket applications on the Monday morning after Lizzy's blistering guest appearance on Rod Stewart's BBC TV Special in October. It was a measure of how far Lizzy had come as a live band since the acquisition of Robbo and Gorham.

"We blew Stewart off," Gorham announces proudly, "because he was miming and we played live and loud in the studio. Afterwards he went up to Phil and said he was so excited watching us that it really made him realise how much he missed playing in a band, because he'd just left The Faces then. Phil was on such a high, because Rod Stewart was one of his favourite singers."

After Rod Stewart and Hammersmith Odeon the plan was to pay a flying visit to Ireland and then return Stateside for a late November/December tour in support of the new album. But while the crew were actually in New York finalising the preparations, word came through from Morrison and O'Donnell's London office that the tour would have to be pulled.

"Me and Big Charlie were just about to leave our hotel to pick the band up from JFK airport," says Frank Murray, "when we heard that Brian Robertson had slashed his hand in a fight at the Speakeasy, and he wouldn't be able to do the tour. As it was so last minute there wasn't time to get a replacement, so we were to forget it and come back to England. It was a big let down, and Robbo had a lot of explaining to do."

Morrison and O'Donnell in particular were furious with Robbo for jeopardising the tour by going on what they assumed was a drunken rampage the night before he was due to leave for New York. But Robbo maintains to this day that reports about the fateful evening's events were grossly exaggerated, and that his injury was more the result of bad luck rather than inebriated bravado.

"At the time I couldn't get a flat, so I was sleeping on a friend's couch for a while," he explains, endeavouring to put the record straight once and for all. "The flat was real small and I couldn't handle staying indoors, so I used to go out all the time. That particular night I went to the Speakeasy for a meal, and contrary to popular belief I was not drunk. I had my steak, or whatever, and then as would usually happen I got up and jammed with the band that was playing – that night it was a group called Gonzales.

"Now Frankie Miller was there that night too, and as usual he was severely shit-faced. He kept nagging everyone to let him get up and have a blow as well, and in the end he jumped on stage, ripped the mike off me and started singing, really out of it. We kind of finished the number as best we could and left it at that.

"After the show I went back into the tiny dressing room and I saw Frankie on his hands and knees about to get bottled by this guy Gordon, the guitar player in Gonzales. So I rushed over and tried to stop it, but he pushed the bottle straight through my hand. It sliced through the nerve and severed my artery, and there was blood pumping all over the place. So I broke his leg. And I broke his mate's collarbone. And I nutted another one of them. And I would've killed the lot of them if someone hadn't hit me on the back of the head with a bottle and knocked me unconscious.

"The next thing I knew I was in hospital. I had to phone O'Donnell up at about six in the morning and break the news to him. They all thought it was because I was drunk, but I wasn't, I'd only had a couple of beers. It was all because of Frankie, and of course he didn't have a scratch on him.

"The doctor actually told me I'd never play again. He told me I'd cut my tendon and that was it. I went back to Glasgow and I was devastated. I kept picking up a guitar, but I couldn't feel my middle finger and my stitches kept bursting open. This happened three times. The third time I went to another doctor to get stitched up again, and he told me I hadn't cut the tendon at all. I was so relieved, but really angry that the other bastards had told me I wouldn't play again."

Whether Robbo would play in Thin Lizzy again was another matter entirely. The timing of the Speakeasy incident was cruel and the band was not impressed, least of all Philip, who according to Gary Moore had been making enquiries about Moore's availability to rejoin Lizzy for a few months prior to Robbo's injury.

"I think Phil had been having problems with Robbo for a while," explains Moore, "and he wanted me back in the band.

We were going to discuss the situation properly when they returned from the States, but I think fate accelerated the situation and the next thing I knew I was going to the States with them."

Isn't that where this chapter came in?

Chapter IV

Pills, Powders & Potions

1977 began with 'Don't Believe A Word' striding up the UK charts to No.12 (No.2 in Ireland), while the new-look Thin Lizzy reconvened in New York to start rehearsals for a 42-date US tour supporting Queen. It was a plum tour to land as Queen were establishing themselves at the time as one of the most successful rock bands in the world with their No.1 album *A Day At The Races*. And it gave the marketing men the chance to come up with the corniest of titles in Elizabeth II's Jubilee Year: 'The Queen Lizzy Tour'.

"It was a great package," says O'Donnell. "Queen remembered supporting Mott The Hoople when they first started out in America, and they understood the benefits of having a happening support band. They obviously felt that as they were moving into the ice hockey stadiums they could do with an opening act who could sell 5,000 tickets on their own, which was what we could do at the time. Plus, Brian May was a big Lizzy fan, so I guess the tour was ideal for both of us."

The tour was due to start in Wisconsin on January 13, and this gave Lizzy the chance to squeeze in at least a week's worth of rehearsals in the Big Apple. Once again Frank Murray and Big Charlie had travelled on ahead to ensure a smooth passage for the band, and as Murray recalls they were quite taken aback by the hospitality they received from their American hosts.

"We had a publishing connection with the Robert Stigwood Organisation, and to welcome us to the States they sent two limousines to pick us up from the airport and drop us off at the Mayflower Hotel, opposite Central Park. We thought it was a nice gesture. But then as we got out the driver asked me if we'd be needing the limos later, so I said, 'Yeah, sure.' I thought, 'How nice of Stigwood.'

"That night Philip and I got in the limos and went to CBGBs to see Talking Heads, then later on to Max's Kansas City to see Mink DeVille. We also went cruising in the limos the next day, and the next night, and the next ... in fact, we had them running us around all week. I mean, we had roadies going to pick up new sets of guitar strings in these limos!

"A few weeks later I got a call from the management in London: 'Er, Frank, what's this limo bill?' So I said, 'Well, the guys just kept picking us up every day – I thought it was complimentary.' Apparently it wasn't, and the Stigwood people were pulling their hair out. The bill was thousands and thousands of dollars."

When the tour finally got underway Lizzy were left in no doubt about the lie of the land. The Queen operation was slick and strict, and everything had to run like clockwork. There was no such thing as playing over your allotted time, as this would mean having to pay overtime fees to the unions. This was what Frank Murray referred to as 'playing with the big boys'.

"We'd met Queen before as we both shared the same publicist and we'd both been tipped as Promising Newcomers, or something, by *Disc & Music Echo* magazine, way back in 1973. They had a reception for us at the White Elephant club in Curzon Street. The only thing camp about Freddie Mercury then was his purple nail varnish.

"Now all of a sudden we were with Queen again and they were superstars, way out of our league. But they were so professional that we learnt a hell of a lot from them. I'd say it was the best tour we ever did. I certainly came of age as a tour manager on that tour, and the whole crew toughened up as a result of it.

"We had many running battles with Queen, mainly over soundchecks and whether or not we could fly our logo. When they wouldn't let us use it Philip would tell us to put it on the side of the stage by the PA. He'd say, 'I'm gonna make sure the kids see the fucking thing one way or another!'

"Queen were also very touchy about backstage passes, they

wouldn't let anyone backstage. Lizzy, on the other hand, let everyone backstage. I mean, every chick in town had a back-stage pass! The Queen people would go insane: 'Who are all these fucking people?!' We'd go, 'Dunno'."

"After a while the Queen people started to get a bit concerned about how well we were going down," O'Donnell claims. "Even on the second night there was a little bit of friction when they told us to cut our set from 45 minutes to 30 minutes. They said it was because they needed more time to change over, so instead of going on at 7.30 and finishing at 8.15 we'd have to finish at 8.00pm. So I said, 'Why can't we go on at 7.15 and still be off by 8.00pm?' They couldn't answer that, so we got our full set back."

"Apparently," says Gary Moore, "Freddie was very intimi-dated by our band. People would tell us afterwards that Freddie would be stomping up and down in his dressing room while we were on stage going, 'Listen to that applause! Get that band off *now*!' One night Freddie's boyfriend, this little guy who acted as his masseur, came into our dressing room and said, 'I just wanted to tell you guys that you were wonderful tonight', before scurrying out of the door. He told us later that Freddie would've killed him if he'd known he'd been in to congratulate us. We thought it was hysterical."

"In certain parts of the States we couldn't get reaction from the audiences at all," admits Brian Downey, "and it was very depressing. We thought we just couldn't compete with Queen. But then we spent a few nights watching their show and we realised that while they were a great band, their show was exactly the same night after night, with no spontaneity at all. That made us feel a lot better, because we knew we could do some great ad-libs and that would at least give us more of an edge than Queen."

"In the end we started getting some great reviews," says Frank Murray, "and that pissed Queen off even more. We'd be at the airport in the mornings reading the previous night's reviews, and we'd all be talking about these great write-ups. Sometimes I'd feel embarrassed for Queen, because they'd be sitting up in First Class and we'd be back in Scumbag Class, but we had all the good reviews."

"Some of the reviews said we blew Queen off, but that was going too far," Downey admits. "I don't remember blowing Queen off on even one occasion. But it was nice to get favourable reports because we were putting in some great performances, especially Gary Moore, and we were easily holding our own with Queen."

"I think the tour was the best thing Lizzy ever did from the point of view of raising their profile," Moore reckons. "And for me it was all very fresh – much better than my first stint in the band. Some of the shows we did were brilliant, although we completely blew our chance at Madison Square Garden in New York. It was the worst show on the tour for us – the only one where we didn't get an encore.

"We actually did an incredible amount of shows in three months, and the travelling was very gruelling. The weather was awful – it was the worst winter they'd had for years – and a few shows had to be cancelled due to severe blizzard conditions. There were certainly a few 'interesting' flights on that tour . . .

"At the end of the tour Phil asked me to stay with the band," Moore reveals, "and that put me in a dilemma. I'd just done this album with Colosseum II, and as I'd formed the band with Jon Hiseman I sort of considered it as my baby. I had a lot of loyalty to those guys and I didn't want to walk out and leave them in the shit. So I decided to go back to Colosseum II, promote the album, give it a year, and if it wasn't working out then maybe we could talk about the Thin Lizzy situation again. Which is exactly what happened."

Robbo, meanwhile, greeted Lizzy's homecoming with the announcement that he was planning to put a band together with ex-Rainbow bassist Jimmy Bain. The two had been living together and writing songs for some time, and the band they envisaged was a hard rock four-piece called Wild Horses.

"The Lizzy situation was all very iffy by now," Robbo explains. "I figured it was the end of me and Lizzy. But I kept the same management and kept in touch with what was going on, and eventually I got wind of the fact that perhaps Gary wasn't going to stick around.

"The first time I saw the boys after the Speakeasy incident was at the Hope & Anchor pub in Islington, where Phil, Gary and a few others were jamming with Rat Scabies (from The Damned) and all that mob. Phil hinted then that I ought to rejoin Lizzy, but it was all a bit strange because I hadn't really been fired in the first place."

With the Robbo situation still up in the air, Lizzy flew out to Toronto in May to begin work on their eighth studio album, a three-piece once more. Scott would simply tackle all the guitar parts on the record himself, and they would confront the issue of a second guitar player nearer the time of the next tour.

A more pressing problem was finding the right producer, but Chris O'Donnell was convinced he had his man in Tony Visconti, who'd made his name working with David Bowie and T.Rex. O'Donnell was actually flying across Texas in the process of setting up another Lizzy tour when he came across an article in a magazine he'd picked up at Heathrow in which Visconti complained that bands like Lizzy never made the most of their commercial attributes. He thought the criticism fair, so O'Donnell contacted Visconti and offered him the chance to do something about it. A hastily arranged meeting with the band followed, and while Philip and Scott hardly flattered themselves by turning up at Visconti's house drunk, a working relationship was decided upon there and then.

Bad Reputation took shape during the rest of May and June, so that by the time Brian Robertson edged back into the frame most of the backing tracks had been done. He claims he was responsible for numerous overdubs – "More than you would notice" – but officially was credited only with contributions on 'Opium Trail', 'Killer Without A Cause' and 'That Woman's Gonna Break Your Heart'. It was a bit of a blow to his ego, but not so anyone would notice.

"I was playing on the Wild Horses angle a lot," he confesses. "I told Morrison and O'Donnell that if they signed Jimmy Bain for management I would do *Bad Reputation* on a session basis. I was trying to look after my friend Jimmy, trying to be clever I suppose. As it turned out I shouldn't have bothered because Jimmy Bain turned out to be bad news. But in those days I was a dickhead, full of stupid arrogance, and of course I knew best."

To teach Robbo a lesson the front cover of *Bad Reputation*

featured the band as a three-piece. "We were trying to put him in his place," explains O'Donnell. Shots of all four Lizzy members did appear on the inner sleeve, though, along with a rather bizarre photograph of a naked girl lying on a bed with her eyes covered with sticky tape and cotton wool. Chris O'Donnell explains again: "Phil was seeing a girl in New York at the time called Carol Starr, a well-known photographer. She took him around a few museums in New York, and at the museum of modern art he came across what was known at the time as 'The Stackawheat Murders'. The girl on the sleeve covered in pancakes and syrup was one of the victims of this rather gruesome and somewhat odd series of attacks.

"Phil went overboard about the case, but I was against putting that picture on the inner sleeve. I said to Phil, 'The kids in Manchester or Birmingham aren't going to understand what that's all about.' I guess it was Phil's way of trying to be subtle.

"A further example of that was the whole idea of the playing card symbols: Robbo was the rough diamond, Brian Downey was the club, he was the spade . . . Phil was a great romantic, he thought everyone would understand what he was going on about. I wasn't so convinced sometimes."

Another curious factor of the *Bad Reputation* package was that it was not a Jim Fitzpatrick creation. After the impressive presentations of *Jailbreak* and *Johnny The Fox*, the plain black cover with the reversed-out images of Lynott, Downey and Gorham (courtesy of Sutton Cooper) came as something of a surprise.

"It was all the result of an horrendous mistake," says Fitzpatrick. "Philip called me in a panic and said he had a week to get the new cover together, but that he was coming to the States (where I was living at the time) and so maybe we could get together and work on something. I gave him my address – 44 East Walk Road, Madison, Connecticut – and arranged to meet him in a few days.

"The next thing I know he's on the phone telling me he's lost. So I told him to head for the sea, and he'd find it easy. But an hour later I got another call from him, telling me he was still lost. So I went through all the directions again, real slowly, and he got Big Charlie to write everything down. An hour later the phone rang again, and it was Philip in another call box. He said he'd asked a cop to direct him to the sea and the cop had said there was no sea in the vicinity of Madison, and in fact there was no East Walk Road in Madison either. It was then I realised that he was in Madison, Wisconsin, not Madison, Connecticut!

"We gave up the idea of trying to get together then, because we just didn't have the time. By this time the deadline was upon Philip, and I think that's why the cover ended up looking like it had been thrown together."

Overall the slick and confident nature of the album managed to disguise the turmoil that had squirmed beneath it. Gorham's guitar work suffered little from the absence of Robbo, while Lynott sounded as assured and teeth-grittingly driven as ever, and Downey's explosive drumming on the title track was quite remarkable, even by his standards.

'Soldier Of Fortune' set the scene by adhering religiously to Lizzy's heatseeking twin-guitar formula, if only by the wonders of modern recording techniques. It was classic Lynott fodder with a stop-start riff during the verses which allowed his typically rich vocal line to hit the listener right between the eyes. As album-openers go, it was in the 'Jailbreak' class.

'Bad Reputation' and 'Opium Trail' were next, both with a sinister edge that seemed to correspond with the menacing blackness of the album cover. With the band easing off the gas, 'Southbound' closed the first side with a lilting sentimentality which captured the romanticism of the author. Gary Moore may claim he wrote the riff ("Phil actually gave me some money for it years later, after much haggling!" he laughs), but the words, the mood, the magic . . . it had Lynott tattooed on its soul.

Side Two spread its wings further. The hard rockers would've gone for 'Killer Without A Cause', or perhaps the slightly breezier 'That Woman's Gonna Break Your Heart', while those in search of their annual dose of Lizzy slush would've settled for the unbelievably laid-back 'Downtown Sundown' and the unashamedly poppy 'Dear Lord', both of which sprang from Lynott's deep religious faith. The latter song even featured the dramatic sound of a 'heavenly choir', although this turned out to be the work of Tony Visconti's wife, successful Sixties singer Mary Hopkin, who made 16 separate recordings of her voice which were then miraculously layered onto the track.

Finally there was 'Dancing In The Moonlight (It's Caught Me In Its Spotlight)' – the rather unnecessary subtitle being added by the band's American record company Mercury to distinguish it from another song with the same title that was on release at the time. They needn't have worried, as the sheer quality of Lizzy's effort was enough to distinguish it absolutely. Featuring the husky, sexy sax of Supertramp's John Helliwell, it was as O'Donnell says, "A truly great pop song!", perhaps Lynott's most memorable achievement since 'Still In Love With You'.

'Dancing In The Moonlight' was released as a single in July and spent eight weeks in both the UK and Irish charts, reaching Nos. 14 and 4 respectively. During August the band (with Robbo officially 'guesting' on guitar) undertook a European Festival tour, which included headlining at the Reading Festival on Saturday 27th (above Aerosmith, Ultravox and the Little River Band among others) and at Dalymount Park in Dublin (ahead of The Boomtown Rats and Graham Parker & The Rumour). It was a time when Lizzy's star was burning bright, but the presence of fellow countrymen The Boomtown Rats on the bill, at a time when they represented Irish interests in the New Wave of rock which was peeling away from the punk explosion, was a sharp reminder to Lynott that he couldn't afford to be complacent.

"Philip was always interested in what was happening at street level," says Bob Geldof, "and he'd often turn up to watch us at this little basement club in Gardener Street called Moran's. This was around early '76. He was very approachable, liked to have a laugh, bought us drinks, and was generally very keen to find out all he could about us. From my point of view there was an instant rapport between us, and I was particularly interested in his legendary escapades with women. He used to tell some great stories, and of course I couldn't wait to join the club!

"He was very supportive and gave us loads of advice. We also got introduced to Ted Carroll (who by this time ran Chiswick

Records), and both Chris Morrison and Chris O'Donnell helped us immensely when we were looking for a record deal. All we had to our name was this shite demo tape, and yet the two Chrises got it to the head of A&R at Phonogram, Nigel Grange, and that was the key to it all for the Rats.

"We also got offered the chance to support Lizzy on a 30-date tour once, through Ted Carroll. As it turned out we had to turn the tour down because our finances were in a terrible state and, in the days before I even knew monitors existed, I had to scream so much to hear myself on stage I couldn't possibly do 30 shows in succession. But the fact was that Philip and the Lizzy organisation were always willing to help.

"Of course, you could look at that two ways: firstly, it was all very noble and charitable because by giving us a support slot he was giving a leg-up to a new band. But secondly, he knew we weren't going to be a threat to him. Or at least that's what he thought.

"When we came to do Dalymount Park I was out to get Lizzy. In fact, I was out to get anyone who we played with, I was totally ruthless. The day we arrived in Dublin we heard that we'd just got into the Top 20 with 'Looking After No.1', and they wanted us to do *Top Of The Pops*. A year before this I was standing outside Dun Laoghaire dole office in the rain, and yet here I was now with a record in the Top 20. I'd always been a loud-mouth, but now I'd finally delivered. Sure as hell, I was going to boast about it from the rooftops.

"To add to all this, the night before Dalymount I'd gone apeshit on the *Late Late Show* on Irish TV and stirred up a shit load of controversy about priests and religion and all sorts of crap. My father went up the wall, I was denounced by my local church, it was all over the papers the next day and all hell broke loose. Philip didn't appreciate that at all, he was a bit brittle about it. He was supposed to be king of the castle on his home territory, but there we were on the telly, in the charts and in all the papers. He was very jealous and suddenly he wasn't so helpful.

"As it happened," Geldof concludes, "we played badly that day and didn't go down an eighth as well as Lizzy. But we made such a noise that Philip was taken aback. It was triumph for the attitude of punk and New Wave, and a victory for the next generation."

Lizzy and the Rats actually finished the year neck-and-neck in some quarters, and Geldof says he still has a copy of the *Record Mirror* in which the two rivals tied for Best Band Of The Year, and he and Lynott tied for the title of Sex God.

"It was uncanny," he laughs, "because there was this picture of the pair of us on the cover, and we looked almost identical. In those days I had a long thin face with a big chin, a big nose and this mop-like hair-do which stuck out all over the place just like his. The only difference was I had bigger lips than him."

Despite having the likes of Geldof breathing down his neck, Lynott was very much on a high in the summer of '77. Not only did he have a hit single and headline the biggest rock festival in the country in August, he also published his second book of poetry, *Philip*. Then in September *Bad Reputation* made its grand entrance, hitting No.4 in the UK charts and emphasising that Thin Lizzy had never been bigger, nor Philip more influential. Adored by fans, admired by contemporaries, accepted by the critics, a natural for the media.

It was, however, a time when those who knew Philip best started to sense a change in his personality. In retrospect it can be blamed partly on the fame that he was enjoying and partly on the drugs he was taking, but whatever the explanation the emergence of Philip Lynott The Difficult Artiste cut no ice with the likes of tour manager Frank Murray, who'd come such a long way with him.

"Philip was one of the nicest guys you could ever meet in your life, he was my closest pal and I loved the guy. I knew him when he was with The Black Eagles and together we went from a tiny community centre in Dublin to Madison Square Garden. It was a brilliant journey, every step of the way. He was my Best Man when I got married in 1973, and he even came on honeymoon with us to Ibiza, with his girlfriend Gail, his mother and Dennis! My wife Ferga designed his clothes for him, I sweated blood for him, and I shared many memorable moments with him – like the night we went to the movies to see *Mean Streets*, and he actually did get 'chocolate stains on his pants' from a box of Maltesers, a line he later used in 'Dancing In The Moonlight'.

"But when we went to America in September '77 to do our first big headline tour he'd become a bit starstruck. He was very unfair to our support band, Graham Parker & The Rumour, with regards to things like soundchecks. He also started to worry about the size of his hotel bed, the colour of the amps, the way his eggs were done, and so on. He'd seen how Queen had made all these 'star demands' on the previous tour, so now he was headlining I suppose the 'Freddie' in him was starting to come out.

"Actually, in certain spots across America the Rumour were really giving us a run for our money. In fact I can remember Scott standing in the dressing room one night while the crowd were calling for the Rumour to do an encore and saying, 'Oh shit, they haven't blown us off again, have they?' Scott came very close to leaving Lizzy on that tour, and Brian Downey told me one night at a club in Boston that he was thinking of jacking it in too. The morale of the whole band was getting low.

"The problem was we'd all been hitting it a bit heavy – smoke, drink, coke and so on. But then Philip started taking tranquillisers; he'd do all this coke to keep him awake until five in the morning, then take a load of sleeping pills to get himself asleep, and then there'd be someone knocking on his door a few hours later trying to get him on the bus to the next town. Consequently he'd usually be in a really foul mood, and he'd be looking for a fight."

"The sheer adrenalin and high-level energy of those tours is something that I'll never forget," says Peter Eustace. "Philip was a workaholic and everyone would just simply have to keep up with him. But the crew did get a chance to party as hard as they worked, and that made the whole tour something akin to a pub beano. It was a riot! Philip used to interview prospective crew members himself, and the first question he'd ask would be, 'Can you fight?' Everyone was shit-scared of Thin Lizzy. Our reputation preceded us, although I'd say that 90 per cent of it was exaggerated. We'd go to a club and people would be expecting us to tear the place apart, yet Philip would go mad if anyone damaged a hotel room, or stepped out of line that way.

"Things did get a little crazy at times though," Eustace continues. "The whole scene with chemicals got way out of hand, and the crew guys would end up spending all their money on the stuff. At the end of the tour, instead of having some money to show for three months hard work, they'd be owing thousands of pounds to dealers. I guess it was the same with Philip. It was OK until he discovered pills, powders and potions."

"America did seem to bring the worst out of Philip at times," says Frank Murray. "One place he always created havoc in was Phoenix, Arizona. The stage at this gig was 'in the round' (circular, and positioned in the centre of the venue) and because of that one of the house rules was that you had to use the house PA. But Philip would always send me in to tell the guy that we wanted to use our PA. Every tour it was the same story: 'You can't use your own PA.' 'OK, we'll refuse to play.' 'Fine. Fuck off.' Then I'd have to go back to Philip and tell him he wouldn't budge, and of course Philip would blame it all on me. Blame the bad news on the messenger, that was Philip.

"Most of the time we had a great rapport between us. In fact, Philip always made sure that the band and the crew were one team, not two separate camps. We'd arrive in a town and all go out and get pissed together – especially when we were rehearsing in Dallas, where every night we ran up huge bar bills at this great club called Mother Blues. It was a gang thing, part of the magic of Thin Lizzy, and a lot of other crews at the time were envious of the relationship between us and Lizzy.

"Yet that *Bad Reputation* tour wasn't the happiest. When we reached Toronto (where, incidentally, the band's show at the Seneca College Fieldhouse in Toronto on October 28 was recorded for an American radio programme called *The King Biscuit Flour Hour*) Philip asked me how I thought the tour was going, and I told him the truth. I told him I thought we were getting all our priorities wrong, and he didn't like that. Plus, he didn't like doing certain drugs in front of me, so I guess I was a real pain in his side whenever I was around. The whole atmosphere escalated to the point where when the tour finished I decided I didn't want to work with the band any more."

It could be argued that part of Lynott's frustration in America was the failure to follow up the huge success of 'The Boys Are Back In Town'. 'Cowboy Song' could only reach No.77 in the October of '76, while 'Don't Believe A Word' and 'Dancing In The Moonlight' didn't even chart. Philip took a long hard look at his record company and decided that with new acts like Dire Straits coming through, perhaps Thin Lizzy just weren't flavour of the month any more.

"More than part of the reason Lizzy didn't have a lot of commercial success in America was that Mercury (part of PolyGram) was crap," states John Burnham. "Unfortunately we had to release all our US product through Mercury, the way all our product in the UK came out through Vertigo, but Mercury was a dreadful company.

"The music business in America is New York and LA. Mercury was in Chicago. It was run by two guys – Charlie Fash and Irvin Steinberg – and they didn't have a clue about rock music. They'd come to prominence when Mercury had been successful with soul music, pre-Stylistics era, but they were non-starters when it came to rock'n'roll.

"Look at the roster we had: Graham Parker & The Rumour – cracking in the UK, nothing in America; 10cc – cracking in the UK, nothing in America; Alex Harvey – same thing; Thin Lizzy – same thing. Mercury just couldn't do anything for rock acts, and that situation prevailed until we signed Dire Straits.

"When we signed Dire Straits Philip realised that they were going to be big, because he could see how much effort the record company was putting into them. He also realised around this time that maybe Lizzy weren't the golden boys at Phonogram any more. So he called a meeting at PolyGram and said, 'Right, now I want everyone to get back behind Thin Lizzy. I don't want to hear another word about Dire Straits. I don't want to hear another fucking word about Mark Knopfler. I've been making money for this company for years, and I want something from you in return. You needed me a few years ago, now I need you. I want to see everyone giving Lizzy their full support.'

"It definitely shook a few people up, although in America I don't think anyone at Mercury was too bothered when Lizzy got out of their deal and signed to Warner Brothers. Still, strange how the band's next album, *Live And Dangerous*, went on to be successful in the States . . ."

Lizzy returned to the UK and finished the year with a run of dates through November and December. The tour, with support from the delightfully named The Radiators From Space, commenced in Newcastle on November 11 and covered nearly 30 shows nationwide, including four in London (Hammersmith Odeon, December 10/11 and Lewisham Odeon, 13/14) and one at The Kursaal in Southend on the 17th.

To help ease the band's passage across the country the record company decided to lay on a limousine for the tour. The swishest of transport would also do nothing to ruin the band's cool rock star image, as they purred up to the backstage door to be swamped by hundreds of autograph hunters and photographers. Only as John Burnham explains, with Thin Lizzy nothing quite worked out as planned.

"The limo thing was a great pose," he contests. "But we could only afford one limo, so there would be all the band, plus a boot full of gear to ferry around in this car – so much gear, in fact, that the boot would never shut properly. They ended up having to hold the boot down with a wire coat hanger they'd nicked from a hotel room, and of course it totally destroyed the look of opulence that swanning around in a limo might have suggested.

"That summed Lizzy up for me – scruffy, in a most endearing way. I told them once: 'You're the smallest-time big band I've ever worked with!' And they were! They were floating along in this big limo, and there was this bit of wire holding the boot together. It pissed O'Donnell off because it didn't look Big Time enough, but for me it was typical Thin Lizzy."

Joining the band on that tour was Terrie Doherty, who worked as Regional Promotions Manager for Phonogram from 1977–81, concentrating on the North West of England. She has never forgotten her very first encounter with Philip, in a dressing room at Liverpool Empire.

"I had a stack of radio interviews set up for Philip," she

recalls, "and so I had to go backstage to meet him. I was very shy and nervous, but I plucked up all my courage and knocked on the dressing room door. This big blond-haired guy (Big Charlie) opened the door and said, 'Whaddyawant?!' So, blushing and panicking a bit, I said, 'I'd like to see Phil Lynott, please.' So he replied, 'Oh yeah? Lots of girls would like to see Phil Lynott – fuck off!' And he slammed the door in my face.

"I didn't know what to do, but eventually I decided to give it another go. I kept knocking on the door and finally this guy answered. I said, 'Er, I'm Terrie and I work for Phonogram . . .', and he went, 'Well why didn't you say so? Come on in!'

"I went in to the dressing room and got a real grilling from Phil. Charlie said, 'Hey Phil, this is the new bird from the record company', and Phil just stood there, eyeing me up and down, like a Sergeant Major inspecting a soldier. He then started walking around me, slowly, while I was sweating buckets. He kept going, 'Hmmm, the new chick, eh? Well . . . hmm . . . yeah . . . well I suppose you'll have to do.' I was terrified, but it was all a big wind-up; they were just testing me, checking me out. It was the Phil Lynott Initiation Ceremony."

One of Terrie Doherty's duties as Fairy Godmother of the North West was to ensure that the band's Manchester gig, a kind of 'second homecoming' for Philip, was one big party. It would involve rounding up all his friends and helping Phyllis turn the Clifton Grange into a Thin Lizzy shrine, with posters and banners and stickers everywhere, in preparation for the after-show shindig.

"Whenever Lizzy played Manchester the motto was: 'The Boys Are Back In Town'," she reminisces. "It was a real event, usually the highlight of a tour for Philip.

"One of the tasks I always had was to ring Steve Coppell (former Manchester United and England player) and get him to come along to the show, with as many of the other United players as possible. I'd get them a row of seats at the front, and Phil was such a huge Manchester United fan he'd be dead nervous. He'd be in the dressing room ten minutes before the show going, 'Terrie! Terrie! Are they here? Is Steve Coppell here? Is he? Is he?'

"The players would then come to The Showbiz afterwards for the party, along with an assortment of actors and actresses, sportsmen like George Best and Alex 'Hurricane' Higgins and all sorts of celebrities, not to mention a few of the more colourful characters on the Manchester scene. There were tons of people there, and Phyllis would declare an open bar and people just served themselves.

"One night the actor Geoff Hughes (formerly Eddie Yeats in *Coronation Street*, more recently Onslow in *Keeping Up Appearances*) got behind the bar and starting playing the barman. Phil called over to him and ordered a drink and Geoff said, as quick as a flash, 'Sorry, we don't serve blackies in here!' Honestly, you could hear a pin drop. Chris O'Donnell and I looked at each other and shuddered. But fortunately Geoff managed to make a joke of it and change the subject before Phil exploded. He'd heard all the black gags before but he was still very touchy about the subject, to the extent where he would never eat at the Sambo's fast-food chain in America, because he remembered being called by that name at school. He had to be in the right mood to even talk about it.

"We had a lot of laughs at The Biz though," Doherty emphasises. "They were the best after-show parties ever, and were famous for being so. They would go on all night and no-one would leave sober.

"The strange thing was, the hotel wasn't anything like you'd imagine it to be if you heard some of the stories about the parties. The rooms were stuffed with beautiful ornaments, trinkets, knick-knacks and a mass of bric-à-brac. There were polished leather sofas with antimacassars on the back, little coffee tables with bowls of fruit on and mannequins dressed in weird costumes standing here and there. If someone had peeked through the window one day they would've thought they were looking at a typical granny's parlour. But then after midnight it turned into the biggest rock'n'roll den in Britain. People would come from all over the country to try to get into the party."

"Phyllis was like everyone's mum, rolled into one," reckons Robbo, "and The Showbiz was like everyone's ideal party place. The only trouble was she could be real strict about certain things: she made me wash my hair once just before we were about to go off to do a TV show. I made a run for it but she grabbed me, marched me to the kitchen and shoved my head in the sink. The next thing I know she's squirting Fairy Liquid all over my head! She said: 'I will not have someone in my son's band going on TV looking like that!' And you couldn't argue with her."

Another major part of Lizzy's promotional visits to the North West was Philip's annual visit to Radio City in Liverpool. The idea of a music biz celeb taking over the station's rock show for an hour had proved so popular that everyone from Phil Collins to Frank Zappa had sampled the delights of ILR knob-twiddling over the years, and the spot became a much sought-after one, especially for record pluggers.

As DJ Phil Easton from the Great Easton Express explains, Philip did the show once in the mid-Seventies, loved it, and returned on every tour thereafter. "He was very good at it," he insists. "He had a very dry sense of humour, a great way of telling stories around the records, and he had a broad and varied taste in music. He'd play Cream, Little Richard, Kansas ('Carry On My Wayward Son' was a favourite of the whole band and crew), UFO, Stevie Wonder, plus a lot of reggae and r&b. I also remember him playing those dreadful Kiss solo albums; I don't think he was a fan, but he was both amused and fascinated by the whole marketing side of Kiss.

"Generally I found his visits to the station to be great for getting an insight into the man behind the myth," Easton adds. "Phil would come in and do my show from 7.00pm to 8.00pm, and then he'd be off to Liverpool Empire to be on stage by 9.00pm. And to be perfectly honest I could barely see the connection between the two guys. I found him such a gentle guy that I couldn't relate him to the larger-than-life stage character I'd see later that same night.

"It was always a pleasure to have him in the studio. He was very funny, very friendly, always courteous and co-operative."

"I've never known an artist who has actually liked the promotional merry-go-round," says Terrie Doherty, "but Phil used to put up with it well, and was always very professional. How would anyone like to be told, right after coming off stage, that they've got to be driven all the way to Bradford for a radio interview, and then be back in Manchester the same night for a show the next day? Phil used to suffer from the fact that the onus for interviews was always on him as the spokesman and frontman of the group. But he always did it with a smile on his face. Well, perhaps it was a grimace . . ."

"Press-wise Phil was very shrewd," says Tony Brainsby. "He'd plonk himself down in my office and work really hard throughout the day, interview after interview after interview. He also took the time to remember things about the journalists who interviewed him, so that if he ever met that journalist again he could go, 'Oh, how's the wife?' or whatever. He realised that that kind of familiarity with people could only endear him to those people. And of course he also realised that if he was nice to the people in my office they would get behind him more, so he'd turn up with bunches of flowers for all the girls and generally be very charming. He was very clever like that."

The New Year began with the mixing of *Live And Dangerous*, a joint effort between the band and Tony Visconti. In between times Lynott began submitting ideas for a solo album to tape, as well as knocking up a few tunes for the next Lizzy studio album, while Decca continued to milk their portion of the back catalogue by releasing 'Whiskey In The Jar' again.

But the most pressing project was the live album, which the band chose to complete at Des Dames Studios in Paris. Or did they?

"The whole Paris thing," confesses John Burnham, "was a bit of a tax scam. We'd never do any work in Paris, we'd just have a great time – hence the picture on the record sleeve featuring a cocaine tray with a razor, a straw and a rolled up fiver. The reference on the back cover – 'I remember Paris' – was also part of that. It was a laugh.

"Actually my most embarrassing moment came when I flew out to meet Philip in Paris. I got a really early flight from Heathrow, got to Paris, checked in at the Novotel, and phoned Philip around noon. He invited me to his room, lit up a huge spliff and started to chop out four lines of coke. And this at a quarter past midday!

"Anyway, not wishing to be thought of as namby-pamby, I took a few draws on the spliff and did two lines of coke. I wasn't really prepared for it at that time in the morning and I probably went green. But then Philip came and sat opposite me on the bed, slipped a cassette of the latest *Live And Dangerous* mixes on this Walkman and I put the headphones on. Philip was really keen to know what I thought of it. Anyway, the first track had just started when the coke and the weed hit me, and I threw up like something out of *The Exorcist*, all over Philip's lap.

"So much for me being macho. It became an on-going joke after that: 'What do you think of the new album?' BLEEUURGH!!'"

By March enough of the live album had been mixed for the band to take time out of the studio to film an accompanying video, also called *Live And Dangerous*. The Rainbow Theatre in London's Finsbury Park was booked for a special one-off gig on the 29th and the result was one of the best live rock videos ever produced; a vision of a band on top form that remains spine-chillingly exciting to this day.

With a running time of just 60 minutes the whole Lizzy show could not be included, but such is the momentum of the chosen footage even tracks like 'Jailbreak', 'Cowboy Song' and 'The Rocker' aren't missed. In fact, the video featured three new songs, never before released: 'Are You Ready', 'Baby Drives Me Crazy' and 'Me And The Boys' (all three "soundcheck-type fillers" according to Robbo). Although potential purchasers should be warned that the track titled 'Call On Me' on some labels is in fact 'Still In Love With You'.

The video opened with images of the road crew arriving at the venue and constructing the stage, to the accompaniment of the live 'Rosalie', which was shortly destined to be the single. The action began with 'The Boys Are Back In Town' and rarely let up until the flashpot finale of 'Me And The Boys' (the B-side of 'Rosalie') at the end. Throughout, the edge with which the band played fully justified the 'dangerous' boast.

Preceding the album by two months, the live version of 'Rosalie' (complete with the 'Cowgirl's Song' section) was released in April '78 and proved a popular success. It reached No.20 in the UK charts, inspired a rare live-in-the-studio performance on the mime-time TV programme *Top Of The Pops*, and the video for the single (taken from the Rainbow footage) was a favourite on Kenny Everett's Television Show.

"At last," says John Burnham, "Thin Lizzy came alive, in both senses of the term. As a record company we tried hard, as did Philip, to get the studio albums to recreate the excitement of the band on stage, but for whatever reason it just didn't happen. Then came the *Live And Dangerous* package and everything fell into place. That album had everything: power, energy, excitement, emotion, humour, melody, dynamics . . . plus something extra, something that most rock'n'roll bands didn't have.

"To me, there always seemed to be a lot of love in Thin Lizzy's music. Philip used the word about men – not in a homosexual sense, but in the true sense – and I felt that he did love the members of his band, the road crew, the guys in the front row. He used to say to me, 'You know you're loved', and I always thought of that as a great compliment. So there was always that aspect of affection around the band, and I think that warmth came across on *Live And Dangerous*. It was a great album, and perfectly timed."

"One of the reasons why we decided on a live album," O'Donnell explains, "was because the sound of those Hammersmith Odeon shows (14–16th November 1976) was so powerful. I always used to get bugged by the fact that Lizzy never had the ability to play that block rhythm sound that many of the great British guitarists made famous – people like Paul Kossoff. Lizzy's sound was always a bit weedy, with these long, fluid guitar lines instead of meaty rhythms. Yet when we listened to that Hammersmith gig from the Maison Rouge mobile recording truck outside we knew they'd got the sound right at last."

The *Live And Dangerous* album was taken mostly from those Hammersmith shows, although for tax reasons it was claimed that some of the tracks originated from the Toronto show on October 28 the previous year. It was also claimed by some that the album had been so polished up in the studio, with Visconti even using crowd noises from a David Bowie concert, that the album was barely live at all. Chris O'Donnell refutes these suggestions strongly.

"*Live And Dangerous* was 75 per cent live," he states for the record. "The rest was overdubs, mainly of vocals and lead guitar solos, just to 'clean' the sound up.

"Tony Visconti said the art of making a great live album was what you did in the studio, so don't be fooled, because most live albums are polished up in the studio. The reason is, most people want to hear quality of sound on records – they don't want to hear muffled solos, or dodgy vocals. So if you've got the means to make something sound better, the listener can only benefit."

It's a reasonable enough argument. The double-disc package of *Live And Dangerous* certainly sounded pristine and powerful, and no matter how much had been manufactured in the studio, from the opening chords of 'Jailbreak' right through to the climactic strains of 'The Rocker' the listener felt they were right there in the front row.

The album was nothing short of a tour de force, up there with all the classic double live rock albums. The sheer brute brilliance of the way Side Three surged through 'Cowboy Song', segued into 'The Boys Are Back In Town' and 'Don't Believe A Word', and then thundered through 'Warriors' and 'Are You Ready', for example, was quite breathtaking.

Then there was crowd favourite 'Emerald' (complete with Lynott's oft-repeated if grammatically incorrect request: "Is there anybody here with any Irish in them? Is there any of the girls who'd like a bit more Irish in them?"), plus the mean bitch that was 'Massacre' and the awesome live version of 'Still In Love With You'. This particular rendition, fraught with trembling emotion, could even be the highlight of Philip Lynott's entire career.

The title of the double album, which Lizzy persuaded Phonogram to sell for the price of a single, came from a suggestion by Chris O'Donnell. "I was talking to Bernie Rhodes about the possibility of doing a gig with The Clash at the Roundhouse, but he was stalling a bit. He said to me, 'We don't just do gigs, we make political statements. Everything we do has to be dangerous, do you understand?' I said, 'Perfectly, Bernie!' I put the phone down, rang Phil and said, 'How about "Live And Dangerous"?' He thought it was great.

"At the time the picture which finished up on the back cover was going to be the front cover, and the title was going to be *Thin Lizzy Live*. This was because Scott and Robbo insisted they had to be featured as equal members of the group. But I rang the record company and said, 'Scrap the group shot, put the picture of Phil on the cover and call it *Live And Dangerous*.' "

The packaging of the album was a significant success. The mass of live pictures – 55 in all – which were splashed across the sleeves made an exciting change from the one or two out-of-focus jobs you usually got with live albums. Just by looking at the cover made you feel as if you were in the middle of a Thin Lizzy concert.

"In those days the record company would tell you that you had a day with a photographer, and you had to get all your photos done in that day," O'Donnell explains. "But I realised that photographs could sell a project, and that a day simply wasn't enough for such an important part of the project. So when Chalkie Davies came to photograph us in the States for an *NME* feature, we kidnapped him. We took him on the road with us for two weeks and made him take hundreds of shots.

"Now in order to see all of them I had to get a couple of those carousels that you slot the slides into, then turn around. It was while I was flicking through all these slides that I began to recognise certain parts of the set from the poses of certain band members, or whatever. I told Phil and Chalkie that it was just like watching a gig, and it was that which gave me the idea to use all of the damn shots in order to create a photographic record of the show.

"Of course," O'Donnell continues, "the record company had kittens, because there were over 70 colour separations that were needed for the sleeve, and in a normal sleeve there's only usually two or three. But I managed to convince them that the record was going to be massive, and that it would all pay for itself.

"Little did we know that *Grease* (the soundtrack to the John Travolta/Olivia Newton-John film) was going to be released at the same time, and we were No.2 behind it for six weeks straight. Still, I believe it was the biggest-selling live album ever in this country, so we didn't do a bad job on it, did we?"

Indeed, everything about *Live And Dangerous* seemed to be spot on, and it remains to this day one of the greatest live rock albums. But at the time certain employees of Phonogram had to bend a few rules to allow the album to reach its full potential. John Burnham, who'd become label manager at Vertigo by this time, was one of them. "My job was to get the album out on budget," he declares. "The artist's manager would come in demanding this and that, and it was up to me to persuade him that my way of thinking was best – and of course my way of thinking was always along the lines of what was cheapest, as that would please my boss.

"With *Live And Dangerous*, Morrison and O'Donnell wanted to market it in three phases. We'd apportion an equal amount of money to each of the phases, and the idea was to keep the record up there in the charts for as long as possible. So we started the first phase of the marketing exercise and the album took off. We then entered the second phase, and the album continued to blaze a trail. So we came to the third phase and the management wanted to make it an even bigger campaign, way beyond our budget. My job was to persuade the management that we didn't need to do this, but I was so into the album that I cheated Phonogram and spent the money that Morrison and O'Donnell wanted. It was the only time I ever cheated Phonogram, but the album was such a success that I got away with it."

While the *Live And Dangerous* campaign hammered away in Europe and America, Lynott took time out to recharge his batteries in the Bahamas. The trip wasn't strictly a holiday as time had been booked at Compass Point Studios in Nassau to allow Philip the option of recording some tracks for a solo album. But all industrious intentions disappeared like a Caribbean cocktail the minute they got there.

"It was great," says Scott Gorham, "sitting there under a ton of sun-tan oil on this beautiful white beach, sucking on a few Bahama Mamas and looking at all the bikinis wiggling past. The trouble was, the last thing you wanted to do was work. Like, 'Who's for the studio and who's for the pool?' Trying to get us to record in the Bahamas was a big-time mistake."

"I couldn't believe how lazy Phil had become," exclaims

Huey Lewis, who'd been invited on the 'holiday' with a view to lending a bit of harmonica to the album. "We were supposed to be in the studio by six, but Phil would turn up at nine. Then an hour or two later he'd be off to a club, and that would be it for the night. That was when I first started to worry about his health.

"We did achieve something though. There was this song he had called 'Tattoo', which I used to called 'Giving It All Up For Love', because that was the hook. I kept telling Phil he was doing it all wrong, and in the end he said, 'Look Lewis, I'm tired of your bellyaching – do the damn song yourself!' "

Lewis did just that, and the song was one of three tracks on the first Huey Lewis & The News demo tape, which actually secured them a record deal in 1980. In 1982 the song was released as a single in the UK but failed to chart, although by this time it had already surfaced on Lynott's solo album, *Solo In Soho*.

Suitably refreshed, Lizzy returned to London and tumbled straight into rehearsals for the forthcoming European tour. The Rainbow Theatre was booked for two days to enable the crew to get to grips with the band's full production, which now included new lights, new flashbombs, mirrorballs and, for the first time, lasers, and those who caught the sessions were introduced to a clutch of embryonic songs, including 'S&M' and 'Waiting For An Alibi'.

With the engine refuelled the band played a short series of concerts in Europe during May, before returning to take their new show to Belfast's Ulster Hall on June 14 (Lynott had jammed with The Boomtown Rats at the same venue the night before), Glasgow Apollo on June 17, Manchester Belle Vue on the 18th and Newcastle City Hall on the 20th, before the crucial visits to Wembley's Empire Pool, on the 22nd and 23rd. The promoter for these latter dates was Harvey Goldsmith, a move which elbowed Adrian Hopkins out of the picture for the first time since the *Jailbreak* tour. But Hopkins was soon restored thanks largely to Lynott's sense of loyalty.

"When Morrison and O'Donnell started talking to the big promoters, such as Harvey Goldsmith and Mel Bush," Hopkins explains, "Philip started to ask a few questions. He said,

141

'Where was Harvey Goldsmith when Adrian Hopkins was losing money promoting us in the early days?' He felt that the fact that I'd stuck with Lizzy through some thin times meant that I deserved his support in return.

"Harvey was really trying hard to woo the band, though. On the opening night of the tour in Glasgow he hung this huge banner from the balcony of the Apollo which read: 'Harvey Goldsmith and Glasgow welcomes Thin Lizzy!' Phil pointed out to him later that the only people who could see it were those in the band ... Then Harvey really screwed it up by presenting everyone with the usual end-of-tour bottle of champagne each ... and charging it to tour expenses! From that day on Lizzy never really worked in the UK without me being involved."

The Harvey Goldsmith tour was quite a daunting step for the band to take, essentially representing another rung on the rock'n'roll ladder. Some folk feared the move into the bigger arenas might be a bit premature. But Chris O'Donnell was adamant it was feasible. "Phil wanted to do Hammersmith Odeon again, because he knew he could sell that out. I argued with him about doing two Wembleys, and in the end he said, 'OK we'll do Wembley, but if it flops you're finished as my manager!'

"In a sense they were magical evenings, but in another sense it was incredibly depressing, because it was the first sign that this thing we had created and nurtured between us had been taken away from us. Phil and I had an incredible bond, a bond that no-one could get near. We worked so hard together that when it began to pay off and we found ourselves backstage at Wembley instead of the Marquee we'd look at each other and laugh. We used to imagine we'd wake up one morning and someone would tell us it had all been a big mistake, that we hadn't made it at all, that it was someone else's gig. It became a running joke, and that's what my abiding memory of Phil is – that little bond that we shared. But that night at Wembley the bond we had perhaps weakened a little, because we sensed that Thin Lizzy didn't belong to our little gang anymore, it belonged to the fans."

Sadly it was to be the last time British fans of the band

were to see the Robbo line-up in action. After the success of the June tour (although Robbo maintains the first night at Wembley was "horrendous"), Lizzy took it easy in July, using the opportunity of a visit to Ibiza for a Bullring Festival to wind down once again. But the following month word filtered through to the British press that the on-off situation with Robbo was probably . . . definitely . . . off.

"The Ibiza trip was a good one," says Brian Downey, "but I seem to remember Robbo getting really badly sunburnt and having to play with a wet towel around his head. He always seemed to be in the wars – broken bones, cuts, bruises, slashed tendons and God knows what else. You never knew if he was going to turn up to the next gig in one piece.

"It did become slightly wearing on us, and we began to discuss replacements. I approached an Irish guy called Jimmy Smith, who played with The Bogey Boys, but he turned the offer down. Phil had one or two other ideas, so when it came to the crunch with Robbo we weren't caught on the hop again."

"I was real happy to have Brian back in the band around the *Bad Reputation* time," Gorham claims, "even though he was a fucking nutcase. He was a great player and a lot of fun to be with. But Phil was always pissed off with him for some reason, and in the end even I had to agree that he was a liability."

"I think Robbo's problem was that he was so aggressive," suggests Terrie Doherty. "He was always on the verge of a fight with someone, and on one occasion he even threatened to punch my lights out!

"It was an unforgettable night, after a gig at the Ulster Hall in Belfast. We were at the most-bombed hotel in the world, the Europa, and there was a lot of Gary Moore's friends and relatives around. They were having a go at Phil in the bar and the atmosphere was really heavy. I also seem to remember another group of people, nothing to do with Moore's mob, in another corner of the bar, threatening trouble against Phil. And then there was Robbo, completely out of it, threatening to beat everyone in the bar up. I tried to cool him down, but he just said, 'If you don't get out of my way I'll punch your face in!' That was enough for Philip, and he grabbed hold of Robbo and tried to make him apologise to me . . . which he wouldn't.

"Lizzy always seemed to get themselves into highly volatile situations," Doherty adds, "and in the end I think the management started to ensure that there was always an element of muscle in the vicinity – minders who'd keep an eye on the boys. But Robbo was the worst for fights, and ultimately that was his downfall."

Robbo's own explanation for his departure is typically blunt and forthright. "It was a case of, if I hadn't have left I would've been sacked," he admits. "I was really just out of control, a complete asshole. I used to drink a lot of whiskey and snort a lot of speed, so I was fired up a lot of the time, like a stick of dynamite waiting to explode, and that caused me a lot of problems. I mean, I'm short-tempered enough, but when I'm on whiskey and speed I'm uncontrollable. And in those days I'd be on two bottles of Johnny Walker Black Label a night: half a bottle at the soundcheck, half a bottle before going on stage, and the other bottle during the gig.

"I just wasn't prepared to change my ways at the time, because I thought I was right. I wasn't, but I always thought I knew best. Of course now with the benefit of hindsight I can see there were a few things I shouldn't have done. I now know what a prat I was. And we all know what a prat Phil was, because he isn't here with us today. But you can only ever see your mistakes after you've made them. By then it's too late."

The rock world was hardly shaken to the core when the name of Robbo's replacement was announced during August. Gary Moore's brave venture with Colosseum II hadn't exactly been an overwhelming success, and in fact at various junctures throughout the year the guitarist's meandering path had crossed that of his old friend Phil Lynott – with each contributing to the other's proposed solo album. This was to be Moore's third stint with Thin Lizzy in four years, but his first as a 'full time' member of the band.

In effect, the new Lizzy made their live début at the opening of the Electric Ballroom club in Camden Town, North London, on August 28. Former Lizzy tour manager Frank Murray had masterminded the re-opening of the venue, an old Irish carousel ballroom, and Lynott had persuaded him to let The Greedy Bastards christen the occasion. Gary Moore explains:

"We were round Phil's one night – Gary Holton (Heavy Metal Kids/*Auf Wiedersehn Pet*) was living there at the time – and I remember saying, 'Wouldn't it be great if you could be in a band with no manager and no record company, and just go out and play for cash?' It just came from a conversation like that. And then Phil came up with the name The Greedy Bastards, and everyone wanted to be in it. Elton John wanted to be in it. Bob Geldof wanted to be in it . . ."

In the event the line-up for that first gig was Lynott, Moore, Gorham, Downey, Jimmy Bain, Chris Spedding, Steve Jones, Paul Cook, Malcolm McLaren and whoever else was around . . . but no Elton John and, at the rehearsals at least, no Geldof. "Geldof really pissed me off," snorts Moore, "because he said he was going to do it, so we all went away and learnt all the Boomtown Rats stuff, and then he didn't show up to any of the rehearsals. He did the gig, got his money and pissed off. Then a week later he was in all the papers complaining that the rehearsals were just like a Miss World contest, with everyone posing around. He wasn't even there!"

"It was a pretty hairy gig, but great fun," says Gorham. "The trouble was, I'd look at the front row and they'd all be working up a mouthful of phlegm, ready to spit at us. It was a disgusting trend that was 'in' at the time, and guys like Steve Jones were covered in saliva. I just hid behind Phil and let his big afro catch all the spit. Man, I didn't want to get involved in that shit!"

The set list at the Electric Ballroom was, as you might imagine, fairly loose: a few Lizzy songs, a few Sex Pistols songs, Stevie Wonder's 'Jesus Children Of America', Geldof's 'Looking After No.1', Spedding's 'Motorbiking', the Sid Vicious version of 'My Way', the old standard 'Route 66' and whatever else came to mind in the beer-sodden melee. It was basically one massive jam session, the ideal escape from the grinding formalities of the music business. As Gary Moore says: "No managers, no guest lists, no messing around – just play the gig, get paid, goodnight!"

On a more calculating level the concept of The Greedy Bastards – who later did two more shows in Dublin – perfectly illustrated Lynott's shrewd re-alignment with the happening punk scene, a move which had ensured that Lizzy were one of the few rock bands to escape the great punk purge. Philip deliberately kept himself in touch with 'the street', and made a fiercely determined effort to make sure Lizzy wouldn't be dismissed with the 'dinosaurs' – the whole generation of rock bands who'd dominated the early Seventies. It was one of his most astute career moves.

"Phil was paranoid that he might be getting left behind by all the latest crazes and stuff," explains Moore, "so when punk came along he befriended Steve Jones and Paul Cook as a way of staying in touch. They were always round his house in Cricklewood (Anson Road, NW2), as were all sorts of strange characters from the punk scene. You'd go round there and the place would be heaving. There'd be Geldof in one corner, Bebe Buell (infamous groupie) lying on the floor somewhere, Sid Vicious and Nancy Spungeon sitting in the other corner ... you know that famous photo of Sid and Nancy in the toilet? That was taken at Phil's house. Phil used to say, 'That fucking Sid, he comes round here shooting up, drops the needle on the floor, picks it up and sticks it straight back in his arm ... it's fucking terrible!' But Phil didn't really have the heart to chuck people out. His was an open house, 24 hours a day."

The day after the Electric Ballroom party Lizzy were preparing to leave for Los Angeles to start another American tour, when Brian Downey announced he couldn't face getting on the flight. Instead Downey headed for Dublin where, official sources claimed, he was going to spend the rest of the summer looking after his sick son. The truth was, he was just as sick himself.

"I was totally exhausted," he admits, "I couldn't take any more. I didn't want to see another stage again, and I certainly didn't want to go to Australia, as had been proposed for the band. There were also a few personal problems in my life at that point as well, and I needed time to sort myself out. But I was being totally unprofessional and I really should have been sacked."

"Phil freaked when Brian said he wasn't going to go on tour," says Moore, "but I knew we'd be able to pick up any drummer in LA to stand in for the shows. We had a few spare days in LA anyway, so we started auditioning. One of the guys we auditioned was Terry Bozzio, but he just didn't fit in with us – he didn't do drugs and he didn't say 'fuck' enough times in a sentence! He wanted $1,500 a week or something, and he wanted to bring his wife Dale on the road. We were like, 'Oh yeah, sure!' So we ditched him and got in Mark Nauseef, who'd been playing with the Ian Gillan Band."

The band put in a few days of rehearsals at SIR studios in LA and then took the *Live And Dangerous* tour across America, opening for Kansas during September and Styx during October. As the trek unfolded its title gave a new definition to the term 'apt'. "One night we were in Memphis," Gary Moore shudders, "and Phil decided that he was going to go out looking for Jerry Lee Lewis, because he'd heard that he didn't like black people. We went to this club but we couldn't find him, so in the end we decided to leave, and I went to call our limo driver who was parked outside.

"Now, this guy was parked on the other side of the road, and he had to cut through this gas station in order to turn around and come and pick us up. But as he drove across the forecourt another car blocked him in, and much to my amazement he started to ram this other guy's car with our limo! Crash! Crash! Crash! He was smashing the shit out of it!

"Now, this other guy was a huge black man, a Barry White-lookalike, and he went insane. The next thing I knew our driver has screeched up outside the club shouting, 'Get in the car! The motherfucker's got a gun!' So we all piled in and the limo sped off at about a hundred miles and hour, chased by the Barry White clone in his car. At one point the other car actually pulled alongside our car, the guy wound the window down and started waving a gun at me!

"So we were careering through Memphis, and to make matters worse there was a police strike on at the time, so we couldn't even call for help. We turned our lights off to try and lose this guy with the gun, but he kept right behind us, going through red lights, cutting across parking lots and everything.

"Finally, we got a little way ahead of Barry White and reached the Holiday Inn ... only to discover that it was the wrong Holiday Inn! So we were standing there cursing the driver when Barry White came screeching into the parking lot, we piled back in the limo, and the chase started again. At the end of it all, when we'd finally shaken this guy off, I told Phil I never wanted to hear a Jerry Lee Lewis record again!"

Other incidents which gave substance to the title of the tour included the night in Oklahoma when Lynott got into a huge barroom brawl over an alluring local lass and was escorted back to the hotel battered and bloody nosed . . . only to return to the bar later that night and end up in another fight when someone mistakenly took a sip out of his drink.

"Another close scrape was when we were in El Paso," Moore recalls, "and the record company took us across the border into Mexico for lunch. Phil didn't have his passport on him and they wouldn't let him back into America. He got pulled in and we had to haggle with the authorities for ages to get him released. It was just a good job they didn't see him five minutes before we got to the border, when he was frantically trying to get rid of all his coke . . ."

Danger signs also flashed on an occasion when Lizzy were in New York, and for a fleeting moment crossed paths with the local Mafia. John Burnham remembers the story in awe. "Lizzy's tour manager had to 'bung' this Italian-American chargehand a certain amount of money for the Mafia. It was an unwritten law, I guess. You certainly didn't argue. But when Philip found out how much money they were having to give to this guy, he went to try and sort it out himself. Rather bravely, and rather foolishly it must be said, he marched into this guy's office and began to complain. When he'd finished the guy simply looked at Phil in amazement, and in thickest Brooklyn declared: 'Jesus Christ, the nigger's a paddy!' "

The outcome of that encounter has been tragically lost in the mists of time, but memories of Lizzy's first trip to Australia in October '78 remain crystal clear, especially for Gary Moore. "The band flew Cathay Pacific from Los Angeles to Sydney, via Honolulu and Auckland," he recalls, "and there was a bomb scare, leading to a five-hour delay, leading in turn to all of us getting extremely pissed. When we finally got going two of our roadies got into a fight on the plane and covered all the passengers in beer. They (monitor engineer George

'Mad Dog' McQuade and guitar technician Andy Moore) got arrested at the first stop in Honolulu and chucked off the flight, as well as sacked by Lizzy. Another guy called Colin Harbour who went to help George was also left in Honolulu because the captain wouldn't let him back on. Honestly, Lizzy's road crew was a circus in its own right.

"Anyway," Moore continues, "we left Honolulu and dinner was served. But Phil had nodded off into his food, and the stewardess ended up taking his tray away from him. When he woke up he caused an absolute shit-storm, demanding his food be brought back.

"Eventually, the stewardess rustled something up for him, and he nodded straight off again, with his mouth open. So Mark Nauseef got out his Polaroid camera and took a snap of me spoon-feeding Phil while he was asleep. Later when Phil woke up again he said, 'Hey, check this out man!' and showed Phil the Polaroid. I thought to myself, 'Oh no, you idiot!', and slithered under my blanket, pretending to be asleep. Then suddenly I heard this frenzy of ripping noises. Phil just said, 'Don't ever take pictures of me again, right?' So Mark replied, 'Why?' And Phil went, 'Because I'm a fucking star, that's why!' It was so funny."

When Lizzy got to Australia on October 18 the wind-ups continued apace. A combination of drink, drugs, jet-lag and full-blooded one-upmanship made the band's first press conference a rich source of lively quotes. "God knows what Phil was on at the time," Moore gasps, "but he was being a real asshole, and I couldn't believe some of the things he was saying. After a while I decided I couldn't take any more of it. This press guy asked Phil if he knew anything about Australia before he arrived in the country, and Phil replied by saying that he knew he had some relations somewhere in the country. So I just couldn't resist it, of course. I said: 'Yeah, a tribe of aborigines up the road!' Everyone cracked up laughing, but Phil looked at me like he was going to kill me. He just mumbled, 'Er, as you can see, Gary's the joker in the band.' The rest of the guys couldn't believe I'd said that, but I guess it was just me getting my own back for some of the things he'd said.

"Having said that," Moore adds, "Phil and I did hang out quite a bit on that tour, despite the tension that was in the air. We spent most of our time at parties, to be honest. We'd be offered things like judging Miss Adelaide contests, or going to these receptions with gangs of leggy models. It was terrible, really."

When the band eventually got to play they saw another side of Aussie hospitality. One particular show which comes to Gary Moore's mind involved an early morning flight to a town called Newcastle, just north of Sydney, a stadium full of people frying sausages, and several thousand flip-flops . . .

"We did a great soundcheck at this place," says Moore, "and it really was bizarre playing with this strong smell of sausages wafting around. But then Phil took a sweetie or two – acid, or something – and by the time we went on stage he was acting really weird.

"Then someone threw a flip-flop at Phil, and of course Phil responded by saying, 'If you're gonna throw those fucking things, at least throw both of them so we can make pairs out of them!' The next thing we knew everyone's throwing these flip-flops at us, and it was like *Star Wars* on stage, dodging all these missiles. God knows what it must've looked like to Phil, with whatever he was on at the time."

At another Australian show guests backstage were treated to a glimpse of the more competitive side of Lynott's nature. Whilst always seeming willing to assist his fellow artists, Philip nevertheless harboured a ruthless streak which manifested itself in orders to the road crew to sometimes subtly sabotage acts on the same bill.

"He'd suggest we gave any band that might be a threat to Lizzy a hard time," laughs Peter Eustace, "perhaps by fiddling with the lights, the sound, or whatever. It's a fairly common practise in the music business for one artist to try to pull a stroke on another like that.

"Anyway, at this particular show in Australia Phil heard that the guy who used to sing with Steely Dan was on the bill. It didn't matter that this guy (David Palmer, who fronted a band called Wha-koo) had left Steely Dan years before and his career was virtually over, to Phil just the mention of Steely Dan was enough to get him going. I remember him walking around backstage with a fish knife, threatening people about running orders and set times and so on. I don't think he was seriously going to use the knife on anyone, but it looked good! If nothing else, Phil knew the importance of image: how to establish it, how to sell it and how to get your own way by using it."

Lizzy did four shows on that first Australian tour, with Whakoo, John English and another Aussie band called Sport completing the bill. The events were co-promoted by four local radio stations along with Phonogram and RCA, and were held at Brisbane's Botanical Gardens on October 20, Newcastle's International Sports Centre on the 22nd, Melbourne's Myer Music Bowl on the 27th and, finally, before the magnificent Sydney Opera House on the 29th.

The Sydney show was the one genuine highlight of the Australian tour. The stage was constructed to the side of Circular Quay, in front of the steps which lead up to the famous architectural triumph, and crowd estimations vary wildly between 300,000 and a million. The event was also filmed by Australia's Channel 7 – "There were two helicopters with cameras," says Gorham, "a couple of boats in the harbour with cameras, cameras on stage, cameras in the crowd, cameras coming out of your ass!" – and the concert was due to be released as a live video in the UK. But while the band even got as far as overdubbing the soundtrack on their return to London, frustratingly the project has yet to be taken to its rightful conclusion.

Gary Moore flew back to LA with Mark Nauseef and stage manager Bill Cayley after the Australian tour, a decision not entirely unconnected with the fact that he'd met a new girlfriend Down Under who just happened to be from LA. The rest of the band returned to London to start work on the new studio album, with a rejuvenated Brian Downey slipping back into the fold on the first day at Tony Visconti's Good Earth Studios in Dean Street, Soho.

"I'd lost loads of weight and cut my hair short," Downey laughs, "and I don't think they recognised me at first. But I think Phil was pleased to have me back in the band, because I don't think it had quite worked out with Mark Nauseef. If Mark had fitted in I think I would've been out of the band for good, but as it turned out I was glad to be offered my job back."

The year finished for Lizzy with a special charity concert at Hammersmith Odeon on December 17, and then two Christmas shows as The Greedy Bastards in Dublin. The latter, featuring the pick-up band of assorted Pistols, Rats and liggers, not to mention support from a young U2, were held at the ill-fated Stardust Ballroom which was to burn down in 1981 claiming 49 lives.

The Hammersmith show was part of Lizzy tradition, a 'thumbs up' to those who'd supported them throughout another tough year. Except this time the gesture backfired amid a hail of poisoned reviews, and one critic even went as far as to suggest that the band must be on the verge of splitting up.

"There's no doubt it was a really bad gig," Gary Moore concedes. "We did a great soundcheck, but when it came to the show it all started to go wrong. I suppose the opening didn't help: we crashed in with the big power chord as usual, complete with the flashbombs, and there we all were cowering up on the drum riser, huddled together like rabbits, afraid we were going to get our faces singed! So much for the big macho heroes.

"Anyway, I'd suggested beforehand that we started the show with 'Are You Ready' for a change, because 'Jailbreak' was getting boring night after night, and so we launched into 'Are You Ready' . . . and it sounded shit. We then went straight into 'Bad Reputation', but it still sounded crap. We were all looking at each other going, 'What the hell's going on?'

"Then came my solo. It was my first gig with the band in London, it was my big solo spot, my moment of glory, I was all ready to let rip . . . and my roadie hands me a guitar with no strap! The guitar just fell to the floor and I felt a complete prat. I freaked and chased the roadie off the stage, kicked him in the nuts and smashed a mike stand with the guitar. I was livid!"

In between extracts from The Three Stooges' routines, Lizzy delivered what was essentially the *Live And Dangerous* set, speckled with new songs such as 'Waiting For An Alibi', 'Black Rose' and 'Back On The Streets', with lead vocals from Moore. The set closed with another new song, 'Get Out Of Here', and the inevitable encore section featured an appearance by Steve Jones, who helped thrash a Pistols-like punkiness into the Frank Sinatra/Sid Vicious standard, 'My Way'. But long before then the dye of a downbeat show had been cast.

"Basically, the whole gig was a disaster and I wasn't surprised we got slagged," Moore declares, adding that he can still remember whole lines from the stinging critiques that followed. "In our defence though, I must say that the tour in general was really good, and that the press just caught us on an 'off' night.

"Typical Lizzy, really. If it wasn't for bad luck we wouldn't have had any luck at all."

Chapter V

In The Realms Of The Black Rose

As one of the hardest working bands in rock, time was always at a premium for Thin Lizzy. Tour followed tour in rapid succession, recording schedules approached like on-coming juggernauts, extracurricular commitments ate into spare days and promotional activities never seemed to cease.

1978 wasn't just about *Live And Dangerous*, the Robbo/Moore saga, The Greedy Bastards and Sydney Opera House. For Philip there was also the chance to guest on Jeff Wayne's *War Of The Worlds* soundtrack as Parson Nathaniel on the track 'The Spirit Of Man'. There was the opportunity to mull over a few ideas with reggae group Third World. Plus, around the '77/'78 time there were a number of sessions for friends: appearing with Bob Geldof as backing vocalists The Dublinaires on the *Blue Wave* EP by Blast Furnace And The Heatwaves; adding some vocals to Johnny Thunders' *So Alone* album; producing the single 'Look At Love Bleed' for Ron McQuinn and writing lyrics for McQuinn's interpretation of 'Banshee' on the B-side; and also producing Brush Shiels' version of 'Look At Love Bleed', as well as the follow-up single 'Fight Your Heart Out'.

All this and more: on December 19 (or possibly the 20th, as not even the family are sure), Lynott became a father for the first time. Sarah Philomena was born in Holes Hospital at St. Stephen's Green, Dublin, the result of Philip's relationship with Caroline Crowther, daughter of entertainer Leslie Crowther, who met Philip while working for PR Tony Brainsby. It was one of the proudest moments of his life.

Also at the end of the year a plan was hatched to publish *A Collected Works Of Philip Lynott* – coupling the poetry from his two previous books, *Songs For While I'm Away* and *Philip* – and there was also talk of some future link-up with Midge Ure and Mark Knopfler from Dire Straits. Finally for good measure there was the chance to secure some major publicity, as Philip accepted an invitation to judge the 1978 Miss World Contest.

"That was a great coup for us," enthuses PR Tony Brainsby. "Great for Phil's reputation as a ladies' man, great exposure for Lizzy, a great night out . . . and all it took was a few timely phone calls to Eric Morley's office. I think Phil was a perfect choice as a judge, and of course as he was Irish the organisers couldn't be accused of being too biased towards the Brits.

"The event was held at the Royal Albert Hall and there was a party afterwards in Park Lane. Phil pulled one of the contestants and disappeared, but not before I'd got him to have his picture taken with Miss Argentina. We got that snap in quite a few of the papers – and around the same time I managed to get a photo of Philip with Marie Osmond (Brainsby also represented The Osmonds) in a few of the papers too. It was an exciting time to be his PR, because it was so easy to sell him."

Lynott's profile was certainly high at the time, and he was very much in demand. The drawback of succumbing to all these obligations was it didn't leave an abundance of time to work on his own material, and this led to some worries about the next Lizzy album.

His solution was to create a 'pool' of songs from his collaborations with the likes of Gary Moore, Scott and Brian, Jimmy Bain, Huey Lewis and ex-Slik/Rich Kids guitarist James 'Midge' Ure. The pool could then be dipped into whenever the need arose, either for solo albums, Lizzy albums, one-off singles, or whatever.

"It was another of Phil's big ideas," laughs Moore. "He was always coming up with stuff like that. 'Hey! (assumes the Lynott accent) I know what we should do, guys . . .' We just went into whatever studio was available whenever we could and recorded everything."

The songs produced during this prolific period ended up on a variety of albums – Moore's solo album for MCA, *Back On The Streets* (released December '78), Lizzy's *Black Rose* (April '79) and Lynott's *Solo In Soho* (April '80). As Gary Moore explains, many of the songs could've been interchangeable.

'Back On The Streets': "We did that live with Lizzy, but it was always going to be my song, and it came out as a single. The album was done over a long period of time, while I had a foot in both camps."

'Don't Believe A Word': "The song was originally written to be like 'Stand By Me', with a real slow tempo. We did it in a very Fleetwood Mac style. In fact, Peter Green was in the studio at the time and he heard it and said, 'It's like something Fleetwood Mac would do', and we were like, 'Er, there's probably a very good reason for that . . .!' Phil would always write a song and go, 'OK, let's try it faster', and that's how the Lizzy version finished up. He was great like that; as far as he was concerned once you'd written a song you could do anything with it. He was very flexible, unafraid to experiment with things."

'Fanatical Fascists': "That was Phil's version of punk. For a while he became very influenced by what was happening on the punk scene, and that was the result. I seem to remember there were a lot of people around at the time who were interested in stealing that song. Gary Holton from the Heavy Metal Kids was one. I just managed to get in first."

'A Night In The Life Of A Blues Singer': "That was recorded at Ramport Studios around the same time as 'Fanatical Fascists'. It was supposed to be for Phil's solo album, but it ended up on the (12″) B-side of Phil's last single, '19'."

'Sarah' (immortalising not his granny this time, but his young daughter): "That was written on an acoustic guitar, mostly by me. Actually, Scott didn't even play on that song – and to this day he still can't play it! It was me, Huey Lewis on harp and a little drum machine, sitting in Morgan Studios. It wasn't even intended to be for Thin Lizzy, it was just something we did, and I thought that it might end up on Phil's solo record. I think it only ended up on *Black Rose* because Phil was a track short for that album.

"I thought it came out well, and I thought Tony (Visconti) did a great job on my solo. He layered about seven guitar tracks on that bit! I can't even remember where I got the melody from – I probably nicked it from Jan Hammer, or someone."

'With Love': "That was recorded at a different session altogether – at Good Earth, with Jimmy Bain. Again, it was going to be for Phil's solo album."

'Flyaway': "A Jimmy Bain song, which ended up being recorded by Wild Horses (the band which also featured Brian Robertson). For a while Lizzy were going to use it, but then I think Jimmy whisked it away for himself."

'Parisienne Walkways': "I remember going over to Phil's flat in West Hampstead one night, and there was this old acoustic guitar lying on his bed. I picked it up and played him the chord sequence and he thought it was really good. He reckoned it sounded French for some reason, so he started thinking along those lines. The first thing he sang was, 'I remember Paris in '49', and of course that related to his father, and his birth date. Not many people sussed that, and that proved how clever he could be with words. There were a lot of personal references in his songs that people never picked up on. He was definitely one of the greatest songwriters in rock.

"Anyway, we recorded the song with Brian Downey on drums, so it was really Lizzy without Scott. I'd actually invited Scott to play on it, but at the time Scott was really lacking in confidence – he'd been pushed to one side by Robbo a lot of the time – and he'd really got himself into a state about it. He thought he was no good, he didn't want to play anything in case he embarrassed himself . . . I don't know, I think Robbo's attitude had intimidated him for too long, and his confidence had been shot to pieces. When I joined the band everyone said Scott's playing got a lot better because I think I gave him the chance to come out of himself again. He was a 50 per cent better guitar player than he was before. I didn't try to overshadow him at all – in fact, I tried to restrain myself most of the time, because I realised that I was just one quarter of the band, not a solo artist all the time. Still, maybe Scott felt playing on my solo album might not be the best move for him, so I left it at that.

"The funniest thing about 'Parisienne . . .' though was watching Phil trying to play the opening notes on a fretless, stand-up bass. He simply couldn't play a fretless guitar, so he had to put chalk marks on the neck to indicate where the frets would be!"

By the time Moore's album, a much underrated opus, hit the record shops in the UK, Lizzy were over in EMI's Paris studios working on *Black Rose* with Tony Visconti. Along with 'Waiting For An Alibi', 'S&M', 'Sarah', 'With Love' and the jerky 'Get Out Of Here' (co-written with Midge Ure), there was a rare Lynott/Gorham/Moore composition called 'Toughest Street In Town' to be pinned down, plus the twin-guitar pop-rock of 'Do Anything You Want To' and the grim-faced 'Got To Give It Up', with its startlingly revealing lyric.

"I remember Tony Visconti despairing of Phil," says Moore, "because he was so meticulous about it. He'd go into the studio early to lay down his vocals, light up a big spliff, and just sing a stream of lyrics off the top of his head. That's how he wrote a lot of his songs, going over and over the vocals, changing the words around, until he was satisfied with what he'd got. So he'd spend six or seven hours just building up one vocal, and Tony would go, 'Yeah Phil, it sounds great! Come in and have a listen.' Then Phil would go into the control room, listen to it and go, 'Yeah, it'll do as a rough, I suppose.' Tony would be pulling his hair out! He had this bottle of brandy and a jar of valium under the desk, and I think they were the only things that kept him going through those sessions."

If anything Lynott's lyrics were cleverer than ever, especially on tracks like 'Do Anything You Want To' when his rhyming couplets hit home with machine-gun subtlety: 'People that despise you/Will analyse then criticise you/They'll tell lies and scandalise until they realise you/Are somebody they should have apologised to/Don't let these people compromise you/Be wise too.' Lynott's ability to bend the pronunciation of certain words, in order to make them rhyme or simply suit a stanza, was a technique he used increasingly and to great effect.

His knack for conjuring violent and vivid visions of the seedier side of life was continuing to prove uncanny too. The squalid, neon-scarred landscape of the 'Toughest Street In Town' was as unmistakable as the sound of an assassin's gun, while the dark, depraved world of sadism and masochism described in 'S&M' was as brutal as a body full of bruises. It was almost as if the author felt he belonged in this kind of neurotic nether-world, mixing with luckless low-lifes such as the hopeless gambler Valentino in 'Waiting For An Alibi', or the defeated junkie drunkard in 'Got To Give It Up'.

The centrepiece of the new project, however, was the title track: 'Roisin Dubh (Black Rose): A Rock Legend'. It was arguably the most ambitious piece of music Lizzy had ever attempted, and it sprawled majestically across the second side of the record in four sections – i) Shenandoah, ii) Will You Go Lassy Go, iii) Danny Boy and iv) The Mason's Apron.

Moore wrote the instrumental parts to the track 'Black Rose', while as usual all the lyrics came from Philip, inspired by a Gaelic poem he'd read at school called *My Dark Rosaleen*, by James Clarence Mangan (1803–49). *Dark Rosaleen* was an analogy of Ireland, and in the same way Philip used 'Black Rose' to represent Ireland, as he delved back into the myths and legends of his homeland with all the misty-eyed romanticism he could muster.

The imagery of 'Black Rose' was most important, and once again the task of representing Philip's grand ideas in pictorial form fell to Jim Fitzpatrick. "The first thing I did was get some roses and spray them black," he explains, "to see if they looked right. But of course, as soon as I sprayed them they died. Then I found a purple rose and drew that, which Philip absolutely loved. But I still didn't think it was quite right. I puzzled over the concept for some time, until one day when I was reading another James Clarence Mangan poem and came across the line, 'I see the blood upon the rose . . .' I thought the idea of blood coming out of a rose was just the kind of surreal imagery the album needed, and fortunately the record company loved it.

"I was very satisfied with the whole *Black Rose* artwork, until one day Phonogram rang me up and said, 'We've just realised that we don't have a picture of the band for the back cover of the album – can you do something real quick?' I had to knock something together at the speed of light, so I drew each member of the band. I was very pleased with my likeness of Philip; I pulled his hair down over one eye like Dennis The Menace, and gave him a bit of a Little Richard look with the little moustache (exactly the image Prince later nicked!) and I was also quite pleased with the way I made Gary and Brian look. But Scott . . . well, he looked like a woman! I still cringe every time I look at that drawing, and I hope Scott has forgiven me by now."

No sooner had Lizzy put the finishing touches to *Black Rose* in February than they were out on the road in America, gearing themselves up for a crucial UK tour which had been booked to take them from March to May. Gary Moore remembers it well. "The day we finished the album was hilarious. We had to be at Teddington Lock at seven in the morning to start filming a slot for the *Kenny Everett Show*, then we had to shoot back to Good Earth Studios to finish the last mix, and then we had to go to a playback party at the Embassy Club, before getting up at the crack of dawn the next morning to fly to Texas to spend three weeks opening for Nazareth! Gatwick to Dallas with a hangover . . . I was as sick as a dog."

After their short stint with Nazareth ("They were hysterical," adds Moore, "they'd come into our dressing room every night and try to kill the vibe by making stupid comments about totally irrelevant things, like they were trying to psyche us out.") Lizzy returned to London to kick-start the promotional engine for *Black Rose*. 'Waiting For An Alibi' was released as a single on February 23 and made No.9 in the UK (No.6 in Ireland), but Philip wasn't prepared to simply sit back and hope the album would follow it into the charts. He was determined that the corporate muscle of Phonogram would get behind *Black Rose* and push it as hard as it could.

"Philip," explains John Burnham, "knew that sometimes record companies simply didn't do albums justice. There's a very non-creative side to a record company, and that's the sales force – reps, who could be 'repping' Johnson's Baby Powder, right? Never mind rock'n'roll, these are the guys you'll find sitting in their Cortinas in Rugby on a wet Thursday morning, cursing the fact that they've got to push their records. I mean, there's a good chance that these guys don't give a shit, right? So Philip recognised this and decided that he had to stimulate the record company in order to get the whole machine revving.

Phil on stage with Thin Lizzy – the neck of his bass guitar
and impossibly long legs were a magnet for photographers. (LFI)

The Black Eagles in the early Sixties:
"To a lot of local kids, Philip was a star even then."

The infant Philip (centre) makes a birthday wish.

The first Thin Lizzy band: Philip, Eric Bell and Brian Downey. (LFI)

Thin Lizzy in the mid-Seventies:
Scott Gorham, Brian Downey, Brian Robertson and Philip. (LFI)

Thin Lizzy on Top Of The Pops with Snowy White (left) on guitar. (LFI)

The rocker on stage with trademark grin and tight leather pants. (LFI)

Phil with Bob Geldof at the premiere of the film *Quadrophenia*, 1979. (Rex)

Phil with bride Caroline Crowther and their daughter Sarah
at their wedding on February 14, 1980. (Rex)

Phil with The Greedies, the Lizzy/Pistols band formed in 1980, left to right: Scott Gorham, Paul Cook, Steve Jones, Phil and Brian Downey.

Phil with Gary Moore during their 1985 collaboration on 'Out In The Fields'. (LFI)

"Philip didn't die of a heart attack," says Jim Fitzpatrick.
"He died of a lifestyle." (LFI)

"In a way it was obvious," Burnham grins, "we went for the girls! We bought all these black roses, and Philip and I went around the PolyGram offices giving these roses out to all the women. Of course they loved it, and everyone was talking about it. Suddenly, people started to put a lot more effort into *Black Rose*. The company got buzzing. It was a huge PR success, and all for the price of a few roses."

The *Black Rose* tour got underway at Brighton Centre on March 29, and presented the unusual spectacle of a band promoting two singles at once – 'Waiting For An Alibi' and 'Parisienne Walkways', which MCA had released earlier in March. Demand for tickets meant that promoter Adrian Hopkins could afford the luxury of booking two nights at many venues, such as Bristol Colston Hall, Newcastle City Hall and both Glasgow and Manchester Apollos. While in London two extra nights were added at the Hammersmith Odeon (April 27/28) to go with the two originally announced (22nd/23rd).

Hopkins has more reason to remember this particular UK tour than simply increased business, however. On at least two occasions the staunchly 'clean' promoter had close scrapes with police drugs squads, but came out of them smiling. "We were playing at Sheffield City Hall (April 18) and I'd sussed that there was a plain clothes officer from the drugs squad sniffing around. There were always drugs squad people around when Lizzy toured; they got friendly with the hall managers and got backstage passes that way. Anyway, I was standing next to this guy when John Burnham came over to me and said, 'Hey, I've heard there's some undercover drugs squad people around – look after these will you?' And he gave me about ten spliffs, wrapped up in toilet paper. The drugs guy next to me nearly choked, but I just turned to him and coolly said, 'Don't worry, he knows who you are and he was just joking.' I then, tiptoed away when he wasn't looking and breathed a huge sigh of relief."

Two days later the band were playing in Bridlington Spa, but Hopkins had arrived the day before to check everything was ready. Naturally one of the most important facilities to check out was the local pub ... "I got talking to the barmaid and asked her if she was going to the show," he explains, "although

I didn't tell her I was involved with the band. So she said, 'Yeah, I'm going with my boyfriend, who's coming down from Hull. It's going to be really exciting because he's with the Hull drugs squad and they're going to bust Thin Lizzy.'

"So I finished my drink and got out of there as fast as possible! I went back to the band and told them that under no circumstances were they to have drugs on them that night . . ."

"So I got this big brown paper bag," John Burnham continues the story, "and everyone gave me their 'stash' to look after. This bag was full of 'goodies', believe me. Anyway, Huey Lewis and I took this bag and started to make tracks, and just as I opened the door to leave 40 cops came dashing in. The timing was unbelievable! Huey and I just stepped outside, closed the door quietly, and were gone. Two seconds later and we would've been caught with the biggest drugs haul of the year!"

"The police were all dressed up as fans, in leather jackets and jeans," laughs Hopkins. "When they made their move they sealed off the backstage area and wouldn't let anyone move for about two hours. They were looking up people's bottoms and everything, wondering why they couldn't find anything. Meanwhile, John Burnham and Huey Lewis are trundling happily towards the next town with half of Bolivia in a paper bag."

"As usual the Manchester shows (May 1/2) were a real high-point for the band," claims Terrie Doherty. "The whole gang was there at the Apollo, and I remember Phyllis turning up with a huge black rose on the lapel of her jacket. She looked stunning. The party afterwards was good too . . .

"Actually, before the boys could make the party that night they had to do an interview with Piccadilly Radio, which I'd set up the week before. Straight after the show I dashed over to Piccadilly to make sure that all the security arrangements were in place and that everything was ready for the band. But first I had to speak to this old commissionaire who was working there. I said to him, 'I'm just here to check on a few things for my band, who are doing an interview later.' It didn't seem to register with him, so I nodded at the big sign in the reception area which said 'Piccadilly Radio Welcomes Thin Lizzy'. He immediately stood up and said, 'Oh I'm so sorry Miss Lizzy, please come in. I honestly didn't recognise you at first . . .' The poor old fool was terribly embarrassed when I told him I wasn't Thin Lizzy at all."

'Do Anything You Want To' was the next single to be lifted from 'Black Rose' (it reached No.14 in the UK during a nine-week run on the chart), released in June along with the 'kettle drum' promo video, while the band fulfilled a number of engagements on the Continent. Although some of these engagements had to be cancelled according to Gary Moore, "as someone made the mistake of letting Phil have a few days off in Amsterdam".

Another 'working' holiday in the Bahamas followed (one of the few achievements of the trip was the backing track to Moore's next single, 'Spanish Guitar'), and then the band returned to America for a series of dates with big name acts. Many observers felt that if Lizzy were ever going to break America in a major way, this was their chance. "We started the tour with Journey," says Moore, "but it quickly became apparent to me that things were going downhill. Phil just wanted to have a good time basically, and it seemed like he didn't give a shit about performing to a consistently high level. It was a shame because it was a great chance for us; if you're opening for Journey then you're playing in front of huge crowds every night, usually stadiums. But Phil was blowing it. It got to the point where the party after the show was more important than the show itself.

"We played three shows with AC/DC – Royal Oak (just outside Detroit), Cleveland and Chicago – and I used to watch Angus Young in awe. I used to say to Phil, 'Look how hard that guy works – that's how we should be!' But it never worked out like that.

"We also played a couple of shows with The Doobie Brothers, and this was just before they had their massive hit with 'Minute By Minute'. They were so big they had their own plane – a DC3 called The Doobie Liner, and their road crew even had one called The Crewbie Liner. It was a family-run airline, and you've never seen anything like it. The plane would be taking off and there'd be Jeff Baxter walking up and down the aisles with a big spliff in his mouth, people doing crazy things all over the place . . . I thought I was going to die! One time we flew through a thunderstorm and the pilot lost the airport. He kept saying, 'I'm sure it's around here somewhere . . .'

"But," Moore pulls his train of thought back from the brink of insanity, "the bulk of our shows were with Journey, and for me they weren't much fun. Phil was becoming harder and harder to work with. You couldn't get him out of his hotel room for a start. I mean, we'd all be waiting in the lobby to leave for the soundcheck and Phil would be arguing on the phone with his girlfriend, Caroline. Our tour manager would be banging on his door for ages to no avail. The rest of us would just have to sit around and wait for him. It got boring and frustrating. I can't tell you how many times our tour manager would have to hold flights while we tried to get Phil in the limo, or how many times we'd catch flights by the skin of our teeth. We were always late for everything. Scott used to call us 'The most unprofessional professional band in the world', and he was dead right.

"One night we were in Cleveland, playing a club near the university there," Moore continues, "and we were all in the lobby of the hotel waiting for Phil to come down again. As usual there was no sign of him. So I told the limo driver, 'Fuck it, go without him.' Now, the gig was only five minutes down the road, and I intended to send the driver back to the hotel again, so it was no big deal. But Scott was mortified that I might do this, and said, 'Well you can take responsibility for this.' So I replied, 'Fine, let's go.'

"Later, when Phil arrived at the gig, I could tell he was pissed off in a big way. He'd been doing amphetamines the night before and he was 'coming down', and that made his mood worse. The look on his face was murderous. He even made the crew move all the equipment on the stage a few inches to the right, just to be awkward. I think before the end of that evening the tour manager resigned, his personal assistant resigned . . . no-one could take it any more.

"So that night we were on stage and Phil was still in a foul mood. By this time he was beginning to make a lot of mistakes on stage, because of the state he was in; he'd forget words, miss bits out, and once he even sang through my guitar solo! I was screaming at him on stage, and he had his back to the audience and was screaming back at me. We were both going, '*Fuck you!*'

"It was quite comical really because the gig was awful. The guys in the front row were shouting, 'Fuck off! You guys suck!' Then the next thing I knew Phil's leather trousers split right up the backside, and he had to go off stage – just behind the drum riser – to put a new pair on. The crew were pissing themselves laughing, because Phil had given them such a hard time that day. There they were, helping Phil into a new pair of pants, while he tried to carry on playing the bass. It was real Spinal Tap."

Chris O'Donnell tends to be more defensive of Lynott in this instance, claiming instead that while he undoubtedly revelled in the excesses of his station, he always managed to send the punters home happy. O'Donnell also feels that in criticising Lynott in this way Moore brings to mind the terms 'pot' and 'black'.

"When he was in the band originally Gary Moore was the most fucked up individual you could ever wish to meet," O'Donnell snaps, "to the point where he'd urinate in his sleep every night, take loads of downers all the time, and get so out of it that even when someone glassed him that time he didn't even feel it. Then suddenly he's eschewing that lifestyle and getting all sensitive about Phil's drinking and drug taking.

"Basically, Phil could always pull the show off on the night, even if what was coming through the stage monitors sounded pretty awful. But Gary just judged a show by what he could hear through the monitors, and he couldn't handle it.

"Plus, Gary was being seduced at the time by Don Arden, who owned Jet Records, and wanted to sign him as a solo artist. And to make matters worse Gary had this girlfriend who was a complete nutter – he was spending all his money on jewellery for her, and all sorts of shit – and she was also telling him that he was too good for Lizzy, that he should go solo."

The friction between Moore and Lynott reached its limit the day Lizzy arrived in San Francisco to join Journey, The J. Geils Band, UFO and a host of other top rock names on Bill

Graham's Day On The Green festival. It was American Independence Day, July 4, 1979, and John Burnham was there with Huey Lewis.

"We got to the site at noon and we were legless by 1.00pm," he recalls. "It was a marvellous set-up, all Astroturf backstage, with peacocks strutting around and waiters with silver trays loaded with champagne and margaritas. However, being the Bay Area there was a lot of drug dealers around as well, and there was so much cocaine on offer it was unbelievable. There were massive lines of the stuff all over the place, lines as thick as your arm. They called cocaine 'snow'. Well, this was like being in a blizzard! I reckon virtually everyone backstage at that gig was on cocaine, and it really did take over the whole day."

"By the time Lizzy came on we were blasted," Huey Lewis continues the tale, "but we couldn't wait to hook up with Phil and the boys after the show. We waited backstage, but the band just stormed off after their set and went straight into their trailer. Boom! The door slammed. We were standing around outside and we heard all this screaming and yelling and pounding coming from inside. It was like there was a murder being committed. Then all of a sudden – boom! The door of the trailer flew open and Gary Moore walked out, straight through the dressing room area, straight through the parking lot . . . *gone!*

"We didn't know what to do, thinking it wasn't the best time to approach Phil. But then another minute went by and Phil suddenly stuck his head out of the door. He goes, 'Hey lads, sorry about that, come in for a drink! Everything OK? D'ya need another drink? Did you enjoy the show? Are you hungry? What can I getcha?' He was the perfect gentleman, and yet his guitar player had just quit and he didn't even know if he was going to have a band for the next night."

Moore was tracked down in LA, and at a band meeting a few days later he agreed to finish the rest of the US tour. When he failed to turn up for a massive show opening for Journey in Reno, Nevada, several days later, even the most obtuse of observers must've guessed it was the end of the road. Chris O'Donnell waited at the airport to pick Gary up, but three flights came in from LA and the headstrong guitarist wasn't on any of them. O'Donnell then had to tell Philip that Lizzy was back to a three-piece again.

"Strangely enough Scott was delighted," O'Donnell remembers, "and he really came alive that night. Of course there were certain parts he couldn't play, but overall the band were great."

"I'd made up my mind to leave the band before then," Moore confesses, "and one night after I'd spent some time working on 'Spanish Guitar' in the studio, I just did a runner. I was hanging around with Glenn Hughes (ex-Trapeze and Deep Purple bassist/vocalist) at the time, and I went to hide at his house in Northridge. I'd just had enough. Plus, there were one or two personal things that came into play, and it all added up to me wanting out there and then. I couldn't stand there watching Phil blowing it night after night, and I couldn't stand the fact that the management were powerless to stop him. They were scared of Phil. In fact, Phil was effectively manager of the band anyway, he was the one calling the shots, and they couldn't control him. No-one could control him, to be honest.

"The thing that pissed me off though was I heard that I got fired from Lizzy. That was bullshit. The last conversation I had was between O'Donnell and myself, and he said, 'Are you out or are you in?', and I said, 'I'm *out!*' But then he went around telling people that he'd said to me, 'You're out.' That is absolutely not true at all.

"Of course the knives came out. They said I was unprofessional, but Jesus, you would've had to have been really unprofessional to get thrown out of that band. I told someone once that they fired me for going on stage with my guitar in tune! I was only joking, but it was a bit like that.

"Looking back I've no regrets about leaving the band," Moore adds after a long, thoughtful pause, "but maybe it was wrong the way I did it. I could've done it differently, I suppose. But I just had to leave."

Moore's abrupt departure created ripples which spread to a number of other issues. For a start there were reports that Lizzy's US label, Warner Brothers, had placed an injunction on the release of Moore's *Back On The Streets* album because they objected to the prominence of Philip's voice on tracks like 'Parisienne Walkways' and 'Don't Believe A Word'. Later reports claimed the injunction had been lifted at Lynott's insistence, but these were never verified. All Moore himself will say about the controversy is: "There was a lot of crap flying around, so I took Phil's voice off 'Don't Believe A Word' and put out a different version."

One thing that Moore is prepared to elaborate on is the rumour that the ill-feeling between the management and himself ran to the extent of a bitter court case. "When I joined the band (in '78) I was on an equal share with the other three," he explains, "because that was the only way I'd join the band. So I bought this flat in Fitzjohn's Avenue, Hampstead, with the money I'd got, just before leaving for the American tour. When I left the band I discovered that they (the management) had put a 'lean' on the flat, which meant I couldn't sell it. O'Donnell even had someone come round and change the locks. I got back from America and couldn't get into my own flat! I ended up taking O'Donnell court, and of course I won the case."

It would be years before Lynott and Moore felt inclined to speak to each other again. In the meantime life continued for Thin Lizzy. The rest of the American tour sprawled into the distance before them, and beyond that there was talk of headlining the Reading Festival and making an inaugural visit to Japan. So as it was agreed that the band should be bumped back up to a four-piece, a replacement for Moore needed to be found, and fast.

Chris Morrison got straight on the phone to Midge Ure. Ure, who'd just joined Ultravox, agreed to help Lizzy out on a temporary basis, and had barely shut his suitcase when he was being bundled aboard Concorde for the trip to America.

"Midge listened to *Live And Dangerous* all the way over on the plane," Gorham remarks in admiration. "As soon as he got to New Orleans (Lizzy were appearing at the Fox Theatre that night) he went straight to his hotel room and he and I sat down and worked out who was going to play which parts. An hour later we were at the soundcheck, ironing out a few of the more tricky parts, and 45 minutes later were on stage doing it for real. Midge was great, he didn't drop a note."

"Both Phil and I agreed that with bands like the Rich Kids, Midge was a latter-day Steve Marriott," says O'Donnell. "He was a great guitar player, even though he never got any credit for it, and he had a great rock'n'roll voice. He was certainly better than the bands he'd been involved with before. Really, he was just a stop-gap in Lizzy, but we did see tremendous potential in him."

So much so in fact that Morrison and O'Donnell immediately snapped Ultravox up for management. Chris No.2 explains: "While we were in New Orleans Midge played me some of the new Ultravox demos, and I thought it was great stuff, really innovative. By pure coincidence someone approached Chris Morrison in London at the same time with a view to managing the band, and Chris liked the tape too. So he called me in America to tell me all about this new band he was interested in, and all I could say to him was, 'Never mind that, I've just heard a demo from a new band called Ultravox and it's brilliant!' "

Ure meanwhile had flung himself into Thin Lizzy with gusto. It had long been an ambition of his to work with Lynott, and while his previous form with teeny heart-throbs Slik hardly groomed him for heavy metal stardom, his versatility was never in question. "I'd been a big fan of Phil's for years," he explains, "right back to the time of the *New Day* EP, when I used to go and see them play in Glasgow as a three-piece. I was interested in them because of their association with Skid Row, who I'd also seen play a couple of times, but from the first time I saw Phil I knew there was something special about him.

"I next met Phil a couple of years later when I found him wandering around Glasgow looking a bit lost. I took him back to my parents' house and my mother cooked him a meal. We dropped him off at his gig that night, I remember. Then three years later I bumped into him again in London, when I was playing with The Rich Kids. We got talking and that led to us writing some stuff together, like 'Get Out Of Here'.

"When I was asked to help Lizzy out I was thrilled, and I didn't find it overly difficult to fit into the band, because I didn't have a wealth of solo parts to learn. The hardest thing was remembering which harmony guitar part went in which song, because Lizzy's songs were similar in structure. I'd learnt all the harmonies with Scott, but it was easy to get mixed up and suddenly find yourself playing, say, the harmony part for 'The Boys Are Back In Town' in the middle of something else.

"Once the initial teething problems were over it was great fun," Ure enthuses. "It was every schoolboy's fantasy to be up there in front of thousands, throwing some serious rock'n'roll shapes. I had woken up in a dream world in New Orleans. It was my first trip to America, my first day as a member of Thin Lizzy, a really big gig as special guests to Journey . . . and that night I ended up bonking (Journey guitarist) Neal Schon's girlfriend! I didn't know who she was at the time, I simply thought she was my welcoming present! Then when I discovered who she was I got a bit worried. The next morning she wanted to travel to the airport with me, but I was trying to push her into Journey's limo before anyone suspected anything. I had visions of Neal Schon sending his bodyguards after me and pummelling me to death. The rest of the band thought it was hysterical, but I was looking over my shoulder for the rest of the tour."

Midge didn't worry that in terms of image he was way out of synch with Lizzy. His short hair and high-fashion clothes were, in his opinion, an irrelevance that didn't affect his freedom as a musician to straddle various fences. "I never think of fences, or barriers between music," he explains. "Playing in a pop band, playing with synthesizers, or playing with guitars . . . why should there be a dividing line between any of it? It's all music, and the only difference is that some of it is good, and some of it isn't. To me, Lizzy were a band who wrote great tunes and just happened to play them loud.

"It was the same with the image. Perhaps in a way I influenced Lizzy to change their style slightly, because instead of me pulling on a pair of rock'n'roll boots, suddenly Phil started wearing designer clothes instead of his leathers, and shortly after I left Scott had all his hair cut off. I don't know whether I was a good influence on them or a bad influence, but it certainly helped to show a different side to the band."

"Having Midge in the band was definitely a bit weird at first," says Peter Eustace, "because he was a square peg in a round hole, there was no doubt about it. He was like a refugee from Devo, an alien from the Planet Zog compared to the others. But Phil was impressed with him. He said he played the best version of 'Whiskey In The Jar' ever, and he also had a great voice, which was of enormous benefit to the band, because backing vocals weren't Lizzy's strongest point."

With Ure easing comfortably into the hard rock role, Lizzy completed the rest of their commitments with Journey in America unscathed. However, they did have to relinquish their spot at the top of the Reading Festival bill on August 25, citing lack of time to rehearse a full set (the US set was just 45 minutes), feeling that they might not be about to give a 100 per cent performance to their British fans. German band The Scorpions were wheeled in as Lizzy's last-minute replacement.

"The T-shirt pirates had a field day," Adrian Hopkins reminisces. "We'd just managed to pull Lizzy off the official T-shirts at two days' notice, but the pirates had all these shirts with THIN LIZZY on them, so they simply added WHERE THE FUCK ARE . . .? across their design. Even I was impressed."

Lynott did appear at the launch party for The Boomtown Rats' new album, *The Fine Art Of Surfacing*, however. Held mischievously at Putney Swimming Baths in South London, the bash inevitably ended up with everyone in the water. Tony Brainsby remembers the occasion particularly well, because he can't swim. "Suddenly Lynott and Geldof chucked me in the pool," he gasps, reliving the dreadful moment, "and of course my heart stopped. Little did I know that Phil was going to dive in straight after me – fully clothed – and haul me out. He had me out in seconds, but it was still the most frightening experience of my life. I nearly died of shock, but Phil and Bob thought it was a great laugh."

Lynott and Geldof shared a similar sense of humour, and at times it was just as well. They never actually got around to writing anything together, but on the one occasion when they did attempt a vague collaboration Lynott ended up trying to sleep with Geldof's girlfriend, Paula Yates. Fortunately, Geldof saw the funny side of it. "Philip was going on about this surfing movie that was coming out," he recalls, "and he wanted me to write a song with him for it. So one night I went to his house, and first of all we were mucking about with this new video system he had. Videos in those days were primeval, and he had to push all this equipment around in a supermarket trolley, so that was funny enough to start with. But then he ended up getting me and (photographer) Chalkie Davies to kneel behind the sofa and pop up on cue singing 'She's So Modern', like a couple of Ronettes, or something. We were pissing ourselves laughing because we'd been doing coke for hours, and he always used to have loads and loads and loads and loads of it.

"Anyway, about 4 o'clock in the morning Paula had gone to bed and that left me, Philip and I think Jimmy Bain. He wanted to do a Beach Boys pastiche for this film, so we went into his studio and we came up with this really poxy song, with him trying to do all the vocal harmonies. It was absolute shite, a complete disaster.

"So there we were, pissing around with this song, and Philip was chopping out more and more lines of coke. I did quite a bit of it, but then all of a sudden I felt terrible and started to shake. I literally fell off this stool I was sitting on and I found myself crawling around the floor on my hands and knees. I decided I'd better get to bed quick, but when I got in bed I was still shaking wildly. Paula woke up and couldn't believe the state I was in, and I ended up staggering to the bathroom and being violently sick everywhere.

"It turned out Philip had given me a line of heroin. I'd never done it before, and it was a fucking long line he gave me, which was very dangerous. But it was all deliberate on his part, because as I had my head down the bog throwing up, he sneaked into the bedroom and tried to jump into bed with my missus! Apparently, earlier that evening he'd taken Paula upstairs on the flimsy premise of wanting to show her his gun collection, but as soon as he'd got her in the room he got his knob out and said, 'This is my biggest gun, darling!' Paula pissed herself. She said: 'For fuck's sake don't be so ridiculous Philip!' So what had happened was he'd thought to himself, 'If I can get rid of Geldof for a while I'll be in.' So he slipped me a line of heroin and nearly killed me!

"Now if someone tried that trick on you," Geldof splutters in between wheezes of laughter, "you'd want to kill them, right? But I couldn't be angry with Philip because he was so sweet about it. He was just trying it on, the way he always tried it on, and to him it was just a laugh. He'd look at you and be chortling away, and you couldn't help laughing as well."

September '79 saw three new releases to tickle the fancy of Thin Lizzy completists. Decca released *The Continuing Saga Of The Ageing Orphans*, a compilation of 11 tracks from the first three albums, remixed and in some cases altered (not necessarily for the better). Meanwhile Vertigo put out 'Sarah' as the next official single (it made No.24 in the UK), and MCA responded with Gary Moore's 'Spanish Guitar' – Lynott's bass lines surviving from the original recording, but his vocals having been substituted for Moore's (although 1,000 copies of the original version were apparently released in Sweden, where else?).

While the Lynott/Moore argument raged on in the pubs of Britain, Thin Lizzy were on the opposite side of the world, enjoying Japanese hospitality for the first time when they arrived in Tokyo on September 29. In return Japanese fans got to see the first-ever incarnation of Lizzy as a five-piece, as Philip had drafted in guitarist Dave Flett (who worked with Manfred Mann) to allow Midge Ure to switch to keyboards when necessary. This also presented the Japs with a spectacle not seen since the demise of Lynyrd Skynyrd – no less than three lead guitarists huddled together at the front of the stage, for certain numbers!

"Dave Flett was the most nervous guy I've ever met in my life," declares Brian Downey. "He used to puke up all over the shop before going on stage. He was a great guy and a brilliant guitar player, but Jesus, he'd be a bag of nerves every night!"

"Flett was just someone who was always hanging around," O'Donnell adds dismissively. "You'd be rehearsing and Dave would be next door. Or you'd be in a bar and Dave would be on the next table. Or you'd be at a party and Dave would turn up out of the blue. If you're in a football team and someone turns up every Sunday, inevitably they'll get a game in the end.

Of course, once you've given them a game you realise why they weren't in the team to start with. That was how it was with Dave Flett, unfortunately."

Midge Ure's main memory of the band's first Japanese tour is the amount of sake that was drunk. That and the experience of walking around Tokyo with someone whose physical appearance alone was enough to inspire awe among the locals. "At well over six foot Phil towered above all these little Japs," Ure laughs, "and what with being just about the only black man in the country you couldn't go anywhere without everyone in the vicinity pointing and gasping. There was me, who'd hardly ever been out of Britain before, walking around this strange far-flung land with one of my lifelong heroes, and having a million eyes watch us wherever we went. Quite amazing."

Midge would remain in the Court of King Philip well into the New Year, but Dave Flett would bow out of Lizzy in December after two special concerts in England to compensate fans for pulling out of Reading. According to Ure, Flett was very much hoping to be offered a permanent contract as Lizzy's guitarist, but he denies he was ever tempted to try to secure the post for himself.

"I don't think I was a good enough guitarist to tell you the truth," Ure declares, "and that's not being coy. I was never a fast guitar player and Lizzy wanted a serious twiddly-diddly guy. In any case, I'd just joined Ultravox and I was incredibly excited by that. I used to bore the band to tears with synthesizer music, and subject poor old Scott to hours of Magazine and Kraftwerk, so they probably wouldn't have wanted me in the band much longer anyway!"

The extra UK dates were at Manchester Apollo on December 16 and Stafford Bingley Hall on the 18th, as Lynott was keen to ensure that it wasn't always London-based fans who enjoyed such privileges. As might be expected just before Christmas they were pretty loose affairs, with both the band and crew enjoying the chance to let their hair down after another stressful year.

"The show at Stafford was a scream, and perhaps my biggest moment of fame with Lizzy," Adrian Hopkins boasts. "They had me and a roadie dressed as two tarts for the bit in the show where Philip used to warn the girls in the audience that if they weren't good they'd grow up to look like THIS! And then they'd launch into 'Bad Reputation' . . .

"Anyway, this night there were thousands of fans queuing outside the venue, and we'd already reached the limit of 8,000 people inside. These were the days of 'rubber walls'. But the Chief Fire Officer from Stafford, the head of police and the venue manager who worked for the agricultural ministry were unhappy with the amount of people we had in, so they came backstage and demanded to see the promoter.

"There I was, in the bar, dressed in a beautiful black dress, stockings, high heels, a headscarf, make-up, the whole bit. They nearly fainted. Later when I went on stage everyone in the band immediately sussed it was me in drag except Phil. When he finally twigged he laughed so much he had to stop the show."

Lynott next surfaced at the Rainbow Theatre later in December, jamming with his new friends Dire Straits. He also joined the ligging likes of ex-UFO guitarist 'Mad' Michael Schenker backstage at Wild Horses' Electric Ballroom show the same month, along with faces from the Manchester United team such as Steve Coppell, Lou Macari, Joe Jordan, Ashley Grimes and Jimmy Nichol. If nothing else, the revelry which ensued prepared the uninitiated for another bout of boys-club madness in the shape of a Christmas single from The Greedies (no longer The Greedy Bastards, according to a linguistically sensitive soul at Vertigo). 'A Merry Jingle' ('Jingle Bells' meets 'We Wish You A Merry Christmas', sort of) was the consummation of a marketing brainwave which brought together Lynott, Downey, Gorham, Jones and Cook . . . or, alternatively, the last breath of a jolly good wheeze. Either way, chart compilers remained undisturbed.

"We did make the *Kenny Everett Show* and the *Top Of The Pops* Christmas Special though," Gorham protests, "and all Steve Jones kept doing was take the piss out of Jimmy Savile. At the top of his voice he kept shouting, 'Now then now then, guys'n'gals guys'n'gals!' In the end Jimmy Savile got really pissed off with it and came over to us. He said, 'Look lads, I'm just trying to do my job. Give me a break, eh?' So Phil said,

'Yeah sorry Jimmy'. But the second he turned his back Steve Jones let out an almighty Jimmy Savile noise and pretended to fiddle with an imaginary cigar. We had hysterics and nearly didn't make it through the show."

Now howzabout that then.

Chapter VI

The Rock Star And The Man

On St. Valentine's Day, February 14 1980, Philip Lynott finally married Caroline Crowther, the mother of his 14-month-old daughter. The ceremony, at the Catholic St. Elizabeth Of Portugal church in Richmond, and the reception at the Kensington Hilton afterwards, were both back-slappingly show-biz occasions, complete with oceans of champagne, flowers and a scrum of paparazzi insisting on one more of 'the happy couple with the proud father'.

Caroline, 20, was the middle child of five born to Leslie and Jean Crowther. She had met Philip when she worked for Tony Brainsby, making the tea. Before that she'd had a number of short-lived jobs, including working as a topless waitress in a Soho clip-joint. She'd also posed nude for the men's magazine *Mayfair* in 1977 under the alias Hilary Stevens, picking up just £150 for the session which the photographer tricked her into believing would be published only in Holland.

Those who hung out with the crowd which included Caroline and her friend Magenta De Vine, who also worked for Brainsby before pursuing a career as a TV presenter, claim that drugs were an accepted part of the social whirl, and that Caroline frequently indulged. These claims shatter the assumption made by many that it was Philip who turned her on to recreational narcotics.

"Phil was just really chuffed to be going out with Leslie Crowther's daughter, and a Mayfair centrefold," says Brainsby. "I don't know if Leslie was exactly chuffed with his daughter going out with a heavy rock star, let alone a black one with his reputation. But Phil was definitely besotted with Caroline, and they made a good couple."

Despite his love for Caroline, Philip continued to pander to the superstud image that even the national tabloids were beginning to perpetuate, and many of those who toured with Lizzy never ceased to be amazed at how loose his principles remained. Not even the birth of his daughter changed him completely, and yet on St. Valentine's Day 1980 everyone did their best to imagine a future through rose-tinted spectacles. Was this, the tabloids wondered, the taming of the Wild Man Of Rock? Philip stood before the cameras and grinned his familiar jaw-jutting grin, keeping his thoughts to himself.

For many of the guests the most memorable moment of the wedding was Leslie Crowther's father-of-the-bride speech, wherein his recollection that, "When Philip asked for my daughter's hand in marriage I said, 'Why not? You've had everything else!' " had them rolling in the aisles. The only guest not choking on his Moet was Best Man Scott Gorham, who had to follow Crowther's highly eloquent and professional oration with some nervous waffle of his own.

"When I accepted the job I didn't really know what was expected of a Best Man in Britain," he complains. "I shit my pants when they told me I'd have to make a speech. I mean, handing the ring over at the church without dropping it was fine. But standing up in front of hundreds of people at the Kensington Hilton and trying to follow Leslie Crowther? It was pretty disastrous. All I wanted to do was get out of that room as quickly as possible."

Two months after the marriage Philip announced he was buying a property in the North Dublin fishing village of Howth, to further strengthen his daughter's Irish roots. Glen Corr, a large bungalow backing on to the beach in one of the area's most exclusive roads, cost him £130,000 at a public auction in Dublin. But at the time his accounts were looking good, and as he'd now passed the 30 years of age milestone he felt it was time to lay some sort of foundation for his family's future in Ireland.

His mother and Dennis were delighted, as it meant they'd be able to keep in close contact with their beloved Sarah. Chris Morrison also had reason to welcome the move, as it meant Lynott would be saving a lot of money in tax.

"In those days," Morrison explains, "tax rates went up to a punitive 83 per cent. On an investment income you were paying an extra 15 per cent surcharge. So for every pound you got back in interest, you were paying out 98 pence! Your money was devaluing quicker than you were making it. So in a way there wasn't a huge amount of incentive to keep money.

"We constructed a way, legally, where Philip could get around that. He was domiciled in Ireland, resident in the UK, and we managed to create a situation where if he wrote a song overseas, or made a record overseas, the income from that was tax free – provided he didn't remit it back to the UK. The money he made in the UK was just as well spent, because why pay 83 per cent out of it in tax?"

By this time Lynott already owned properties in London, most notably The Walled Cottage at 184 Kew Road in Richmond, Surrey. Situated opposite Kew Botanical Gardens and surrounded by a third of an acre of land, the £250,000 house had five bedrooms, three reception rooms and a 40 ft Granny annexe at the bottom of the garden which was converted into a home studio. But after the buzz of shelling out for Glen Corr Lynott decided to invest more of his royalties in real estate, and looked at the possibility of setting his mother and Dennis up in business in Dublin, allowing them to leave Manchester for good. For his mother's 50th birthday he bought her a beautiful house called White Horses, overlooking the sea near Howth. And he also spent £235,000 in 1980 on a hotel called The Asgard, which was situated on Balscadden Bay in Howth, and which his mother intended to hire out for functions such as weddings and birthday parties. Sadly, the hotel was to burn down on the August Bank Holiday of that year.

"We got a phone call at 3am," says Phyllis, "and we all dashed to the hotel. We stood there watching the firemen try to put it out, but it was too late. Philip stood with his arm around me and said, 'Never mind ma, I'll buy you another one.'"

Just a month before the burning of The Asgard Philip had become a father for the second time. Cathleen Elizabeth was born at Holes Hospital in Dublin on July 29, 1980, spelling her first name with a Catholic 'C' instead of a 'K' at Philip's insistence, and taking her middle name from Caroline's elder sister. Phyllis admits that there was some disappointment that the second born wasn't a boy, but that relief at the child's good health was ample compensation.

"Both the girls were gorgeous and he adored them," Phyllis glows, "we all adored them. Plus, what with Dennis and I settling back in Dublin, we hoped that we could be one big family every time Philip was home. That was what Philip wanted, he loved the family atmosphere."

"He was a natural father," Dennis stresses. "He loved kids and he was very gentle. He would spend hours rolling around on the floor playing with them. He loved older people too, and if he was at a party he would make an effort to go round and speak to all the old people. He would deliberately avoid the hanger-on types, and sit with the quieter, shyer people – because he was actually quite shy himself. He could get embarrassed in a second, and he'd hate things like people swearing in front of his mother. He'd even hate it if something sexy came on the TV while we were all watching it. You wouldn't believe it, but I would see him blush regularly.

"Sometimes," Dennis adds wistfully, "I think that it would've been nice for his fans to have seen the other side of Philip. They'd see the rocker up there on stage, but they wouldn't see the man who'd come home and play with the kids, or pamper his beloved dogs, or mess around with his grandmother and have her in hysterics. That was the real Philip to me."

"We used to love it when Philo came home to Dublin," says Smiley Bolger. "He'd ring me up from London on a Tuesday and say, 'I'll be home on Thursday – get the boys together!' So I'd go down to the Bailey and put the word around, and Philip would get back to town and it'd be party time. We'd always have these impromptu gigs around the town, with whoever was around. Philip loved it. A few drinks, a few songs, a few bob in his pocket, cheers.

"As all friends have, I had good times and bad times with Philip. But nine times out of ten were good. Some of the best were just sessions drinking up at the Baggott Inn. We'd talk about football, he'd ask how your mother was (even though he'd never met her), and he'd be very free with his knowledge; he was always advising other people, younger bands, how to get their careers together. I used to listen to him and think he'd make a great teacher.

"What we had there was the first real Irish rock star," states Bolger. "Before Philo we had Van Morrison, but he was a more cool-headed kind of guy. We had Rory Gallagher, but all he ever wanted to do was make it to 65, still playing the guitar. Philip was different. He was the party man. He was into the grace of the black man, the cool dude, the almost pimp-like guy who wore sharp suits and lived this on-the-edge existence. He had the looks. He had the style. He had the ideas. He used to say, 'Give me half an idea and I'm away.' And you'd hear things cropping up on Lizzy records that came from conversations you'd had with him in the Bailey bar.

"You'd also see within him the distinction between the rock star and the man. I thought he was a natural rock star, but he always referred to that side of him as 'me act'. Sometimes the 'act' would swallow him up and in quieter moments at the Baggott or the Bailey he'd admit to being sick of himself. But the man always shone through in the end, and it was at times like that you felt he was a special human being, and it was a privilege knowing him. We were so proud that he was a Dubliner."

"I would argue that Philip was, and still is, the only true rock star ever to have come out of Ireland," states Bob Geldof. "Van Morrison was never considered a rock star because he didn't look like one, and nor did he want to look like one. And on the last U2 tour Bono admitted that he set out to be like a rock star because that's what his fans want him to be. He clearly stated that he was dressing in a certain way, talking in a certain way and acting in a certain way purely because he felt it was what he should do.

"But Philip was a rock star to the very core of his being, and therein lies the tragedy. He couldn't be anything else, it was that or nothing. He was totally wrapped up in the whole trip.

"An example of that was when we were invited by Sting to the premiere of The Who's *Quadrophenia* in London. Philip phoned me up and asked me how I was getting there, and when I told him I was probably getting a taxi he was horrified.

He said, 'It's a fucking premiere and you're in the charts, you can't turn up in a taxi, man!' He told me he was hiring this great big white limo for the night, and insisted on coming all the way down to Clapham, where I was living at the time, to pick me and Paula up.

"So we arrived at the premiere in this ridiculous stretch limo and I felt a complete prick getting out of it, very self-conscious. Philip, in complete contrast, was very comfortable. He flung the door open and stepped out in such a majestic fashion you'd have thought he'd been born in the back seat of a limo.

"It was the same when you went round his house," Geldof adds with a grin. "I don't think he'd ever answer the door without being dressed in the official gear – the leathers, the studded belts, the full Monty. He lived the mythical rock star existence, and it was a huge mistake because ultimately it was his downfall.

"In Ireland of course people loved that whole image, because they didn't really have anyone else like him. The Irish were very proud of him, even though a lot of people cringed when 'Whiskey In The Jar' was a hit, because it's such a corny song, the kind of thing you only sing at closing time when you're really pissed! But even that didn't matter, because Lizzy were absolutely steeped in Irishness, far more so than the Rats. I thought it was a load of bollocks and I despised the whole idea of selling the 'paddy' angle. But I did like Lizzy and would've been prepared to admit so even at the height of the New Wave, when it wasn't trendy to like anything other than The Clash or The Stranglers or whatever.

"To me, from *Jailbreak* onwards Lizzy were cool, they were the ultimate 'lads' band when they did stuff like 'The Boys Are Back In Town'. Philip was the classic rock star in every sense, and the fact that he was from Crumlin was all part of what made him unique."

Lynott certainly never forgot where his roots were and always keenly anticipated returning home. He took one of his greatest pleasures in looking after his family. Timothy Lynott remembers one time when Philip was visiting home as if it was yesterday.

"I used to work at this flour mill down on the quay," he

explains, "and I used to cycle to work for the 3 o'clock shift. This particular day Philip came to the house in a big white limo and gave me a lift. We put my bike in the boot and off we went. It was incredible, this beautiful white limo pulling up at the mill, and me getting out. People couldn't stop staring at me for the rest of the day!"

Lynott loved to spoil his mother and Dennis too, and on several occasions paid for them to be flown to America to taste a bit of life on the road with Lizzy. Limos would run them around, the best hotels would be booked and they'd be wined and dined at the finest restaurants.

Yet the VIP treatment that Philip loved to bestow on his mother and Dennis wasn't merely confined to displays of ostentation in public. Lynott loved to buy his family presents, and would always be on the lookout for Dennis The Menace merchandise for his own Dennis. He would also buy duplicate items of clothing or jewellery for Dennis whenever he splashed out on himself, and would never forget to send a bunch of roses to his mother at Christmas or on her birthday – the amount of roses corresponding with his mother's age, plus one orchid.

"Basically," says Dennis, "he was the perfect son. He had his wild times when he was touring the world, but when he came home he was just like any loyal, loving son visiting his mum. He became a kid again."

The assertion that there were many sides to Philip Lynott is the most common reflection on his character of all. The diamond geezer, the complete bastard. The easy-going drinking pal, the moody ogre. The joker, the sulker. The simple Irish boy watching TV with his granny, the international Playboy raging around the world in a chemically-induced frenzy.

But his talent as a writer and musician was just as multi-faceted, and this was possibly something many critics wouldn't have accepted until the release of *Solo In Soho*, in April 1980. The album had taken two years to come to fruition, recorded at a number of different locations by a roll-call of friends and associates, and it provided the perfect antidote for the driving hard rock of Thin Lizzy.

Few albums polarise opinion among Lynott's fans more

profoundly than his solo albums. For some they were an unnecessary distraction, for others they were fascinating glimpses behind the Johnny The Fox façade. Yet whatever they were, they certainly allowed Philip to clear his head of a tangle of ideas, and in theory at least allow Lizzy to continue without wandering too far from their chosen path. Self-produced (with Kit Woolven) and self-indulgent, they served a purpose.

Delays over the announcement of Lizzy's new guitarist allowed Lynott to complete work on the album in the early months of 1980. Unsurprisingly, it was mostly recorded in London's infamous red light district (at Tony Visconti's Good Earth Studios), where the depressing proximity to a lot of the capital's down-and-outs inspired the deliberate double-meaning in the title. But there were a handful of remnants from the visits to Compass Point in Nassau, including the calypso-flavoured 'Jamaican Rum' and the rallying cry for black culture that was 'Ode To A Black Man'.

The latter track was really a tap on the shoulder for the complacent black man, as Lynott nurtured the opinion that none of the new generation of black artists were 'saying it for black people'. Bob Marley came in for a bit of stick in the lyrics, as did Stevie Wonder, but the track avoided the kind of blinkered bitterness which fuels the violent political aggression of those who spew black supremist dogma from rap records today. Lynott was always far more subtle, far more articulate, far more persuasive.

The title track of the album hinted once again at the author's biological roots, sliding along on a reggae theme with loose-limbed lubrication from Brian Downey on drums and old friend Jerome Rimson on bass (who impressed Lynott by having played on the original recording of 'Dancing In The Street' by Martha & The Vandellas). And there was more experimentation on 'Talk In '79', a bass/drums/rap vocal concept which was written from the perspective of a music journalist, with name checks for flavours of the month such as Sham 69, Generation X and The Stranglers.

'A Child's Lullaby' was the sequel to 'Sarah', corny but charming, while 'Tattoo (Giving It All Up For Love)' was made of the kind of pop that day-time radio thrives on. Yet it was another track which the BBC chose as the theme tune to their flagship pop show, *Top Of The Pops*.

'Yellow Pearl' was a synthesized conspiracy between Lynott and Midge Ure, a product of their time in Japan together when they encountered the Yellow Magic Orchestra. Brian Downey also played on the track, as did Ultravox's Billy Currie and Visage's New Romantic socialite Rusty Egan, and once again it provided the opportunity for Philip to veer away from a guitar-orientated sound and make a stab at a new direction. It was later released as a single in March '81, and swiftly re-issued as soon as it became the *Top Of The Pops* theme (whereafter it reached No.14 in the UK).

"Just as Steve Jones and Paul Cook had been Phil's link with punk, so I became his connection to the po-faced electronic scene that was blossoming," Midge Ure explains. "Phil had the only 7-track studio in the history of the world at the bottom of his garden (it was an 8-track studio but he never managed to get one of the tracks to work), so when I had my 24-track studio built at home I used to invite him over to have a dabble. He loved it because I had an engineer working in there, so he didn't have to worry too much about working the new technology, he could just mess around with a few ideas."

Midge has no recollection of contributing to either Lynott's second solo album or Thin Lizzy's *Chinatown* despite being credited on both, but he suggests that if certain recordings were kept for future use then they came from the experimental sessions at his home studio in London. He can, however, trace the origins of 'Yellow Pearl' back to Lizzy soundchecks, when he'd play with the tune on the keyboards.

"I was never a keyboard player by any stretch of the imagination," he admits, "but Phil kept me in there for a while, even when the new guitarist came in, just to add an extra dimension to the sound. At rehearsals and soundchecks I used to play around with this riff I had, and Phil had obviously clocked it, as when he started doing his solo album he called me up and suggested we worked the idea up into a proper song.

"I actually have no idea what the song is really about," Ure laughs, "except perhaps that, as a thin outline, it's a comment on the thought of Japanese technology taking over – a twist on the Yellow Peril idea. The imagery of all the Sony Walkmans in the video was definitely inspired by our trip to Japan, because it was there that we saw Walkmans for the first time. It was a very techno time, because Phil was building his home studio around then, and I was introducing him to a lot of the new electronics that were revolutionising the art of recording, so everything tied in.

"The funniest thing about the record, though, was the way Phil insisted on trying to get every word to rhyme. If you listen carefully you'll hear that some of what he sings is complete nonsense, stuff that came off the top of his head and just happened to rhyme. It still makes me laugh today."

Fortunately Lynott didn't venture too far into the realms of New Romanticism, although 'Girls' (co-written with Jimmy Bain) was indeed another guitar-free zone. If part of the idea of doing a solo album was to exorcise his fear of the rapidly advancing keyboard technology, then tinkering with moogs and string machines on tracks like these certainly achieved that.

'Girls', which was originally going to be a Wild Horses single, was also earmarked as the title of the album, according to Jimmy Bain. One idea Philip had was to "have a song about girls of different nationalities", but in the event Philip's strategy was to get a group of girls with different accents to read from a script he'd written, and then edit the extracts into one long piece which could be phased in and out of the track. Again, experimentation was the buzzword.

Perhaps the nearest *Solo In Soho* got to Thin Lizzy was 'Dear Miss Lonely Heart', the first single released in March, and another product of the dangerous liaison with Jimmy Bain. The hook had been driving Lynott around the bend for months, and he finally off-loaded it with some relief into a chord sequence that Bain had worked out. The lyric, meanwhile, was a slice of pure Lynott mischief: an Agony Aunt on a lonely hearts column dishing out her replies to the wrong people.

Finally there was 'King's Call', written about the death of Elvis Presley (and also commemorating Martin Luther King). It was one straight from Dire Straits' back-pocket, although few eyebrows were raised as Mark Knopfler contributed both to the track and to the promotional video which accompanied its release as a single in June.

"We really did think 'King's Call' was going to be a hit," says Alan Phillips, who worked as Product Manager at Phonogram between 1977–82 and dealt with both Lizzy and Dire Straits, as well as Rush and Status Quo. "In fact, I thought it could have even been a No.1, that's how strongly I felt. When it relatively flopped (it only made No.35 in the UK) I think one or two people began to have sneaking doubts about the whole Philip Lynott Solo idea . . ."

Back in February, around the time of Lynott's wedding, Thin Lizzy finally announced the name of their new guitar player. Terence Charles White, known as Snowy since the age of five and a seasoned session player who'd worked with artists as varied as Peter Green, Linda Lewis, Al Stewart, Cockney Rebel, Pink Floyd and Cliff Richard, had actually agreed to join Thin Lizzy the previous November but for contractual reasons had to remain anonymous until the New Year, when his stint on Pink Floyd's *The Wall* tour was completed. His official appointment not only ended months of speculation, it also ended Lizzy's tradition of excluding English musicians. White was born in Devon.

"Phil and I had actually been aware of him since 1977," Gorham explains, "since we saw him play with Pink Floyd at Madison Square Garden in New York on the *Animals* tour. We were quite surprised to see this other guy on stage with Dave Gilmour, but even more surprised when this other guy got a solo spot! Snowy was firing off some great shit, and Phil and I were going, 'Who the hell is he?'

"We ended up holding the auditions for our new guitar player at Shepperton Studios," Gorham continues, "but they were going nowhere. It was so boring that whenever we had a break I'd go wandering off around the other sound stages, to see what was happening. In one studio I found Cliff Richard rehearsing, and who should be playing guitar but Snowy White!

"So I invited Snowy down to our studio for a blow, just for a bit of fun, and he came along and jammed. It sounded great, so as we were getting close to our deadline for finding a new guy we asked him if he'd be interested in joining full-time. From

Cliff Richard to Thin Lizzy (via Pink Floyd) in one easy move!"

"Although I wasn't perhaps the most obvious choice for Lizzy," Snowy admits, "I didn't have any qualms about joining the band because when I discussed the idea with Phil he did seem keen to let me have the space to do my own thing. We discussed the fact that I wasn't a hard rocker, and I never made any promises about wearing studded belts and jumping around on stage. He was quite happy to have somebody who, as he put it, could be more of a musician."

White remembers making his live début with Lizzy in Ireland during April, as part of a transitional Lizzy line-up that included Midge Ure on keyboards and occasional guitar. "It was funny really," he laughs, "the band were there at the shows trying to be all macho and cool, and there was Midge in all these weird fashion clothes, putting on his make-up. I thought he was very brave."

"Sad but true," admits Ure. "But I was a young man then . . . well, that's my excuse."

As the new line-up took shape Lynott decided that the band would need a more permanent keyboard player, his opinion having been swayed by Ure's contribution as well as the whole *Solo In Soho* experience. Word of Lizzy's requirements was put out in the usual manner, and the grapevine quickly stretched to Manchester, where an old friend of Philip's, bar owner Joe Leach, claimed he had the ideal man for the job.

In fact, Darren Wharton was hardly a man at all at just 17 years old. His only experience of playing before live audiences was doing cover versions in the discos around Manchester – "the Tiffany's circuit" – and that for only a couple of years. But Leach convinced Philip that the lad had enormous talent, and the pair of them were invited to London for the day to audition.

"We arrived at Good Earth Studios and they were working on the track 'Chinatown'," Darren remembers. "I was very nervous, but Scott and I went to the pub and told jokes for an hour, and that settled me down a bit. When we got back to the studio Phil asked me to play a bass part on a mini-moog – the descending run on 'Chinatown' – and I did it first time. I could see he was impressed.

"As we left that day Phil asked me to learn a few Lizzy songs. He only wanted three or four songs, but I wrote their whole set down in a book and learnt the lot. It was an easy set to learn because most of Lizzy's repertoire was just in A minor or F sharp minor, and in any case, on tracks like 'Jailbreak', 'Are You Ready', 'Waiting For An Alibi' and 'Don't Believe A Word' there weren't any keyboard parts at all. Phil just wanted an underlying pad, a texture, to fill out the sound on those tracks.

"Anyhow, a week later I was invited to Shepperton Studios, where the band were working on their full production, and I joined in with the rehearsals. They put me up at the Cunard Hotel in Hammersmith and I'd go back there every night and dream that I was a proper member of Thin Lizzy. Then the next thing I knew Phil was saying, 'Oh by the way, we're playing in Scandinavia next week . . .' "

Wharton's first gig with Lizzy was in Oslo, followed by dates in Copenhagen, Stockholm and Helsinki. As would be the case throughout the 'Chinatown' tour he was 'hidden' at the side of the stage, but then he accepted this as part of his apprenticeship.

"As the tour progressed I noticed that Phil had 180 lights on him, and I had one on me," he laughs. "I spent a lot of time stumbling around in the dark! But for the first few months I was very much on trial, as I don't even think they knew what they wanted to do with keyboards in the band. I just kept my head down and did as I was told, and in return Phil was like a father figure to me, taking me under his wing and teaching me the ropes. All the guys were looking out for me as I was so young, and the atmosphere was a really friendly one."

There were also the inevitable wind-ups on the keyboard kid, and one particular running joke was that tour manager John Salter was gay and fancied him. Wharton winces at the memory: "Phil was always saying to me, 'John likes young boys, and he's got his eyes on you.' I was terrified! John went along with the gag throughout the whole tour, and one night he even sneaked up to my room and got into my bed! Of course, I was the last person in the entire Thin Lizzy organisation to realise that the whole thing was only a wind-up."

As Lizzy announced a series of UK dates to take them through May and June, they were already trying out the new show in Ireland. One particular concert for April 3 (Maundy Thursday) in Bundoran had to be switched to Enniskillen on the same day, after the Canon of Bundoran had proclaimed that it would be sinful for young people to go to a rock gig instead of church on that particular day. But further concerts during April at Kilkenny Savoy, Tralee St. John's Hall and Cork City Hall (with Sweet Savage supporting, the band that included future Dio/Whitesnake/Def Leppard guitarist Vivian Campbell) went ahead without a hitch.

It was most unusual that Lizzy should be on the road in advance of the release of their new album, however. Lynott had 'Dear Miss Lonely Heart' out as a single (inevitably it was also slipped into the new Lizzy set) and by mid-April *Solo In Soho* was in the shops as well. A single called 'Chinatown' was released in May, and fans were also introduced to a new song called 'Sugar Blues' on the B-side (the song was recorded live in Cork the previous month). But as the 'Chinatown' tour opened with two nights at Newcastle City Hall on May 1 and 2, the *Chinatown* album was still languishing in Good Earth Studios.

Nevertheless, those who made it to the City Hall were in for a special treat. Apart from 'Chinatown' and 'Sugar Blues', plus another new song entitled 'Sweetheart', the set featured a tumultuous encore of 'Rosalie' and 'Emerald' with Brian Robertson guesting on guitar. Wild Horses just happened to be playing Newcastle Poly the following night, and the impromptu reunion proved that there were no hard feelings between the two former protagonists.

Dates for the rest of the UK tour were still being shuffled around as the band kicked off in Newcastle, and fans in Edinburgh and Dundee found themselves going to see the band a day later than they'd expected. But the Glasgow Apollo show, always a favourite for the band, remained intact on May 6, and produced the first moment of farce on the tour. Adrian Hopkins remembers: "We were backstage before the show and John Salter the tour manager, said, 'I'm starving, I haven't eaten all day.' So I said, 'Well, why don't we go for a Chinese as soon as the band hit the stage?' So Salter said, 'You can't leave the venue, you're the promoter!' But I argued that as soon as the band hit the stage my job is done.

"Anyway, the very second Lizzy hit the first power chord John and I sneaked out to this Chinese restaurant up the road. We had a lovely meal and a bottle of wine or two, and then as we walked back to the Apollo we saw all the kids coming out. 'Perfect timing', I said, 'they won't even know we left the venue.'

"The minute we walk through the door the venue manager came screaming up to us – 'Where the hell have you been? We nearly lost the show tonight because of you!' I couldn't believe it. It turned out that Phil had noticed one of the bouncers beating up a kid in the audience and he stopped the show. He locked himself in the dressing room and said, 'Until Hopkins sorts it out I'm not playing.' So everyone went looking for me. The roadies searched all the local pubs but they had to go back to Phil and tell him I couldn't be found. So then Phil said, 'Right, get me John Salter immediately!' But of course, no one could find John either. We were probably on our second bottle of wine by that time.

"Phil gave us both a real caning for that," Hopkins grins, "although he used it to wind John up. He winked at me as he was shouting at him, and then he actually ended up literally kicking John's arse. John complained later: 'You drag me out for a meal, you admit to Phil that it was your fault and I still get the kick up the arse!'

"Phil could hardly contain a smirk as he pointed out to John that as tour manager he was responsible for everything."

More farcical fun befell the band when their convoy of trucks was stopped by police during the tour. The officers were amazed to find the lorries packed with highway artefacts such as Belisha beacons, bollards, a set of traffic lights and a rolled-up zebra crossing, and it took some time for the crew to convince the thin blue line that the articles were merely stage props.

A more serious brush with the law in 1980 came when drug squad officers posing as gas board officials tricked their way into the Kew Road house. Lynott's clothes were searched and a quantity of cocaine found, although it is believed it was found in a jacket that Big Charlie had recently borrowed. Some sources claim that Big Charlie was offered money to take the rap, as it was feared that a successful prosecution against Lynott might mean a prison sentence and therefore perhaps the end of his career. But when the case went to court Lynott pleaded for mercy and, with the highly regarded George Carmen QC expertly representing him, escaped by the skin of his teeth.

After Scotland the 'Chinatown' tour passed through Liverpool, Leeds, Preston and Sheffield to Stafford Bingley Hall on May 13. Due to Philip succumbing to a bout of flu and laryngitis the following week shows in Brighton, Coventry, Leicester and Southampton had to be rescheduled. But the break did ensure everything would be OK for the crunch shows in Manchester on May 25 and 26, and in London at Hammersmith Odeon on the 28th, 29th and 30th, and the Rainbow Theatre on the 31st and June 1st.

To those in attendance at most of the shows, however, it was plain that Lizzy weren't yet firing on all cylinders. There was, of course, a new guitar player, a new keyboard player, a new stage production, a new set and at least one new haircut (Scott's) to contend with. But accepting all that, Lizzy still seemed to be unusually lacklustre.

Most of the blame fell on Snowy. Great guitar player, but no Brian Robertson or Gary Moore when it came to excitement on stage. The late Bill Cayley, Lizzy's stage manager at the time, always claimed the road crew had to stand in the wings and prod Snowy with broomsticks to get him to move on stage.

"I remember watching the first gig we did with Snowy," Chris O'Donnell claims, "and he just stood there facing his amps, as if he was daydreaming. He wasn't the best choice of guitarist, but then Phil was always impressed by his peers, and the fact that he'd played with the likes of Pink Floyd made him an attractive proposition. Snowy was a musician's musician, and Phil thought that by getting him in the line-up he'd be impressing a lot of other musicians.

"Sadly, Snowy had no identity for Lizzy's audience. He was

faceless and boring. Then again, Snowy was great to work with. He was very professional, very punctual and very keen. If the band had to be in the lobby at a certain time, Snowy was there five minutes before, just to make sure. Snowy lightened Phil's load on the 'Chinatown' tour, simply because you could rely on him."

"Phil knew what he was getting when he chose me," White argues in his defence. "He knew I wasn't an extrovert. Although having said that I did have to work a lot harder on stage with Lizzy than I did with Floyd. There was a certain amount of blood, sweat and tears involved with Lizzy, whereas with Floyd I found I could drift away and wake up at the end of the show!

"One of the main reasons why I didn't move around much on stage was because Phil's bass was so loud, if I didn't stand right in front of my amps I couldn't hear my guitar. The quietest spot on stage was in front of my stack; a few feet to the left and I was gone.

"But the criticism just went in one ear and out the other," White continues. "I may be quiet but I'm hard-headed as well, and I can take it. One review of a show at Hammersmith Odeon said I looked like I'd rather be outside cleaning the windows, and I thought that was brilliant! That reviewer really hit the nail on the head."

White did have to temporarily leave Lizzy during the summer to fulfil an outstanding commitment to Pink Floyd, rejoining the band for six concerts at Earls Court between August 4–9. But his absence proved useful in that it afforded Philip the time to oversee the final mixes of *Chinatown*.

The lengthy delay in the completion of the album, coupled with the early establishment of a title, also meant that for once Jim Fitzpatrick could put some thought into the artwork. "I even had a proper budget to work to!" he recalls. "And a strong concept to work around, and a reasonable deadline. I don't know what went wrong, but for a moment there Thin Lizzy were almost well-organised! Although I have to admit that I thought the back cover of the album was better than the front cover they chose. Something had to go wrong.

"But Philip," he continues, "gave me a completely free rein.

He was of the opinion that his face was so well known – he was practically an icon – that we didn't need to put his photograph on every cover. The record company was keen to use photographs of the band, but Philip felt it would be best to play on the mystery of some elaborate piece of artwork instead. That was a good piece of thinking."

The record company, meanwhile, were also preparing to push the boat out for *Chinatown*. Product manager Alan Phillips: "We did some spectacular black silk jackets, hand embroidered and everything, and they cost us a fortune. Then we did all these posters in the Chinese style of the album's artwork, and all these colourful and elaborate displays which looked fantastic. On stuff like press advertising, point of sale material, jackets and all the other marketing gimmicks, we must have spent £50,000 on *Chinatown* – a substantial amount in those days.

"In addition to that you've got to consider the cost of singles. Every time you release a single you have to have a video (the promo for 'Chinatown' featured the band mooching around in suitably sleazy surroundings). So that bumps up your expenditure. But then you have to promote the single, because the single promotes the album. It's all interconnected.

"If you get a hit single, the budget will increase. If you get another hit, it'll go up more. If you get three hits then you can usually do a TV campaign. *Live And Dangerous*, for example, was TV advertised and probably cost Phonogram at least £500,000. *Chinatown* wasn't as successful, but the company still didn't stint on it."

'Killer On The Loose' did provide Lizzy and Vertigo with another hit single during the autumn. Released in September it reached No.10 in Britain (No.5 in Ireland), and also came in a special double-pack version which featured two more live tracks on the B-side: 'Got To Give It Up' from Dublin in June and 'Chinatown' from Hammersmith in May.

Yet the single also caused a storm of controversy, due largely to unfortunate timing. Britain was transfixed by the so-called Yorkshire Ripper case at the time, as the police hunted a man who'd brutally murdered a number of women, mainly prostitutes, in the Leeds/Bradford area. In such a highly charged climate many observers attacked 'Killer On The Loose', accusing Lizzy of glorifying rape.

Lynott countered by pointing out that the song was merely warning women about the dangers of walking the streets alone at night ('I'm not trying to be nasty/I'm not trying to make you scared/But there's a killer on the loose/Or haven't you heard?'), yet the knee-jerk reaction of an assortment of women's groups and other moral crusaders put enough pressure on the band to make them agree to drop the song from their live set.

"It was no big deal," Gorham shrugs. "We had plenty more new songs that we wanted to fit into the set anyway."

'Killer On The Loose' was actually one of the best songs on *Chinatown*. The album finally emerged in October, but in general the new material lacked the punch and panache of the now notorious single.

If Philip had deliberated over the mix for too long, then it seemed inversely proportionate to the time he'd spent on composing the material. Tracks like 'Sugar Blues' (sugar being a Lynott synonym for cocaine) and 'Having A Good Time' were as dispensable as anything the band might've knocked up in a lazy soundcheck. Meanwhile 'Sweetheart' was a meek regurgitation of the guitar-harmony gimmick, and the reggae-tinged 'Hey You', a tale of cruel disorientation in the city jungle, didn't quite make the grade.

The defiant chorus of 'We Will Be Strong' was more like the real Lizzy, and with 'Chinatown' itself Lynott managed to capture something of the essence of the Oriental mystery that exists beyond the neon of the inscrutable immigrant quarter. But it was to America that Lynott turned once again for his best lyric, a cutting condemnation of white colonialism of the Red Indians called 'Genocide (The Killing Of The Buffalo)'.

'Did you know the redman used to roam this land?/Now the souls of lost warriors blow across the sands . . ./Did you know the redman very well?/Did you know the hunting ground before it became a hell?' Lynott was at once aggressive and emotive, seething through gritted teeth yet touching a nerve of melancholy. It was arguably his finest achievement on an otherwise agonisingly average album.

"A lot of *Chinatown* was made up in the studio," admits White, "especially Phil's lyrics. He used to leave his lyrics until the very last minute and then go into the vocal booth and sing from the top of his head. It was very time-consuming, because he'd be forever changing bits."

Perhaps it was a simple lack of ideas that drove Lynott to repeat a verse from 'Ode To A Black Man' in the tearful ballad 'Didn't I' ('There are people in the town/That say I don't give a damn/But the people in this town/They could never understand'), but even more likely is the theory that wires simply got crossed due to the timing of work on *Solo In Soho* and *Chinatown*. Both albums were being recorded around the same time at Good Earth with co-producer Kit Woolven, and some tracks that were actually meant for the Lizzy album ended up on the solo record. Such shifty manoeuvres ruffled the feathers of Snowy White in particular, who felt he should've been paid as a session player to record tracks for the solo album.

By the time *Chinatown* was released Lizzy were in Japan. Their arrival was marked by the kind of wildly ecstatic scenes that the Japanese seem to bestow upon anyone with hair past their ears, and first-timers like Darren Wharton were completely taken aback by the deluge of gifts offered by the fans. "It was just one big scrum of screaming girls," he recollects, "and they followed us everywhere. We even got asked to leave our hotel, the Tokyo Hyatt Princess, because the staff couldn't cope with the hundreds of girls that would hang around in the lobby night and day. Not to mention those who made it up to our rooms . . . It was certainly the closest I ever got to being a member of The Beatles."

Wharton also recalls hanging out with actor Jan Michael Vincent and US duo Hall & Oates in Tokyo, and with some amusement he recalls the time the band were taken out for dinner by representatives from their record company. "It was an authentic Japanese meal, with all the traditional trappings, so of course the table was only about a foot off the floor. Now, everyone in Lizzy was wearing these ridiculously skin-tight trousers, so no-one could sit down properly. We were all struggling like hell to get our legs under this tiny table, totally red-faced and short of breath, and I think it completely ruined our macho image for the night. The geisha girls who were serving thought it was intensely funny."

After Japan Lizzy headed for Australia, arriving on October 25. First stop was Sydney, where the band had one or two unexpected encounters with fellow celebrity tourists from Britain. Wharton, the pallid teenager on his first trip Down Under, relives the experience: "We stayed at a great hotel in the King's Cross area, and we bumped into loads of famous faces. There was Dick Emery, Rolf Harris, Patrick Mower and Suzanne Dannielle (who Scott and I beat in a pool contest one night), and even Arthur Lowe from *Dad's Army*. It was almost surreal.

"One day I was in the sauna (which was on the roof) when I noticed Captain Mainwaring sitting next to me. We got chatting and I told him all about Thin Lizzy, to impress him. He asked me how long I'd been on the road, and then he asked me if I was missing home. I told him I was, and he just looked at me as if I was Private Pike and said: 'Stupid boy!'"

Lizzy's show in Sydney's Chinatown district was equally memorable, perhaps the only occasion on the tour when they might claim they almost brought the house down. Scott Gorham takes up the story: "For obvious reasons we couldn't take all our flashbombs and stuff through the airports, so we had to hire some pyrotechnics expert in Australia to set up all the explosions for us. This guy told us that the fireworks he'd be using were pretty powerful, so for the first explosion we ought to stand well back from the front of the stage.

"Anyway, we finally walk on stage and I immediately spotted these long candlesticks lined up at the front of the stage, with tin-foil wrapped around them. It all looked a bit dodgy to me, so I stood back by the drum riser. Then we hit that first power chord to go into the opener 'Are You Ready' and . . . B-A-N-G!!! These bombs went off and blew every speaker on stage!"

"It blew big holes in the ceiling," Wharton elaborates, "hit Snowy in the chest and completely knocked him over, blew the PA and temporarily deafened everyone, and just left a key-board sound and the acoustic drums. We didn't know quite what to do, so we stopped playing and went back to the dressing room for an hour or so while all the equipment was sorted out."

"It was," concludes Gorham, "the shortest set we ever did. Imagine the scene: 'Ladies and gentlemen, would you please welcome . . . Thin Lizzy!' B-O-O-M!!! 'Thank you and goodnight!' "

By all accounts Lynott was as impressed with Australia as the other members of the band, but there did seem to be a simmering discontent within him around the time of the tour which led to him summoning Chris Morrison to join him Down Under. Morrison had started to take more of an interest in the management of Ultravox, and while Lynott liked to be known for his supportive attitude towards up and coming artists, his competitive edge could slice through the niceties when he felt his own status threatened. Lynott watched Ultravox have an enormous No.1 single with 'Vienna', and sensed some of his thunder being stolen.

"He could be incredibly two-faced," says Midge Ure. "He'd be your best friend, but at the same time he'd be trying to talk his manager out of managing you. After the success of 'Vienna' he accepted that Morrison would be stupid to let us go, but at first he was not happy about it at all."

After Australia Lizzy spent a short time in New Zealand before returning home for a break, and then heading out to the States once again. As 1981 swung into view the band obliged their Scandinavian fans with a string of dates in Sweden, Norway and Denmark, but then burrowed out of sight to concentrate on recording for most of the rest of the year.

Lynott also completed his second solo album, provisionally entitled *Fatalistic Attitude*. The task was akin to slotting together a huge jigsaw puzzle, as the individual pieces had been gathered over a long period of time. And the guest list also hinted at the disjointed nature of the project, with many names (Ure, Knopfler, Bain, Lewis, etc.) recurring from the first solo record. "We did that album everywhere," explains Wharton, who played on the whole shebang. "Whenever we got a spare minute, wherever we were, Phil would whack up the multi-track and we'd do a bit more on it."

Simultaneously, work began on a new Lizzy opus. The

band used Odyssey, Morgan, Battery and Townhouse studios in London, fitting their sessions in at every convenience. Although Lynott did take time off to return to Dublin during April, where he and old friend Smiley Bolger attempted to out-naff the Eurovision Song Contest (being hosted by Dublin thanks to Johnny Logan's triumph the previous year) by holding their own Alternative Song Contest.

"We had this big bash at McGonagels and everyone got into the spirit of it," says Bolger. "One band was called The Rubbers, and they had a Pink Floyd spoof song called 'Another Prick In The Dail'. And there was another guy who had a song called 'Behind Every Successful Woman There's A Simpering Wimp'. Philip and I did a version of the 'Mountains Of Mourne', changing all the words around and playing tin whistles and things. We were so bad we were brilliant, and we won it hands down!"

No less than four versions of 'Mountains Of Mourne' appeared on Bolger's 1981 Ireland-only single 'What 'Bout Ye!!', three of them featuring Philip in some capacity. Meanwhile back in the UK Vertigo dipped into the market during March with *The Adventures Of Thin Lizzy*, a compilation album, and again the following month with the double A-sided *Killers Live* EP (which matched 'Are You Ready' and 'Dear Miss Lonely Heart' from Dublin in June 1980 with 'Bad Reputation' and 'Opium Trail' from Toronto in October 1977). Even while Philip kept a low profile the product kept coming.

In fact, Lizzy would only play a handful of shows during the summer of '81, and Lynott openly admitted that, with *The Adventures Of . . .* album going gold (100,000 copies) in the UK, he intended to treat those gigs as the last of the 'greatest hits' sets. The band warmed up with shows in Scotland, Jersey and Guernsey, and then braced themselves for two major festivals, Milton Keynes Bowl on August 8 and Slane Castle in Ireland on August 16, which would be watershed shows for Thin Lizzy.

Ironically, the Milton Keynes show was a disaster. The bill was weak (Judy Tzuke, Paul Jones' Blues Band and Ian Hunter), the event wasn't well advertised, the attendance was embarrassingly low and the wisdom of shoving Lizzy into such a situation reflected unfavourably on their management. Snowy White even goes as far as to say that he didn't feel Lizzy were "genuine festival-headlining material".

"The band were atrocious that day," Peter Eustace recalls in horror. "Scott had a nightmare, he couldn't play at all. Philip was really pissed off at the poor turn-out, and I don't think he could wait to get off stage. The gig was a major blow for us, a real Black Hole for Thin Lizzy."

To compound the frustration, it came hot on the trail of Lizzy's worst showing in the UK singles charts since the early Seventies. 'Trouble Boys', written by Billy Bremner from Rockpile and backed with Percy Mayfield's 'Memory Pain', was recorded at Odyssey Studios and released in August. It could only stumble to No.53 (No.30 in Ireland), and to this day neither the remaining band members nor the management can explain why it was released at all.

"Everyone hated the damn song," spits Wharton, "but for some strange reason Phil liked it, so . . ."

Morale was low, but Slane Castle managed to lift the band's spirits. It was home territory (just 30 miles outside Dublin), the weather was kind, the crowd was massive and the bill, which included megastars-in-waiting U2, was imaginative. "It was, however," Peter Eustace laughs, "a day of one-upmanship between us and U2, as is usually the case when you get two Irish bands together. We were headlining, but they were determined to steal the show and tried a number of old tricks.

"For a start, we had the idea of hiring a helicopter to fly Phil to the venue, because it was a long way out to the stage. Unfortunately, we were told that all the helicopters in the area would be at this air show on the day of the gig, so we gave up the idea. Then on the way home from the castle we got lost and ended up at the airfield where they were having the show. To cut a long story short we managed to persuade someone to let us hire a helicopter for the next day.

"Unknown to us, U2 had tried the same thing and failed. They wanted to upstage Lizzy by making a big entrance, so when they saw Phil flying into the arena in this helicopter they flipped. It was during Hazel O'Connor's set, and the helicopter circled really low, so everyone could see Phil's grinning face at the window. The crowd went crazy, and U2 were left in no doubt as to who was the biggest Irish star of them all.

"When they got to play they tried to fire off all these massive explosions, but none of them worked. It was very embarrassing for them, because they'd clearly planned their big-show strategy meticulously. But they got their come-uppance and by pure accident Lizzy came out on top."

Revived by the success of Slane, Lizzy returned to London to continue work on the new album. At around the same time a free flexi-disc with *Flexipop* magazine featured an out-take from Lynott's second solo album sessions called 'Song For Jimmy' (a Hendrix tribute, despite the misspelling), and rumours also abounded that Philip was about to take the part of Hendrix in a new American movie. But according to Chris Morrison the idea didn't get beyond the first stages of discussion.

Renegade was the next project on the production line, and it was launched in November after a decision was made, wisely, to delay the release of the second Lynott solo LP until later the following year. The management were anxious not to repeat the marketing mistake of *Solo In Soho*, which pre-empted *Chinatown*, and determined to ensure the maximum impact for the new record.

The album, co-produced by the band with Chris Tsangarides, was originally going to be called *Angel Of Death* (indeed Jim Fitzpatrick even got as far as drawing an apocalypse scene for the cover), the title taken from a track co-written by Lynott and Darren Wharton, itself inspired by readings from the Prophesies Of Nostradamus. It was to be Wharton's first songwriting credit, and it grew from the seeds of a fast, fluttering keyboard riff that Lynott overheard in rehearsals. But while the track opened the album in dramatic fashion, Scott Gorham in particular objected to the title.

"Sometimes Phil would throw everything at the wall when he was looking for album titles," Gorham explains, "just to see what would stick. But I thought *Angel Of Death* was too heavy metal for words, and I hated it. I mean, how much more corn do you want? There were great big hunks of butter dripping off that sucker!"

Gorham also had reservations about some of the other

inclusions on *Renegade*, as did Darren Wharton. In particular, Lynott's jazzy acknowledgement of Fats Waller ('Fats', originally Snowy's idea) was greeted with a few worried frowns. "I remember 'Fats' going down on tape and thinking, 'Whoa! What was that?' " Gorham gasps. "But then after 'Dancing In The Moonlight' became a hit I was forced to admit that maybe I was thinking too one-dimensional, that maybe those pop songs had their place on Lizzy albums. Apart from anything else, trying out different styles on the records kept it interesting for us, because after you've recorded X amount of albums with the same band you don't want someone to go, 'Hey, let's do another rocker.' Suddenly, the oddball ideas sound far more interesting."

"Despite the fact that I got to do a piano solo," adds Wharton, "I thought 'Fats' missed the mark. So did 'Mexican Blood', and one or two others. I think Phil was going for a slightly different sound on that album and I got a little concerned because I thought he was straying too far away from the band's winning formula.

"But then Phil refused to be restrained as a songwriter, and he was always keen to experiment. You have to admire that in a musician. Perhaps it worked, perhaps it didn't. At least he tried."

Like *Chinatown*, *Renegade* tends to get swept under the carpet when rock historians review Lizzy's recording career. But while most fans would agree that both the Snowy White albums lacked the firepower of some of the earlier releases, it does seem unfair that an album which contains such stirring rock tunes as 'Renegade', 'Hollywood (Down On Your Luck)' and 'It's Getting Dangerous' is regarded with so little enthusiasm.

The mellower side of White's guitar playing certainly came through on *Renegade*, and especially on the title track, which also boasted another classic Lynott lyric, based on the glorious loner-against-the-world theme. This, coupled with the creeping influence of Darren Wharton's keyboards, ensured that the album continued the evolution of Lizzy's sound.

"The track 'Renegade' remains my favourite Lizzy song," says White, "I am still very proud of my contribution to that piece. In fact, I think the whole album was better than *Chinatown*. I think it proved that Thin Lizzy were a lot more song-orientated than most heavy bands, who usually tend to be riff-orientated."

With a songwriting credit for 'Angel Of Death' and two solos on the album, *Renegade* also marked the emergence of Darren Wharton as a full member of Thin Lizzy. The artwork for the album, unfortunately, suggested otherwise. The original sleeve was to feature a group shot superimposed on a mountain at night with a red sky background. Then the idea was changed to a picture of a red flag, with individual shots of each member with the flag for the back cover. The session was shot success-fully (by top fashion photographer Graham Hughes, who'd worked with Robert Palmer), but then at the last minute the record company claimed that due to the shape of the lay-out for the back cover, they'd only be able to fit four square photographs into the design.

"It was a horrible excuse and it hurt me a great deal," Wharton admits.

The creative and artistic merits, or otherwise, of *Renegade* could be examined at length, but the bottom line will remain that the album was a commercial failure. The single, 'Hollywood', didn't even reach the UK Top 50, despite useful exposure on prime-time BBC television (when, as guests on the Saturday evening *Jim'll Fix It* programme, Lizzy entertained a granny who wanted to play keyboards in a rock band). The album endured the poorest chart position since *Fighting*, making a measly No.38 just eight months after the *Adventures Of . . .* compilation had made No.6.

So what was going wrong? Alan Phillips, Lizzy's product manager during this undoubtedly shaky period, expounds his theory. "Marketing Lizzy wasn't always easy because they some-times fell in the middle ground between what was metal and what was pop," he muses, "and that pleased neither audiences. I think it started with 'Sarah' and then became exacerbated by Phil's solo material.

"In truth, although *Solo In Soho* was full of good songs, I think it did Phil harm. Very few band members actually make a successful transition to a solo artist – even Freddie Mercury, one of the biggest stars from one of the biggest rock bands ever, didn't really achieve that. I suppose you could say that Phil Collins is the exception that proves the rule.

"Phil obviously wanted to get that record off his chest, but it didn't sell particularly well and it didn't do him any favours, because it took him in a direction which the hardcore Lizzy fans didn't want him to go. It was too 'showbizzy' in a way. But then that was his decision, because I certainly don't recall there being any kind of A&R input from Phonogram. Phil was incredibly strong-minded – bright, astute, charming and hungry for success – and he was pretty much allowed to do as he pleased, creatively.

"Perhaps that was a mistake," Phillips concedes. "By the time *Renegade* came along I think his fans were confused by what had preceded it, and that affected sales. There were Lizzy singles, Phil Lynott singles, the *Top Of The Pops* theme, more Lizzy live EPs, Mark Knopfler, all the synthesizer stuff and New Romantic connection with Midge Ure . . . on the one hand it went to show how versatile and productive Phil was, but on the other hand it begged the question: Was it right for Thin Lizzy? Was it right for Phil to be associated with *Top Of The Pops*? What kind of message was that sending to the fans?

"I suppose when you realise that all this was linked to an increase in activity in the illegal chemical stakes, it becomes easier to explain the muddle that Phil seemed to get himself into," Phillips opines. "Everyone knew that Phil was getting heavily involved in drugs, and that didn't help.

"When it became obvious that sales were slipping we were extremely concerned. Lizzy were an important band for Phonogram, not just from a commercial angle, but from a prestige angle as well. So we were trying everything and anything to reverse the trend and boost sales; the idea to use Graham Hughes on *Renegade* was borne of the compulsion to try something different. And then of course when the singles weren't selling well either, we'd put out another format which we hoped would appeal to the hardcore fans – which usually meant live tracks on the B-side. Of course, the idea of using different formats has been perfected over the past 10–12 years, but in those days we were still experimenting with anything to try to return healthy sales figures."

After routining material at Nomis and John Henry's in London, with full-production rehearsals at Shepperton as usual, Lizzy marked the release of *Renegade* with a batch of UK shows in the run up to Christmas, including a show at Hammersmith Odeon on November 27 which was recorded and used for several future B-sides.

In the New Year Lizzy visited several old stomping grounds: Germany, Ireland (including dates in Belfast on February 17 and 18, and Dublin on the 20th) and Scandinavia. The Scandinavian shows remain significant if only because drummer Mike Mesbur from support band The Lookalikes had to stand in for Brian Downey, the victim of an over-zealous bouncer in a nightclub.

"We were in this club in Denmark and I lost my cloakroom ticket," Downey explains. "When we came to leave the guy wouldn't give me my jacket because I didn't have the ticket, so I jumped across the counter and grabbed the coat. The next thing I know this bouncer has knocked the shit out of me. I remember being woken up on the floor by some copper saying, 'Take that coat off please!' Fortunately, my passport was in the inside pocket, and that kept me out of jail. But I had a black eye for days and they sent me straight back to England to get it seen to."

Downey was back in action by the time Lizzy continued their European tour in March, but shortly afterwards it was the turn of Scott Gorham to take time out. He collapsed with 'exhaustion' after a show in Portugal and had to return home to London, forcing the band to play the following night of the tour, on March 9 in the Real Madrid soccer stadium, as a four-piece.

Back in the UK the next shows were rescheduled from the end of March to the end of April. Kicking off at Oxford New Theatre on April 22, the tour motored through Birmingham Odeon (23rd) and Manchester Apollo (24th), and included visits to Sheffield City Hall (26th), Newcastle City Hall (27th) and Leicester DeMontfort Hall (29th), before hitting the capital for two appearances at the Dominion Theatre on April 30 and May 1. These London shows were actually filmed for release as a live video, but according to Chris Morrison they were captured on video film, as opposed to cinematic film, and the final quality was too poor for release.

"We actually spent time overdubbing and editing the footage," says Wharton, "but Phil wasn't happy with it. He'd just shaved his moustache off at the time and he hated the way he looked. I think that had something to do with it."

The *Renegade* shows were actually something of an improvement on the *Chinatown* tour, with more effort and imagination being put into the stage production in particular. The shows started with the ominous sound of a booming bass synth, rumbling eerily through the darkness until spotlights picked out two enormous red flags billowing before wind machines either side of the stage. Strobe lights flashed and smoke poured on to the stage as Wharton steered into the 'Angel Of Death' intro, and then lighting pods manned by roadies actually hidden inside the tubular frames were mechanically raised at the rear of the set, and the lights swept the audience to great effect.

"It was like something out of *Star Wars*," says Wharton proudly, "really spectacular. I could hardly believe it was me up there, opening the show night after night."

The *Renegade* tour is not remembered with much fondness by many of those in the band's inner circle, however. Peter Eustace reflects on it as a time when things were "rapidly spinning out of control", while Snowy White claims the memories are so painful he's managed to blot them out of his mind altogether.

"There was a lot of pressure on Philip on that tour," explains John Burnham who, after a spell working with Huey Lewis in America, had returned to the Lizzy camp as a driver. "When Robbo was in the band, or Gary Moore, the audience had someone else to watch, someone who would take the show by the horns and really whip up the excitement. But with *Renegade* who was there? Darren Wharton was pretty faceless, and Snowy White was so quiet it was unbelievable. Philip didn't have anyone to help him share the burden of the spotlight."

The drug abuse got worse, as Lynott continued to push his body to new limits of endurance. His asthma attacks became more regular, his stamina sometimes wavered and his performances became more erratic.

"Like anyone else who takes drugs Phil ran hot and cold," says Adrian Hopkins, "and I saw both sides of him on that tour. I'd see him stripped naked in the dressing room looking terrible – no weight on him, covered in sores and very fragile-looking. Then half an hour later I'd see him up there on stage looking like a king. This was a man who'd be slumming it with some very seedy, nasty people involved in drugs. But this was also a man who, when we were waiting for our flight at Jersey airport, sat my five-year-old daughter Sarah on his lap and sang 'Sarah' to her.

"I began to feel the need to protect Phil," Hopkins adds. "At one stage I was probably the only 'clean' person on the road with Lizzy, and I used to specifically note these shady characters who used to turn up backstage in areas like Liverpool and Bristol. I knew they were drug-pushers and I made an effort to stop them getting passes. One night Phil had a go at me for turning these people away. He said, 'They're my mates!' But I said, 'No Phil, they're not your mates.' I got some stick for standing up to him like that, but to this day I feel that what I did was morally sound."

"We used to have patrols at our concerts," says Peter Eustace, "with people scouring the audience for the dealers. We knew some of the dodgy faces to look out for. We'd also have people going through Phil's luggage and throwing away all his chemicals. The tour manager would flush anything he found straight down the toilet, but it was like fighting a losing battle because Phil would always get more."

Chris Morrsion claims both he and O'Donnell "tried a few times to put a stop to the substance abuse that was happening, but the bottom line is you really can't stop someone doing that stuff if they don't want to." Morrison also acknowledges that he felt some sympathy for Lynott's predicament, almost going as far as to suggest that drug-taking in rock'n'roll is inevitable.

"The lifestyle is such that there's short periods of intense activity and long periods of total boredom," he asserts. "Touring involves lots of sitting around. Making records means lots of sitting around. Making videos means lots of sitting around.

Most of rock'n'roll is boring, and the only high you get is that two hours on stage every night. You get a huge adrenalin surge and then . . . what? Go home to bed? Most people simply cannot do that, and that's how they end up on drugs. That's definitely how Phil got onto them."

After the *Renegade* tour the band regrouped in Ireland to commence preparing material for the next studio album, but the atmosphere of frustration created by Lynott's increasing unreliability was hardly conducive to productivity. Soon there was friction in the air. Snowy White's dissatisfaction, in particular, had been building up all year, throughout the *Renegade* sessions.

"I'd begun to lose interest in Thin Lizzy a long time ago," White confesses. "It wasn't too bad for the first year – I enjoyed the travelling, the increase in profile and the money. But then I started to feel uncomfortable, and I think they started to feel uncomfortable with me. I discovered that while everyone was trying to broaden the band's scope, it just wasn't happening. Lizzy was just being Lizzy, repeating the same things over and over. It's a problem all successful bands have – being tied to a certain image, a certain kind of song, a certain performance live.

"I could've coped with that, as a professional, if it hadn't been for Phil's continual downward slide. During the *Renegade* period we never seemed to get any work done. I'd arrive at the studio at one o'clock and Phil wouldn't turn up until ten o'clock, by which time I was ready for bed. Some nights he'd turn up at midnight and want to work all through the night. Other nights he wouldn't turn up at all. And the annoying thing was that if Phil wasn't in the studio there wasn't a lot you could do, because he was in charge of everything.

"Phil wrote some great songs, he was a great performer and when you stripped away certain things he was a great guy, but I didn't have much of a relationship with him after the first year. We had no social contact. I'd usually pass him on the stairs at the hotel, as I was going down for breakfast and he was just getting back from a night of . . . whatever. I used to say to him, 'If I tried to live like you I'd be dead in two days', and I was serious. But I don't know if he ever took any of the warnings seriously. Perhaps he was too far gone by then.

"The crunch came in Ireland. I'd told O'Donnell I was only prepared to go if Phil was going to turn up on time, because I didn't want to spend two weeks sitting in a stuffy little studio on the off-chance that Phil might turn up. O'Donnell said it would be OK, but it was the same old story. It became insulting. Nothing got done. I seem to recall a song called 'The Sun Goes Down' that Phil was toying with, but apart from that . . . I was just watching Phil go down the plug-hole."

Snowy remembers playing his last show with Lizzy at an open-air festival in Ireland during this period, and deciding it would be his last about halfway through the set. Back in the studio, one of Snowy's last memories of being a Lizzy member was meeting a young kid in the studio next door. His name was John Sykes. "I remember thinking that he had all the credentials to be a Lizzy guitarist," says White, "and I definitely felt he was far more suitable than me. I didn't quite guess that I was talking to my successor at the time though!"

Back in London after the miserable sessions in Dublin, the band received notice of their forthcoming recording schedule. White looked at it and balked, unable to imagine another bout in the studio with Lynott. "I just decided I wasn't going to turn up," he explains, "and that was most unusual for me because I've always been very conscientious. The next day Chris Morrison phoned and said we ought to have a chat. I walked into his office and he just looked up and said, 'It's over, isn't it?' I said, 'Well, yes it is.' To be honest I was quite relieved."

At around the same time Chris O'Donnell also threw in his hand. Like Snowy and many others in the Lizzy camp he'd had enough of watching the deterioration of the band, and especially its leader. However, his assessment of the last two years is considerably more forthright. "*Chinatown* was absolute garbage, and when Phil brought in a keyboard player for *Renegade* that was it for me," he groans. "A once brilliant band was turning into a pile of crap before my very eyes. Yet I felt distanced from it all. I thought it was like driving a coach down a mountain without any brakes, and I had to get out."

Morrison decided to stay on board, however, and Lynott

decided to carry on working, despite the uncertainties of a band without a guitar player and half their management. July had brought the release of a new Lynott solo single, 'Together', and by way of promotion Philip put together a group – billed as Philip Lynott And The Soul Band – for a brief June/July tour of Ireland, featuring drummer Robbie Brennan and keyboard player Trevor Knight from Auto Da Fe, Darren Wharton on keyboards, Jerome Rimson on bass and Gus Isodore on guitar. He decided to play six-string rhythm guitar himself on the dates (which included a show in Dublin on June 29, filmed for an Irish TV documentary, *Renegade: The Philip Lynott Story*, and a jam with Paul Brady and Rory Gallagher at the Punchestown Festival on July 18), and while the set was intended to consist of solo material only, Philip was forced to include Lizzy songs such as 'Whiskey In The Jar' on several occasions.

The next taster from the heavily delayed second solo album was 'Old Town', released in September and accompanied by a promo video which depicted Philip wandering around Dublin, one particular scene on the Ha'Penny Bridge having since been commemorated with the plaque at Merchant's Arch. The album, its title disappointingly changed from *Fatalistic Attitude* to *The Philip Lynott Album*, finally followed in October.

It was actually less experimental than the first solo album, and probably more cohesive as a result, but it was still little more than a plaything for an artist increasingly keen to play. Stitched together from sessions at Compass Point, Odyssey, Good Earth and Windmill Studios in Dublin, and produced once again by Philip with Kit Woolven, it was a patchwork of simple ideas drenched in the moist-eyed emotions of a soppy, sentimental fool. Lynott was the warrior-turned-wimp, the little boy from Dublin once again, a great big softie at heart.

'Cathleen (A Beautiful Irish Girl)' was the height of twee. Naturally enough it was a follow-up to 'Sarah' as a dedication to his youngest daughter, but apart from the humorous postscript ('Now shut up and go to bed') it was a little too sickly-sweet. And 'Growing Up', a continuation on the 'little girl' theme stroked with the soothing sax of Mel Collins, also suffered from too much of a soft-focus approach.

All ten tracks on the album were composed by Lynott, with Jimmy Bain earning co-writing credits for 'Old Town' and 'Ode To Liberty (The Protest Song)'. The unmistakable influence of Mark Knopfler also shone through on the latter, as did the Midge Ure synthesizer on 'Together'. But Lynott kept the reins tight in his hands throughout, and with tracks like 'The Man's A Fool' showed just how effortlessly accessible his material could be.

In September Philip Lynott And The Soul Band played a few shows on the Continent, and then during October and November they switched to Scandinavia for another string of easy-money gigs. The line-up was similar – Downey/Isodore/ Rimson/Wharton/and Jimmy Bain on 'second keyboards' – but the atmosphere was tense and foreboding, far from the lazy fun of the Irish dates earlier, and for several members of the entourage it marked a dangerous downturn in Philip's career which they weren't prepared to witness. Long-standing live sound engineer Peter Eustace refused to do any more solo tours after Scandinavia.

"It was an evil tour," he shudders, "a very unpleasant experience. Jimmy Bain couldn't get any heroin and he was climbing the walls. Phil was out of it too, and he was an absolute pig to the whole crew. He treated us abysmally. Then halfway through the tour he came up to me and said that he realised he'd been treating the crew badly, but from now on he was going to turn his anger on the band, and give them the same treatment. Then he started to give the band a hard time for no reason.

"Unfortunately he laid into Gus Isodore one day, and he wasn't going to take it. He'd pushed Gus too far, and suddenly this rather nice chap switched into streetwise-kid-from-Detroit mode, and threatened Phil with a broken bottle. Phil loved brinkmanship, pushing people as far as he could, but he realised this time he'd gone too far. I remember the shouts from the dressing room: 'Sorry man, cool it! I was only joking, honest!' I think it must've been the only time Phil ever turned white."

The solo band reunited for some shows in Ireland between December 27 and January 2 that Christmas, but then with the

New Year came new incentives to switch the attention back to Thin Lizzy. By then a new album had been recorded, but speculation over the band's long-term future still tended to cling. Lynott, adhering religiously to the script, insisted the new Lizzy was going to be bigger and better than ever. More objective observers suggested the band wouldn't see the year out. Only time would tell.

Chapter VII

Is This The End?

So did Philip Lynott want to break up Thin Lizzy, or not? The answers, it seems, has been blurred by the passage of time through some very fragile memories.

Some suggest that Philip never wanted to pull the plug on Lizzy. Others insist he'd had the idea of going solo full-time for quite a while. A whole variety of people claim it was their idea to make the band's 1983 tour their last, while an equally vociferous faction claim that it was Philip's idea all along.

One who definitely wanted out was Scott Gorham. During rehearsals for a show in Ireland on the *Renegade* tour he pulled Lynott over to the side of the stage and confessed that he'd had enough. "I was just standing there, watching the crew set up the gear for the billionth time, and I suddenly thought: 'Oh God, do I have to go through all this again?'"

Gorham shakes his head with the pain of remembrance. "I couldn't conceal my feelings anymore, so I told Phil I was calling it a day. Now all this panicked Phil, so he spent some time trying to convince me that everything was going to be OK. Phil had a way of talking me into anything, and I fell for it yet again. He persuaded me to do one more album and one more tour, and I was like, 'Oh . . . shit!' It was very difficult to deny Phil something if he wanted it that bad."

Chris Morrison saw the sense in keeping Lizzy together and wringing one last payday out of the name. After all, the band's financial position at the time was hardly enviable. "The *Renegade* album hadn't done well at all," Morrison explains, "and I realised we were on the verge of bankruptcy. Fortunately I did a deal with the bank and we managed to claw back 50 per cent of the debt, but it was still looking dodgy.

"After *Jailbreak* (which sold about 1.5 million copies) there was a period where we made lots of money, but the band spent it all. We'd do tours of America where we'd 'drop' $100,000. Philip would insist on flying between gigs, with a limo waiting for him at each end. He would insist on a certain quality of hotel. He would insist on the rock star lifestyle. I would have endless rows with him about how much it was all costing, but he didn't care.

"In those days it was costing about £500,000 a year to run Thin Lizzy. Philip was very insecure about the people who worked for him, so we had to have everyone on a retainer. Every person on that crew was on a bloody retainer, and the wages bill was enormous. I work with bands today which cost £50,000 a year to keep together, so imagine how much £500,000 was 15 years ago! There was so much wastage it was untrue, but Philip couldn't see that until towards the end, when money became so tight that he went, 'Oh, I see what you mean.'

"An example of how difficult it was to keep Lizzy working was when Chris O'Donnell left the company on the eve of a tour," Morrison continues. "The band's trucks had been impounded with all the equipment because they hadn't paid the trucking company. If we'd have gone on that tour then we'd have lost another £30,000, so I cancelled the tour. I then had to rework all our finances so that I could pay the trucking company off, get the band on the road, and work it so that we made some of that money back. I cut everything back to the bone, and we eventually made a £12,000 profit.

"It was nail-biting stuff," Morrison pleads. "Then we came to do *Thunder And Lightning* and Philip insisted that the record had a gatefold sleeve. The record company were against the idea for cost reasons, but I managed to persuade them to do a gatefold for a limited edition. Philip said it wasn't good enough and got really upset. He said he was going to leave the band.

"Now, he often cried wolf like that, but this time he convinced me over a period of about three days that he was genuine. I had to sit down with him and persuade him that he should at least complete *Thunder And Lightning* – which, to help ticket sales, we could then present as a Farewell Tour.

"I said, 'If you break the band up now you'll be left with a £250,000 debt. Your tax isn't paid, your finances are all over the place and you're not in a position to set yourself up with anything else. Plus, with ticket sales as they are on the new tour we'll lose another £20,000. However, if you're smart about it you'll do the tour and we'll think of a way of wiping out all the old debt'.

"I had the idea of getting all the old guitar players back for a few shows, taping it, and then persuading the record company to accept a live album as our commitment album. That way I thought we could clear our debt and Philip would be able to start something new with a clean slate."

Of course, Lizzy wouldn't really split up. They would simply take a long break, give each other some breathing space to sort their lives, and then reform. Few of those engaged in the author's enquiries would actually admit to such cold-eyed calculation, but such was the unspoken philosophy.

"The truth was," Tony Brainsby admits, "the whole Thin Lizzy idea was running out of steam, and it needed a kick. The tour we'd announced for the spring of '83 was selling very badly, so something had to be done."

With the benefit of hindsight it might be suggested that such skulduggery shouldn't have been necessary. The choice of John Sykes as Snowy White's replacement had rejuvenated the band enough to have some observers suggesting this was the best line-up since Robbo left, while the *Thunder And Lightning* album that emerged in March '83 was fresh and powerful, and arguably Lizzy's best studio album since the glories of 1976.

Sykes, young and handsome with a massive mane of mousy hair, was the archetypal Guitar Hero-in-the-making. He, or someone of his calibre, should've joined the band when Gary Moore left (for the third time). Suddenly, Philip saw the folly of the Snowy White years.

The link between Lizzy and Sykes was provided by producer Chris Tsangarides. Sykes had just left the Tygers Of Pang Tang, and was in the process of fulfilling his contractual obligations to MCA by recording a solo single entitled 'Please Don't Leave

Me', at Lombard Studio in Dublin. Tsangarides was producing the session, and of course he'd co-produced *Renegade* with Lizzy.

"I asked Chris if he'd approach Phil for me," Sykes explains, "to see if he was interested in playing on the song. Basically, I was always a big Lizzy fan. So Chris got in touch and Phil was into the idea. He brought Brian (Downey) and Darren (Wharton) with him as well and before I knew it I was in Thin Lizzy without Scott Gorham!

"By the end of the session Phil asked me if I was interested in joining Lizzy, and I sort of said, 'Well . . . yeah!' I'd also been offered a gig with Ozzy Osbourne around this time, and I almost took the job. But I got on so well with Phil that I decided to go for Lizzy. So Phil gave me 'the wink' and we went out to this Pink Elephant Club and did a bit of this and a bit of that, and generally got to know each other.

"We flew back to London after that, and it was pretty much a day or so later that he rang me and officially offered me the gig. We went straight to The Boathouse (Pete Townshend's Eel Pie Studios, near Kew Bridge) – I don't think I'd even met Scott at this point – and Phil said, 'Just play anything, let it rip.' I think he just wanted to get me involved in the writing of something on the album, so I just blasted away with this guitar riff and Phil built 'Cold Sweat' around it."

Lynott and Sykes quickly struck up a close working and personal relationship. Besides the relaunch of Lizzy, the two appeared on the TV programme *Razzmatazz* (with Downey on drums) to promote the 'Please Don't Leave Me' single, and also on Channel 4's *Gastank*, where they performed 'Growing Up' and 'The Man's A Fool' with co-presenters Tony Ashton and Rick Wakeman.

The majority of *Thunder And Lightning* was, however, written before Sykes joined. The haunting 'The Sun Goes Down' was conceived by Darren Wharton during pre-production at Zero's in Dublin, while 'This Is The One' was the marriage of a Lynott riff and a Wharton chorus. The keyboard player also secured two more credits: 'Heart Attack' (with Lynott and Gorham, who always hated the title) and 'Someday She Is Going To Hit Back' (with Downey and Lynott).

"That 'Someday . . .' track was an unusual one," Wharton

states. "Scott and Brian wanted to do it at half-tempo, but I wanted to do it up tempo. We ventured into the realms of jazz chords there, and it was all my fault. We were taking jazz chords – 11ths, 13ths, minor 9ths and augmented 5ths and weird chord structures – and copying every note of the chord with guitar harmonies. It was really unnatural for the guitar, and that's why it sounded so strange."

The title track was much simpler. Imagine being hit on the temple by a scud missile. Quite frankly, it was one of the fastest and heaviest tracks Philip had ever tackled, the nearest Lizzy ever got to heavy metal. Yet the macho heroics in the lyrics were strikingly familiar: the dude-in-bar-fighting-over-chick scenario was one many of those who toured with Lizzy had witnessed on more than one occasion, especially in America.

The rest of the album veered between the brilliant and the almost brilliant. The single, 'Cold Sweat', was so typical of Lizzy at their swaggering, bombastic best you could easily forgive the regurgitation of the gambling theme (*à la* 'Waiting For An Alibi'). Meanwhile 'Bad Habits' was another from the commercial top drawer, a Gorham/Lynott composition that showed how Lizzy could lighten up considerably without losing their hard rock edge.

Finally, there were the two tracks written solely by Lynott. 'Baby Please Don't Go' had a touch of the 'fillers' about it, plus a title dubiously close to that of Sykes' solo single (released the previous September). But then 'The Holy War' was a masterpiece in its own right, a whirl of incisive guitar harmonics lashed onto an aggressive bass line, while Lynott growled the words with a venom which told us how much he meant it.

Lynott got his gatefold sleeve as well, although only on early copies of the album, which featured a four-track 12″ EP of 'Emerald', 'Killer On The Loose', 'The Boys Are Back In Town' and 'Hollywood', recorded live at Hammersmith Odeon on November 27, 1981. Otherwise the cover of *Thunder And Lightning* was its least attractive feature, resorting to the kind of tired clichés that had been recently stirred up by the revivalists of the so-called New Wave Of British Heavy Metal.

"The cover was awful," declares Jim Fitzpatrick (who, you

might have guessed, had nothing to do with it). "But then that's how things were going in the music industry at that time. I was getting about £5–6,000 for an album cover at this time, but then came the cut-backs, and there was a new guy at the record company who didn't want to spend that kind of money.

"I actually did the most beautiful design for *Thunder And Lightning* – a very Celtic design with triple spirals and a stone levitating out of the ground, with a flash of lightning there. Philip loved it, but the record company wanted something else. The record company always seemed to want to force the band downmarket, whereas Philip always wanted to go upmarket. No-one ever went bust underestimating the intelligence of the American population, but a lot of record companies do underestimate the intelligence of their audience. I don't think they could imagine these tough, rocker-type kids liking something artistic and perhaps sensitive. They didn't want anything too romantic or too sophisticated, they wanted leather jackets and motorbikes and 'The Boys Are Back In Town'."

So Fitzpatrick's efforts went to ground and the *Thunder And Lightning* cover ended up looking like something the Blue Peter team might've prepared earlier. But in the charts it fared well, and reached the highest position (No.4) of any Lizzy album since *Black Rose* (No.2). And 'Cold Sweat', released ahead of the album in February with two more tracks from the 1981 Hammersmith concert cropping up on the B-sides of some formats, also grazed the Top 30.

"We got 'Cold Sweat' in at No.28," Morrison remembers, "and we got a slot on the BBC's *Breakfast Show*, and *Top Of The Pops*. Unfortunately, Philip turned up at (*TOTP* producer) Michael Hurll's office the worse for wear and ended up swearing at a stage manager. Hurll wouldn't stand for it and he bounced us off the show, the result being that the single only went up one place the following week. If we'd had done *Top Of The Pops* it would've shot up, but we couldn't move it more than one place. A typical Lizzy disaster."

The idea of announcing that the *Thunder And Lightning* tour would be Lizzy's last wasn't such a disaster, on the face of it. Within days of a press announcement the rest of the tickets for the tour, of which there were quite a few, were eagerly snapped up. The trouble was, with their best line-up and album for years in their artillery, plus the high of playing to packed venues all over the country, as fans paid them one final homage, Philip soon began to change his mind about the whole 'farewell' business.

"Once the good reviews started to flood in, and once Phil started to see the fans flocking back in their thousands, he didn't want to stop," says Sykes. "Scott wanted to pack it in, but he was the only one. I think Phil felt I'd given the band a new spark, and after the Snowy years that was something it really needed. He wanted to keep the band going from then on, but he felt that as the press had already jumped on the 'Lizzy to split!' story, he'd have to give it at least a couple of years before he could do another tour. That was the plan."

The tour began on January 26 with a special concert at Hitchin, filmed for the BBC's *Sight & Sound In Concert* show (simultaneously broadcast on radio and TV). It was John Sykes' début with Thin Lizzy, real in-at-the-deep-end stuff, but he passed the test with flying colours, not to mention flying hair.

Two days after Hitchin Lizzy went to Newcastle to perform live on Channel 4's *The Tube*. Once again the band sounded hot, but off camera those who encountered Lynott got a completely different, and quite shocking, perspective of him. A visitor to Lizzy's dressing room found Philip jumping around with a small metal tin like a pencil case. In it was evidence of heroin use. For a Dr. Jekyll who used to look down on such indulgence, this open display of his addiction in front of friends confirmed the emergence of a sad and tragic Mr. Hyde.

The bulk of the UK dates were in February and March, crowned with a string of four Hammersmith Odeons (March 9, 10, 11 and 12). The strength of the new album was reflected in the fact that six of its offspring were included in the set, almost making distant relatives like 'Jailbreak' and 'Suicide' seem jaded by comparison. But with Sykes playing every solo as if it was his last, even old dogs such as 'Cowboy Song' and 'The Boys Are Back In Town' seemed to have retained a bite to match their bark.

The last of the Hammersmith shows realised Morrison's idea of a gathering of the guitar-playing clans. As the main set reached its climax, out of the wings stepped Brian Robertson to contest one more duel with Scott Gorham on 'Emerald', 'Rosalie' and 'Baby Drives Me Crazy'. Then Gary Moore waltzed on to lead Lizzy through 'Still In Love With You' and 'Black Rose', before Eric Bell joined the party for 'Whiskey In The Jar'. Finally, the whole ravenous pack fought over the carcass of 'The Rocker' until the bitter, feedback-swamped end.

"It was chaos," says Bell, "a quite appalling mess if you actually listened closely to what was being played. In fact it was a turning point in my life, and after that I never wanted to hear those songs again. But I suppose the point was it was a good way of burying Thin Lizzy forever."

"There was," adds Downey, "an amazing amount of alcohol consumed in the Odeon bar that night, it was a truly spectacular piss-up. We were still there at five o'clock the next morning, they couldn't get rid of us."

Next stop on the lingering farewell tour was Ireland, and emotional nights in Cork on April 5, in Galway on the 6th, Belfast on the 8th and in Dublin on the 9th and 10th. The shows at the RDS in Dublin were also filmed and intended for release on video, but this never materialised. John Sykes thinks it's probably just as well. "In Dublin Phil turned up late and it was quite obvious he'd had one too many in the afternoon, or whatever. He was quite unpredictable at the best of times, but when he was buzzing on something he could lose it altogether.

"This night he was all over the place. So halfway through one number I'd had enough of him hitting bum notes and I turned to him and said, 'What the fuck are you doing?' The next thing I knew he'd thrown his bass to the floor and walked off stage, leaving us to get through the rest of the song as best we could without him. At the end of the song I had to go backstage and apologise to him before he'd come back on, but then he was all smiles again and we turned it into a joke."

"That last Irish tour was sheer madness," says Peter Eustace, "bottles of port and brandy all the way. I particularly remember the show at Cork City Hall. There was a lot of mixed emotion, with the newer members of the team feeling sad that it was coming to an end, and those of us who'd been there for years feeling quite elated. I just remember a sense of carefree abandon, and Phil loving the fact that I had a whopping hangover the next day."

The end was in sight, although first there was a batch of dates in Scandinavia to undertake, three extra shows in Britain in early May and also a trip to Japan to negotiate. A case of tying up loose ends. "That tour was originally only supposed to be three months, but it ended up lasting nearly a year," says tour manager John Salter, who also worked as the band's agent. "And I could have put more dates in too, because the offers were still flooding in. Everyone wanted Lizzy to play in their town on their last tour."

The Scandinavian leg of the tour was particularly successful, confirmation that Sweden was Lizzy's third home after Ireland and England. However, the trip almost ended in tragedy, when Lynott's powerful Mercedes 450 was involved in a motorway crash between Gothenburg and Stockholm. Photographer Denis O'Regan, a passenger in the car at the time, recalls the incident which very nearly ended Thin Lizzy's career several months prematurely.

"There'd been some serious partying going on the night before and no-one could get John Sykes out of bed," O'Regan remembers. "Consequently, when he finally emerged we were very late, so Gus (Curtis, Lynott's lackey) set off at full pelt in the Mercedes. It was pretty hairy stuff, and I was especially concerned about Philip, because he was sitting in the front and he never wore his seat belt. Anyway, we stopped at this store to get some orange juice or something, and I noticed something strange: Philip put his belt on when he got back in the car. I'd never seen him do that before, and when I thought about it later I found it a bit spooky.

"So Gus went bombing off down the motorway again at 140 mph and it was in the middle of a torrential downpour of rain. We were in the fast lane and a van came through on the slow lane, with a Saab behind it. The Saab then moved into the middle lane to overtake, but so did the van, so the Saab veered into the fast lane to avoid the van and we ploughed into the back of it. We all came to a standstill way down the motorway, and there was debris everywhere. The emergency services arrived and sprayed the entire area with foam, and Gus and I were taken to hospital. It was a miracle that no-one got killed, and not only that but the gig went ahead that evening without a hitch."

After Europe Lizzy headed for the Far East. The band arrived in Tokyo on May 17, and set about preparing for their appearance at the city's Sun Plaza. It was a show Peter Eustace will never forget, but once again it was for the wrong reasons. "Phil couldn't get any heroin in Japan," he sighs, "and he was in a bad way. When it came to the gig they got the start of the set completely wrong, and suddenly Phil just stopped playing. We all looked at one another, and I thought he was going to collapse and have a breakdown. It was one of the most chilling moments of my life. Everyone knew something was very wrong, except the fans who seemed to think it was part of the show. They didn't know whether to clap or not.

"Then Phil started mumbling something to the audience. He was saying, 'You're fucking GREAT! We're fucking SHITE!' He went into this weird, rambling monologue, and I for one was most disturbed by it, because over the years I'd got used to him being so on the case. The whole ugly episode was a real watershed for Phil.

"In the dressing afterwards he continued to ramble on. He was talking about giving all his money away to the famine victims in Africa. I'm not sure he really knew what he was saying. Later, as we drove back to the hotel in the limo, I was trying hard to cheer him up and steer his mind back to the real world, when he suddenly turned to stare at me. He just said, 'Jesus Peter, no more heroes.' The look in his eyes, the way he said it . . . it was an admission that he'd lost it.

"It was inevitable I suppose," Eustace adds, "but once Philip discovered heroin that was it. I used to think that he probably found it a great release, because it meant he could turn off and have something more powerful than himself doing the business. He could go into the golden slumbers just as The Stranglers described in the song 'Golden Brown'. Phil knew what that song was about. He'd really met his match with heroin.

"On the crew we all thought Phil was scared of success, and it seemed as if he couldn't relax into the idea of being successful. Once you've arrived where do you go? All you know is that there's all these young guns breathing down your neck. Drink gave him an escape for a while, but over the years as he became more successful and more materialistic he lost touch with his crowd. In the end heroin allowed him to relax into the idea of being at the top. But it was hardly an ideal solution."

Lynott pulled himself together eventually, but those on that final Japanese trip remember seeing an unusual side to him. He was edgy and moody. Even back in London Lynott found it impossible to relax. With 'down time' on his hands he decided to form a band for a batch of gigs he'd been offered in Sweden, a series of outdoor festivals during July and August known as the Folk Park Tour. Both Sykes and Downey agreed to go along for the ride, and the line-up was completed by rhythm guitarist Donal 'Doish' Nagle (from Irish band The Bogey Boys) and keyboard wizard Mark Stanway (from Magnum).

"I got to know Phil through being connected with John Sykes," Stanway explains. "The Tygers Of Pan Tang had supported Magnum and John and I ended up writing some stuff together. When John joined Lizzy I was invited to a show at the Manchester Apollo, and we all ended up at the Britannia Hotel, which is where I was introduced to Phil.

"When Phil suggested we put a band together for the Folk Park Tour I was delighted, because Magnum were in limbo at the time. Also, the chance to work with Phil was a dream. We had one day's rehearsal, and that was really difficult for me because a lot of his solo stuff which we were going to play had tons of keyboards on it.

"Phil didn't want to do any Lizzy songs on the tour, but in the event the fans demanded it and we did five or six: 'The Boys Are Back ...', 'The Sun Goes Down', 'Sarah', 'Still In Love With You', 'A Night In The Life Of A Blues Singer' and even 'Whiskey In The Jar'. We also did 'Parisienne Walkways', 'King's Call', 'Old Town' and a few others from his solo albums. The band gelled well and for three weeks we really enjoyed ourselves."

In some places the promoters craftily advertised the group as Thin Lizzy, although the truth was a name hadn't even been decided upon. Back in the UK Lynott had suggested in the press that the band was called The Three Musketeers, and then changed it to The Four Musketeers. But according to Stanway they were never billed as such in Sweden. "They were just names Phil was throwing around," he shrugs. "Basically it was just the Phil Lynott Band, having a laugh for a few weeks. Although when we got back to England John and I did spend a lot of time at Phil's house writing some stuff and talking about the possibility of doing something more permanent. Phil even asked me to play keyboards with Lizzy at Reading; I don't know what was wrong with Darren, but he seemed to want me in the band. Unfortunately, as Magnum were playing the festival as well I simply didn't have enough time to rehearse, so I had to decline the offer."

The Big One, the show that Lynott considered to be Lizzy's genuine finale, was indeed the band's appearance at the Reading Festival on Sunday August 28, where they were to headline above Little Steven, Ten Years After, Steve Harley, Climax Blues Band, The Enid, Sad Cafe, One The Juggler, Twelfth Night and Opposition. To heighten the emotion of the event, the festival was being touted as the last to be held on the traditional Reading site.

"It was quite an occasion," Adrian Hopkins assesses, "Lizzy's last UK show, the end for the Reading Festival, a real tear-jerker for some. I decided I'd have some special T-shirts made up for the weekend, so bearing in mind that I also worked with Ian Gillan (who was fronting the Saturday night headliners, Black Sabbath, at the time), I used this design which had Ian and Phil arm-wrestling on the front. It was supposed to be a Clash Of The Titans-type thing. The only problem was we couldn't get the two together for a photograph, so we had to use an artist's impression of them. Phil ended up looking like Joan Armatrading and Gillan like something out of The Sweet."

The festival itself was a roaring success. Friday's bill was the weakest of the three but still proved an interesting mix of progressive rock (Pallas, Pendragon, Solstice), glam (Hanoi

Rocks) and reggae (Steel Pulse), with Big Country winning the day over headliners The Stranglers. Saturday was more hard rock based, with Black Sabbath presiding over Marillion, Magnum, Suzi Quatro, Heavy Pettin', Stevie Ray Vaughan, Mama's Boys and others. And then Sunday came and . . . was this the end?

It might have been a bad omen for Lizzy when a few of their flashbombs went off before they'd even appeared. The crowd cheered wildly but it was simply a case of premature adulation. Five minutes or so later when Lynott eventually sauntered on stage, the schoolboy grin etched across his ample chin suggested that nothing, let alone an errant bang or two, was going to spoil the party. He even decided to resurrect 'A Night In The Life Of A Blues Singer' for fun, and those close enough could see him chuckling uncontrollably to himself as Sykes and Gorham frantically tried to out-do each other with every solo.

"Well," he wheezed with me later, "it was our last British show, so we were all out for as much glory as we could get!"

The running order was slightly different from the set that had seen the band through the earlier UK dates, but generally the idea was to showcase the newer songs at the beginning, before slipping into 'greatest hits' territory towards the end. The concluding song of the set was again 'Black Rose', before the inevitable protracted encores urged the show down the back straight. To close, Lizzy took 'Rosalie' on a brief jaunt through 'Dancing In The Moonlight', and then melted into the sublime melancholy of 'Still In Love With You'.

"I'll never forget that moment for as long as I live," Sykes promises. "I watched the tears roll down Phil's face as he sang the words. Whenever he sang the line, 'Is this the end?' the crowd shouted 'NO!' He was really touched by that."

For Thin Lizzy, the end finally came in Germany the week after the mud and mayhem of Reading. The Monsters Of Rock concept, nurtured annually at Donington Park since 1980, had been expanded to take in a number of large festivals across Europe in 1983, and Lizzy found themselves lining up for their last shows alongside, amongst others, Motorhead, Meat Loaf and headliners Whitesnake. They were, according to John

Sykes, "token gigs, for us to let ourselves down lightly", but they remain historic.

The penultimate show was in Kaiserslauten on September 3, where the Lizzy line-up almost featured two different faces. Gorham and Downey failed to show up on time, and Lynott made provision by offering the gig to two old friends. "Phil walked into our dressing room," says Robbo, who was playing with Motorhead at the time, and said to me and 'Philthy Animal' (Motorhead drummer Phil Taylor), 'Scott and Brian haven't turned up – do you want to do it instead?' Me and Philthy said, 'Aye, fucking great!' Philthy was a massive Lizzy fan, that's the only reason I got the job in Motorhead.

"So we sat down in the dressing room with a little cassette and learned the set. It didn't take long because Philthy knew most of the songs anyway, and all I had to learn were the new songs. But then about two minutes before they were due to go on Scott and Brian appeared – they'd got lost on the autobahn, or something – and we lost our big chance."

Lizzy's last ever show came on September 4 in Nuremburg. Emotions ran high. "I watched the show from the side of the stage that night," says Robbo, "and there was a wee tear in my eye. In my opinion the Sykes line-up was the best Phil had had since I left, and it was so sad to think the band were breaking up. I was upset, me. They played great, too. They wanted me to come on and jam with them, but I said, 'No way, you're playing way too good for me!' I was just glad they were going out on a high note."

To conclude the burial, Lizzy presented Phonogram with another double live album. As Chris Morrison had planned, the album would fulfil their recording commitment to Phonogram, and provide a souvenir of the last tour, in particular the unique Hammersmith jam, for the band's loyal fans. It was released in November and entitled *Life* (or *Live* if you read the logo design a different way; Lynott later likened this play on words to the original Tin/Thin Lizzy gag, although even he admitted he wasn't the best at choosing titles!).

The album wasn't entirely culled from the Hammersmith shows in March. Some of the performances were recorded in Dublin, others in Glasgow on the farewell tour, and 'Renegade' (the only track featuring Snowy White, who was not invited to the Hammersmith jam: "It didn't bother me because I'd decided long before that there was no way I wanted to be involved") was even taken from the 1981 Hammersmith show. Inevitably, there were also additional recordings made in the studio during the mixing stages, principally to polish up the backing vocals.

The basic breakdown was: the newer songs ('Thunder And Lightning', 'Baby Please Don't Go', 'Holy War') on side one, the mellower songs ('Renegade', 'Got To Give It Up') on side two, the singles ('The Boys. . . .', 'Cold Sweat', 'Killer On The Loose') on side three and the more indulgent tracks ('Black Rose', 'Still In Love With You') on side four. There was at least one exception to the rule on each side, but generally the song selection attempted to ensure that the album wouldn't back-track across too much familiar ground.

Life was never going to be a match for *Live And Dangerous*, but the weak overall sound of the album surprised even the most partisan of fans. Lynott's mix was depressingly poor, especially where the lead vocals were concerned, and the incisive edge of the *Thunder And Lightning* performances (a blistering rendition of 'Are You Ready' aside) seemed to have been blunted.

"The recordings were OK but the mix was so muddy it was awful," Downey complains. "Phil was in the studio night and day mixing that record and he wouldn't give himself a rest. Consequently, whenever I popped in to have a listen it was worse!"

"Philip insisted on mixing the album when he really should've let someone else do it," Chris Morrison confirms. "He wasn't in the best of health at the time and I shouldn't have let him do it. Not only was the finished mix rough, but it took forever and it cost a fortune. The album should've been ready to come out around the time of Reading, but instead it crept out at the end of the year when all the furore about the band had died down."

Scott Gorham's verdict on 'Life' is even more damning: "I was so mentally sick I was on auto-pilot for that album. I didn't care about the mixing, I was completely gone by that point. To this day I've only heard one side of it."

It was always going to be difficult to know where to draw the line for Thin Lizzy, especially after months of drawn-out farewell shows and a maze of options product-wise. But perhaps the chapter should've been permanently closed at the end of the festivals, when the euphoria had subsided and reality kicked back in.

"After Germany," Darren Wharton concludes with regret, "we simply said goodbye at the airport, and that was it."

Back in Dublin Lynott spent a few miserable weeks at Glen Corr, contemplating his next move. He'd spend hours walking up and down the beach which stretched past the bottom of his garden in Howth. He needed time to reassess not only his career, but his whole life, as his marriage had begun to go awry. Caroline had moved back to Corston, near Bath, to be closer to her family, and the Crowthers had closed ranks, anxious to shield Sarah and Cathleen from their father's unconventional lifestyle. For the first time in years Philip felt he was losing his grip on his own destiny.

"Philip used to go up and down but he was never depressed," says Jim Fitzpatrick, his companion on many of those beach strolls. "This time, however, he definitely was depressed. He told me he was running on empty and I knew exactly what he meant. He didn't want to finish Lizzy and he was heartbroken that the band had split up.

"I realised then that Philip's health wasn't as it should be. I even started organising football matches on the beach to try to get him involved in something physical, because I'm a fitness fanatic and I find physical exercise the best way to get rid of any stress. I thought Philip could run all his frustration out, clear his head and get rid of all the crap that had built up inside him. Plus, I was worried about the drugs. Not the dope, but other stuff. I used to see people giving him speed and coke and all that shit. I once threw a bag of shit out of the window of the car – I just found it lying on the seat! It was beginning to concern me."

Fitzpatrick tried to talk some sense into his long-standing friend (and now neighbour – the artist had bought an apartment just along the beach from Glen Corr), but the battle was an uphill one. From the time that Lizzy split up to Lynott's last visit to Ireland in late '85 he felt Philip slipping slowly away, deteriorating shamefully. "I saw his mind begin to go the more he got into drugs," he says sadly. "In the early days we used to have the most stimulating conversations – on politics, religion, music, everything. The only thing we really disagreed on was politics, as Philip had a very idealistic view of Ireland; he saw Ireland through green-coloured spectacles and thought that if the British left Northern Ireland everything would be fine. I couldn't accept that, and we'd spend hours swapping our opinions and formulating our theories on our country.

"But then during his last three years Philip became very slow in the head, and he wasn't the same person I once knew. That spark had gone. And then it began to show physically; he started to put on weight, and that bothered him immensely, because he was very proud of his appearance.

"I tried to help Philip, but he'd con me. I said, 'Look, I'll buy you a bike if you'll cycle up Howth Hill every day. You'll be fit again in no time.' In the end he bought two bikes – one for him, one for Caroline – and he'd ring me up and tell me he'd been out for rides. But every time I saw him he looked worse, so I knew he was lying.

"Then later he got very withdrawn. I used to take my family around to the house – at that time I had a daughter of 14 – and suddenly I began to feel it wasn't a good idea at all. Before I would've trusted Philip with my life, but then I saw signs of what I presumed was heroin – bits of silver paper with burn marks underneath – and I thought, 'Whoa! That's not on at all!' I began to get very uncomfortable around him. Heroin was one word that was never mentioned around Philip, but you knew it was going on.

"The big problem was," Fitzpatrick adds, barely able to contain his anger, "that there was a sort of coterie around Philip that kept people like myself at a distance. We began to feel . . . not excluded, but . . . pushed into the background. They managed to isolate Philip from his real friends, because they didn't want people like me giving him hassle about drugs while they were trying to keep the party going.

"Drugs, to me, distort the personality. I saw a very truthful person turn into a liar, and I didn't like it at all. I saw a creative genius losing his mind, and I reacted against that as well. As a person he was 90 per cent wonderful, even if he did have a dark streak that I didn't like. With women, some he'd treat like queens, others he'd treat terribly, especially groupies. But mostly he was a fabulous human being, a 'giving' person, and to see all this being destroyed before my eyes made me very angry.

"I always thought I had this great influence over him – in fact he pretended I had this great influence over him – and I used to be quite proud of the fact that I could walk along the beach with him and try to guide him through his life. I wouldn't lecture him, just attempt to point him in the right direction. We talked about drugs, and I distinctly remember that his attitude to heroin was 'once you're on it you're dead'. So I couldn't believe he was doing that stuff. Drink, yeah. Pills, maybe. Cocaine, probably. But heroin? Chasing the dragon? I couldn't believe it."

Lynott had in fact been tempted by smack many times over the previous five years or more. He managed to keep the subject taboo, but those closest to him couldn't avoid catching wind of what was going on.

"I first saw Phil and Scott doing heroin at the Welbeck Mansions flat in West Hampstead, but I didn't know what it was at the time," Robbo reveals. "Then when I found out it was heroin I just kept well out of the way. I didn't touch that shit until much later – until Wild Horses days – and then I only tooted (snorted) it, and only for a short amount of time. To be honest, I didn't like it. But I noticed that Phil and Scott had really got into it, and especially Scott.

"A while later I went up to Glasgow to do some guitar parts for the *Life* album, because the Hammersmith gig didn't really work out too well, and Scott was out of his face. He was in the toilet doing heroin, and I caught him. I knew then that the situation had got out of control."

Some observers tend to lay the blame for Lynott's attraction to heroin at the feet of Gorham, citing speculation that the Californian had already been mixed up in the smack scene long before moving to London. Charged with such allegations, Gorham opens up and defends himself vehemently.

"It is true that I had done heroin in LA before I came to England," he admits. "In fact, moving to England was great for me, because it got me away from that whole scene. I managed to stay away from drugs for a while, but then as we started to play the same halls over and over again, and play the same tunes over and over again, and do the same shit over and over again, the drugs thing started to creep back into my life.

"The heroin thing started to rear its head in Paris while we were doing *Black Rose*. It just seemed readily available over there and the dealers seemed to like hanging around us. Because I'd done it before, it wasn't a great barrier for me to break once again.

"I remember Phil telling me he'd been doing some heroin while we were in Paris, and I was like, 'Hey, gimme a blast of that!' It snowballed from that. I didn't get Phil into heroin – he got into it on his own – but I certainly didn't try to discourage him. I heard Jon Bon Jovi once say, 'Why didn't the rest of the guys in the band stop him?' That's bullshit. I couldn't stop him. I was doing it too!

"The problem was," Gorham continues, "he started associating with a lot of people who were into that scene, not just me. Therefore he never had a part of his life which kept him away from it – it was always right there on his table, right in front of his face, all the time. It's difficult to quit when you've got it so readily available in front of you night and day.

"It wasn't just smack we were doing either, it was everything. It was the real downfall of Thin Lizzy. And we knew it, and everyone else knew it, but it was like a trap that you had no way of avoiding. We were living the image of the rock'n'roll band to the full, and it has to be said that we loved every minute of it."

Nevertheless Lynott knew he was dicing with death, and his songs were littered with confessions and warnings about the futility of drugs. 'Opium Trail' from *Bad Reputation* was a blunt admission of indulgence ('I took a line that comes from the golden States of Shan/The smugglers' trail that leads to the opium den'), while 'Got To Give It Up' from *Black Rose* went even further, acknowledging the vice-like grip of dependence: 'Tell my mama and tell my pa that their fine young son didn't get far/He made it to the end of a bottle sitting in a sleazy bar . . . /Tell my sister I'm sinking slow/Now and then I 'powder' my nose . . .' Of course, Lynott would claim that he was merely assuming the personality of another character, but having written the words in the 'first person' the song was too confessional for comfort.

'Sugar Blues' from *Chinatown* contained perhaps the most disturbing disclosure of them all: 'Now I'm not the type to worry/Especially if it's concerning my health/Oh no, I never worry/I'd much rather do something else/But I'm changing my point of view/Ever since I caught me the sugar blues'. While the title 'It's Getting Dangerous' from the *Renegade* album said it all for some people.

"It was all there in black and white," muses Smiley Bolger, "staring us in the face. It was so obvious we couldn't see it."

Chapter VIII

On Manoeuvres With Sergeant Rock

Philip had big plans for John Sykes. He saw the dashing guitar player from Blackpool as the spark for a brighter future, a sidekick with the panache of Robbo and the flair of Gary Moore, yet irresistibly younger and hungrier, with the rock world at his feet. Never one to relinquish the possibilities of a useful association, Lynott nurtured his relationship with Sykes as a father might nurture his gifted son.

In the weeks after Reading, Germany and all that jazz, Lynott lounged at home considering his next move. There was talk of a Sykes/Downey/Stanway band, effectively Lizzy without Scott. There was mention of an offer for Philip to join what was only referred to as a "name band". There were also stories of him helping out in the studio with the likes of Junior, Auto Da Fe and Clann Eadair. And, according to Robbo, there was serious talk of putting a band together with Philthy Phil Taylor.

"We discussed it in detail," he says, "a trio with The Animal on drums. But every time Philthy and I went to Phil's house to rehearse he just couldn't get it together. We'd have our gear set up ready to go, and Phil would be upstairs lying in bed. We'd wait around all night, but Phil wouldn't come downstairs. In the end Philthy said 'Fuck this!', and that was that."

Whatever happened, Lynott wanted to remain in Sykes' slipstream, and invited him to stay at the Richmond house for long periods. Mark Stanway, still unsure of his future with Magnum, also frequented the Kew Road residence, and the three of them began to formulate a number of working ideas. When Brian Downey was persuaded to lay down his fishing rods

233

and return to the drum stool (after Lizzy he'd sold his house in Banstead, Surrey, and retired to Ireland for tax reasons), Lynott decided on a short-term strategy involving all of them.

Then Sykes dropped a bombshell. Various members of the Whitesnake camp had been so impressed with his performances on the Monsters tour they urged band leader David Coverdale to secure his services for their next campaign. So much money was being mentioned Sykes had to take it seriously. "I told Phil right from the off what was happening," he declares. "I got a call from Coverdale's manager, Ossie Hoppe, and he told me he wanted me to go to Munich, where they were doing *Slide It In*, to check the whole situation out. I told them I would.

"So I explained the situation to Phil. At that time Phil was busy sorting out a few personal things with his wife and stuff, so I said 'Look, I'm just going to check this thing out, OK?'

"To tell you the truth I was never a big fan of Whitesnake, they were too bluesy for me, but I met Coverdale in Munich and we had a good time and talked about the chance of working together. I told him, 'Look, I'm not the sort of guy that's going to take being ordered around, and I don't want to be told what style to play, so if that's what you're looking for then I'm not the guy for you.' I was pretty strict with him, and we left it like that.

"Then I flew back to England and a couple of days later I got a call from the Whitesnake people saying Coverdale wanted me to join. So I said, 'No, I'm going to stick with Phil.' But then the next day they called again and made me a tempting financial offer. I still turned it down. Then they called again the next day and said, 'Well how much do you want to join the band?' So I put a price on my head which I thought was way above what they'd pay, and they came back and said, 'OK, you've got it.' I thought to myself, 'Oh shit, I suppose I've got to join them now!'

"So I went to Phil and told him that I'd had an offer I couldn't refuse. It was a really emotional moment. I was standing there with tears in my eyes, and he was sitting on his bed with tears in his eyes, and we just hugged each other and blubbed like babies. His attitude was: 'I'd never hold you back

– I wish you well', whereas it could have easily been 'Fuck you!' He was a real gentleman about it."

"Sykes leaving was actually a bit of a kick in the teeth for Phil at the time," says Mark Stanway. "However, I'd written some stuff with a guitar player called Laurence Archer and I told Phil about him. He was good, really good, in the John Sykes league. As soon as Phil got to hear Laurence play he got all his old enthusiasm back.

"Unfortunately, Phil was like that for much of that period. He'd work flat out for a week and be bursting with life, then he'd go into a depression and we'd sit around twiddling our thumbs for a week. He was very unreliable, and you always felt he needed something new, something like Laurence coming into the band, to keep his interest alive."

Laurence Archer, a 21-year-old with fast fingers and vast potential, had been on the periphery of the Lizzy family for some time. His stepfather Reuben, who fronted both Lautrec and Stampede – bands which also featured Laurence – was a teenage friend of Mick Lawford, a one-time Lizzy tour manager who ended up as Grand Slam's wardrobe man. Laurence then joined Wild Horses, who were still being managed by Chris Morrison, and it was around that time that he started to hang out with John Sykes.

"There were a lot of good gigs going for guitar players at that time," Archer recalls, "and John and I were both getting offers. Lizzy were looking for someone, so were Whitesnake, so was Ozzy Osbourne. Anyway, during Wild Horses days I went down to Odyssey Studios to see Phil, and he'd set up this little stack all ready for me to play. He gave me this guitar that he'd bought for Gary Moore, and we jammed around for a while. It was a dream come true for me.

"After that we were doing a residency at the Marquee and Phil came down one night for a jam. Afterwards he offered me the Lizzy gig, but I turned it down because, stupidly, I really thought that Wild Horses were going to do something, and that Lizzy were on their last legs."

They kept in touch and when Mark Stanway mentioned Laurence's name in the wake of Sykes' departure another piece of the new jigsaw seemed to snap into place. Archer, who was going through "a lot of political shit" with Polydor on behalf of Stampede at the time, hadn't played for two months when Philip phoned him. He'd also just returned from a cycling holiday and had cut off all his hair.

"But the next thing I knew this limo had pulled up outside my door with Mark Stanway in it, and I was whisked off to Stringfellow's before I had a chance to blink."

Archer and Stanway followed Lynott to Dublin where, with Downey providing the rhythm, the tentative group began work on a set. They routined some material at Glen Corr, then spent some time at Clink Studios (a converted prison just south of the Liffey), and then booked themselves some rehearsal time at Howth Community Hall. But Downey wasn't happy, neither with the music nor the people who'd started to hang out with Philip again. Downey's condition for rejoining Lynott was that the new outfit would make a clean break from Lizzy and carry no passengers from the past.

"As far as I was concerned the band wasn't as good as the one we had before anyway," he states. "I said to Phil, 'What's the point in doing a second-rate Lizzy?' He was adamant that the band was going to be good enough given time, but I couldn't see it. That's where we parted company."

To further complicate things Magnum had finally picked themselves up after being dropped by Jet Records and had lined up a new tour. As Stanway was still officially a member of the band he felt obliged to honour the commitment. It left him in an awkward predicament. "I was actually going to leave Phil and concentrate on Magnum full-time," he says, "but after losing John and Brian in quick succession, plus being right in the middle of some domestic trouble, I don't think he could've taken me kicking him in the teeth as well."

Stanway did the Magnum dates and dragged Laurence Archer along too, but to placate Lynott they'd both pledged to return to his court afterwards and apply themselves unerringly to the new band. On their return they were introduced to their new colleagues, rhythm guitarist Doish Nagle and drummer Robbie Brennan (ex-Skid Row and Auto Da Fe), and almost immediately were rehearsing for a low-key Irish tour in early May, designed to break in the band gently.

"For a while," Philip told me later, "I was thinking about getting away from the hard rock thing altogether. If I was going to play aggressive music again I wanted it to be sincere. The thing about *Thunder And Lightning* was that I found a good 50 per cent of it was sincere aggression, whereas the other 50 per cent was really concocted. So when Lizzy finished I dabbled in a few different environments – doing silly things with Junior and producing bands like Auto Da Fe – just to get away from it all and recharge my batteries. Then I jumped up in Nottingham with Mama's Boys and I started to get the feel to play heavy again, and then I jumped up with Magnum at the Marquee and I definitely got the taste for it then! After that show I thought: right, let's get this show on the road!"

A plethora of names were considered before the Irish press inadvertently christened the band Grand Slam. There was Reactor Factor, Catastrophe, Hell Bent On Havoc (an astonishingly naff suggestion), Slam Anthem and just plain Slam (the title of a song Lynott had in mind). Nothing seemed to work, until one Irish journalist writing an introductory piece on the band for Dublin's *Evening Herald* offered his editor the headline Grand Slam. It stuck.

With songs like 'Nineteen', 'Sisters Of Mercy' and 'Military Man' up his sleeve, Lynott paid for some studio time out of his own pocket in the pursuit of a recording contract. Demos were put to tape at Lombard Studios in Dublin and at Rock City in Shepperton, and Chris Morrison began to test the water with a few phone calls to old contacts. Caution was the response.

It has to be said that Lynott was cautious too, taking nothing for granted. At rehearsals at E'ZEE Studios in North London during late May he had earned the title of Sergeant Rock, a reference to his almost overbearing strictness and dedication to rehearsals drill rather than his marching jackboots and the shiny buttons on his tunic. As a witness to the way he barked his orders at the top of his voice and stomped up and down as if inspecting an unruly parade, I can vouch for the validity of the nickname.

"It's a bit awkward at the moment," he confided to me during a mid-afternoon break, "because I'm still working on my bass parts and formulating some of the lyrics, so I can't really have a go at them too much if they get things wrong. I have been chasing them up a bit though, but once I get myself sorted out I'll be on their backs even more!

"In fact," he added, taking a slug of something that smelt like a derivative of household bleach, "I'm being too harsh on them at the moment, but I know that the critics and the supporters will be even harsher if they're not performing at their peak, so I'm not letting up."

Philip stood up and strode over to where Robbie Brennan was firing an air rifle at a tin can. He ripped the gun off his drummer and then turned to shoot out several of the wall lights in the studio. Shaking with mischievous mirth, he sat back down and continued: "What I'm concentrating on is creating certain atmospheres, because I just don't want to come in and rehearse blatant riffs. I dunno, I just want . . . The Who had it, you know one minute they could be really crap and the next minute they'd be brilliant. The Stones were like that too sometimes; you'd listen to them and they'd sound like the same old Stones, but then they'd go (snaps fingers) and they'd be off on a different tangent. I thought it was very important to have that tangible thing, and that's why we do a funk song called 'Harlem', just to try to get another feel."

Lynott and the others had been rehearsing at E'ZEE between two and ten pm six days a week, a regime no doubt enforced with one eye on the bank balance. They'd worked up a number of new ideas, including the funk theme of Nagle's which Lynott had titled 'Harlem', a Lizzy-esque rocker from Archer's Stampede days called 'Dedication', and a light-hearted fusion of Procol Harum's 'Whiter Shade Of Pale' and Bob Dylan's 'Like A Rolling Stone', which Archer had constructed with 'Parisienne Walkways' in mind. However, Lynott revealed that Grand Slam's set would include some Lizzy numbers.

"When Lizzy started we did 50 per cent of other people's material just like most new bands do," he argued, "so I adopted that attitude and thought if we were gonna do other people's material we might as well do Lizzy's! We soon got tired of that though, because it started to seem like we were another version of Lizzy. So when we did our first dates over here (England) we made sure we had our own material sorted out. Now we only do two Lizzy numbers: 'Sarah', which Lizzy never did live anyway, and 'Cold Sweat'."

The inevitable comparisons with Lizzy was one subject Lynott was keen to play down. He pointed to the fact that Grand Slam had made an attempt to eschew the established Lizzy sound of twin-guitar melodies by going instead for one lead guitar player and one rhythm player. But even he had to concede that the indomitable strength of his identity as a musician would mean the ghost of Lizzy being shackled to his ankles forever. "I don't feel I have a God-given right to success because of what I've done before," he stressed, however, "and I want Grand Slam to be successful for itself and not because it's Philip Lynott's band."

Bravely, he acknowledged that for many music business insiders the name Philip Lynott was regarded with some scepticism in the light of his 'bad reputation' in Lizzy, rather than as a free ticket to ride. It was partly for this reason that he felt the future of the band lay in America. "My face has been seen around too much over here," he chuckled in his slow, deep way, "and familiarity does breed contempt. I'm just not fashionable here any more!"

He may have been right. The caution expressed by those record company executives already approached was even duplicated by the editor of the magazine for which I conducted the E'ZEE interview, and I had a fight to get the original article published in July '84. Alarmingly, it suggested that while Thin Lizzy was nothing without Philip Lynott, some people felt that Philip Lynott was nothing without Thin Lizzy.

"There was no reason for us not to get a deal," says Archer defiantly, "apart from a political one. We were a band of good musicians, we were getting a good response from the kids and the songs were shaping up well. But we kept running into people who didn't want to know Phil.

"Somewhere, in every major record company we approached, there was someone who'd had a run-in with Phil in the past, and he was blacklisted. For example, EMI were really interested in us, but one of the A&R men there had been knocked out by Phil years previously, when this guy was a journalist and had written something nasty about him. It seemed like everyone was trying to get their own back on him.

"And then there was the drug reputation, which put a lot of people off. It was crazy. The band's Volvo estate car had been seized by police after a couple of drug raids (in which Phil was not directly involved), and it was a marked car. So when we did our first British tour there would be police waiting for us outside the venue every night. In Preston, during the World Snooker Championships, we were partying with Jimmy White and Alex Higgins, and we came out of the gig to see six police cars surrounding us. It was ridiculous, and also a little scary, as Phil had a habit of forgetting where he'd put things . . ."

Lynott had in fact been charged with possession of cannabis in May after being arrested at Dublin airport and strip searched. One of the detectives involved in the arrest claimed there were tell-tale track marks on his arms, indicating recent heroin injection. But officials found only a tiny amount of dope in the lining of Lynott's coat, so tiny in fact that when the case went to a Dublin court the following September Judge Gillian Hussey decided to accept Lynott's solicitor's appeal for leniency. Lynott claimed he regretted his connection with drugs and solemnly proclaimed he wouldn't make the same mistake again.

"I am not going to do anything to hamper this man's career," Judge Hussey said. "As long as he is only using these drugs himself and not giving them to others he is only destroying himself. I wish he would give them up."

This time he was not charged.

Grand Slam's first crucial test came in mid-June, with showcase gigs at the Marquee on the 18th and 19th. All the tiny toilet gigs around the country had simply been a preparation for the London début, as Lynott knew that a battery of record company representatives would be in attendance. He particularly wanted to impress on stage so he could claim the band had secured any future deal through the merits of their live show "rather than because we make good demos or take good photographs".

Lynott looked overweight and tired at the Marquee, but the band were scorching. A packed house, a healthy press and

A&R turnout, stifling June temperatures . . . conditions certainly conspired in favour of the band, and they responded with the strongest of intent. The set began with the shrill, dipping note that crashed into 'Yellow Pearl', naturally sounding much heavier live. As would be the pattern for future shows, 'Nineteen' followed and raced into 'Sisters Of Mercy' (or 'Sisters Of Murphy' as Philip would have it), a real gem hewn from the same rock as 'Emerald'.

'Military Man', like 'Sisters . . .' another mini-epic of changing moods, came next and highlighted the depth of Lynott's songwriting ability, while the slinky street swagger of 'Harlem' pushed Slam's boundaries even further. This preceded a touch of nostalgia in the shape of crowd-pleasers 'Parisienne Walkways' and 'Cold Sweat', and then two more new songs, 'Crazy' and 'Dedication'.

The show was completed by a light-hearted 'Dear Miss Lonely Hearts', incorporating snatches of 'Some Guys Have All The Luck' and 'Every Breath You Take', with encores of 'Whiter Shade Of Rolling Stone' (the Procol-Dylan mutant) and the brand new 'I Don't Need This' bringing the evening to a close. Overall Slam had showcased seven new songs, and while there was still some evolution to endure before the band would be able to boast an entirely original repertoire, the start they had made was highly impressive.

The problem was, no-one was prepared to gamble on a renowned drug addict embarking upon a new mid-life career. Despite Lynott's admirable and extensive efforts to prove the contrary, Grand Slam were always going to be a poor man's Thin Lizzy in much the same way that the fresh endeavours of many established 'names' are unfavourably compared to previous glories.

Unperturbed, Lynott continued to put an amazing amount of effort into Grand Slam, slogging around the country throughout the rest of the summer and autumn playing anywhere and everywhere. "Lessons in humility" Philip called the shoe box shows.

"Basically," says Mark Stanway, "all we wanted to do was get the band sharp for when we played the Marquee, because we knew that's where we were on show to the industry. Phil was in workaholic mode and we'd play pubs for no money, but it was fun and served its purpose. The band was certainly tight – we knew the set backwards – and I think that's why we ended up getting so pissed before we went on every night!

"Honestly," he adds with an air of incredulity, "I don't know how we managed to play perfectly well after the amount of booze we got through. For a Magnum show I could only ever have a pint before a show, because there was a lot of playing to do. But with Grand Slam we used to go on stage in some terrible states. I could hardly stand up some nights. But then it was that kind of music; not technically demanding to play, just more like one big groove that you got into. Most of the time a gutful of beer and a few joints actually helped.

"The trouble was we went too far. We were animals, and it nearly cost me my marriage. Night after night after night . . . sleep was something you'd fit in now and again. It was an amazing existence, and everywhere we went drinks would be free, because Phil was so popular. Coke, speed, joints, champagne . . . anything you wanted, you could have it. I did more partying in 1984 than I have done in the nine years since!"

Stanway saw at close quarters the chaotic nature of Lynott's existence, as he struggled to revive his ailing marriage, struggled to control his drug habit and struggled to resurrect his career with Grand Slam. It helped him understand why Philip was such a complex character, a hard shell with a soft underbelly. "He couldn't escape," says Stanway. "There'd be photographers from the *Sun* standing outside his front gate all night. He was under a lot of pressure, so in the end I invited him up to my house in Wolverhampton for a couple of weeks, and that was the first time that I'd seen him look really healthy and straight.

"I had a family, and Phil really revelled in the family atmosphere. I mean, he'd even wash up! He was in a normal family situation and he was a kitten – warm, gentle, relaxed and the kindest guy you'd ever meet. OK, so he'd light up a joint after the kids had gone to bed, but other than that he was Mister Normal. Seeing that side of him made it even more difficult [for me to understand] the way he'd behave when he was back in the spotlight, abusing himself like there was no tomorrow."

Stanway knew Philip was doing heroin, as indeed was Doish Nagle and Robbie Brennan, who was himself being prescribed a heroin substitute by a rehab centre. Neither was the keyboard player an angel when it came to illegal substances, but he could barely disguise his contempt for his colleagues' flirtations with smack. "It was obvious Phil was on heroin because he was always throwing up," he explains. "But he tried to hide it from me because I threatened him that if I ever saw him doing it I'd tell his mum.

"All the same, I used to see him doing it regularly. I hated it. I remember doing Status Quo's 'End Of The Road' gig at Crystal Palace Football Club. We were being ferried from the dressing room to the back of the stage in a van, and Phil, Robbie and Doish were 'chasing the dragon' as we pulled up to the stage. I just thought, 'Oh no, how could they do that at a time like this?' It was so disappointing."

The gig with Quo on July 14, at which Slam slotted onto a bill beside Little Steven, Dave Edmunds and Chas & Dave, came during a week of recording at EMI's studios in Manchester Square, in which the band completed work on Archer's 'Dedication', among other tunes. This pattern would be followed throughout the rest of the year, with repeated bouts of gigging virtually merging the dates into one long tour, with short studio spells squeezed in between. The one break Lynott allowed himself was during August, although even his fortnight in Marbella was interrupted by an impromptu gig at a nightclub, with Nagle and Brennan flying out to join in the madness, which according to witnesses began at 4am with a shambolic 'Boys Are Back In Town' and went rapidly downhill from there.

One fan who followed the band right around the country during this time was Sue Peters. She'd originally met Lynott at Lizzy's Hitchin show the previous year and had got to know him well enough for him to offer her the chance to mastermind the launch of a Grand Slam fan club. Peters and her friend Christine Loughlin jumped at the idea.

"Philip wanted fans to run the fan club, because he felt that Lizzy's fan club, which was run by the Lizzy office, didn't quite get it right," says Peters. "So Christine and I came up with a number of ideas: everyone would get a personal answer within ten days, regular photocopied newsletters which would be right up to date, and things like that.

"We got thousands of letters and Philip was really pleased. We'd take everything round to his house and he'd sign everything, answer questions, do whatever we wanted him to do. He wasn't keen on us mentioning Lizzy in the newsletter – he'd say 'That's my past, let's talk about now' – but generally he was very helpful. He didn't want it to be called a Fan Club, though. He hated referring to people as 'fans' as he felt it was a bit condescending. He preferred to call it a Supporters Club (although after Grand Slam folded it became The Philip Lynott Appreciation Society).

"Philip genuinely loved close contact with his supporters," continues Peters. "For example, any member of the club who turned up at a gig and showed their membership card could get taken backstage to meet Philip. In fact, a lot of people told us that they'd never been in a fan club before that treated them so well, made them feel as if they were being taken notice of. Philip would never leave a gig without talking to the fans. He'd insist that people came backstage, had a drink, had their photo taken with him, did whatever they wanted to do. He wouldn't leave a gig until everyone had got what they wanted from him.

"I remember one Lizzy gig at Hammersmith Odeon when it was snowing, and Philip opened the window of his dressing room and passed this bottle of brandy out to the fans waiting by the backstage door, so they could keep warm while they were waiting to get in."

The notion of Lynott as a man-of-the-fans can be seconded by rock hack Dave Ling, who as a punter-cum-cub reporter found himself shut out of Lizzy's post-gig party at Carlos and Johnny's Wine Bar in the Fulham Road, after the final *Chinatown* show at Hammersmith Odeon. Lynott arrived late and spotted the teenager outside waiting anxiously. He proceeded to invite him in, ply him with drinks and introduce him to the other members of the band, insisting that he was well looked after.

"He really did care," says Sue Peters. "We used to get hundreds of letters and cards and drawings of him, and we'd pass them all onto him. After he died Phyllis had us sorting through all his old stuff and we came across everything we'd ever given him. He'd kept everything."

Peters and Loughlin did encounter the darker side of Lynott during 1984 though. "To start with he was a right bastard," Peters admits. "He'd shout at us and all sorts. It got to the stage where one night at the Marquee both Christine and I decided we'd had enough. We both walked out. But then Robbie Brennan took us to the pub and told us the score. He said: 'Look, he's doing it on purpose, so don't let him get to you. If you walk out on him now you'll never get back with him. But if you just tell him to fuck off he'll love you forever, because then he'll know that you're genuine and you're not just hanging around him because of who he is.' And he was right."

"In fact, Philip always took great care of us," she adds. "After gigs he'd say to someone, 'Make sure me girls get home alright.' Or if we were very late he'd take us to his house and make us up beds on the sofa. He'd be running around with quilts and pillows, making us cups of tea ... like a mother, really. It was all because we'd passed that first test. Robbie said he did it to everybody. He'd push you to breaking point to see what kind of person you were, but once he decided he liked you he'd do anything for you."

"Phil was very intimidating," Stanway adds, "a roadie's nightmare. All the roadies that had worked for me for years, they're all back with me now, dropped me like a brick when I was with Phil. He'd order people around like they were dirt. I think 90 per cent of it was a wind-up, to see what he could get away with. To me he wasn't a bastard, he just exercised the authority that people allowed him to have.

"Towards the end though his moods were unbelievable, almost psychopathic. It was just down to the heroin. And it was terrible rehearsing with him, because if he was on the gear he'd carry on playing the same thing for two hours, and you had to stay there with him. He'd be in a trance and I used to wish I had a sequencer, so I could switch it on and go down the pub. He wouldn't have noticed.

"Near the end of Grand Slam," Stanway concludes, "Phil

really went to pot. He'd forget his words, he'd put more weight on, he seemed to lose pride in his appearance, and he just wasn't as meticulous as he used to be when it came to recording. We had a lot of ups and downs over the drugs. I mean, I couldn't stop him doing smack, but I was blowed if I was going to stand around and watch him do it."

"The worst thing about getting close to Phil," says Laurence Archer, "was the feeling in the back of your mind that he was going to go too far. Mark and I panicked several times at the house when we couldn't hear any movement from his bedroom. You'd always hear him stomping around, but on the occasions that it went quiet we'd go dashing upstairs and he'd be lying there turning blue. Mark and I literally shook him back to life one day.

"At one stage I actually got Phil off heroin for three months," Archer proclaims, "but every day a courier would arrive with a package for him. Phil and his entourage was a pretty lucrative coup for all the drug dealers, and they'd tempt him by sending him stuff all the time. Trying to keep someone clean while there's packets of stuff turning up on the doorstep night and day is pretty difficult. The strange thing was, Phil was always going on at me about the dangers of smack. He'd be forever saying, 'It's really bad news, don't do it.' Then five minutes later the boot would be on the other foot, and I'd be saying to him, 'For God's sake, you've got to give that shit up!'"

Archer became quite close to Lynott in the year they worked together, to the point where the young guitarist virtually moved into the Kew Road house after splitting up with his first wife. Lynott also took Archer along with him when he was a guest on Virgin's inaugural flight to New York (Philip also appeared in a TV advert for Richard Branson's new airline), a bonding experience if ever there was one. "Sixty crates of champagne, a plane full of celebrities and, if you knew the right people to ask, any drug you could possibly want," the guitarist reminisces. "There was Holly Johnson, Steve Strange, Boy George, Bonnie Langford ... everywhere you looked there were famous faces, and most of them were 'having a good time'. At one point the captain actually asked everyone to move down the cabin as the plane was using up too much fuel in an effort to stay upright!"

Despite the madness of such lost weekends, Archer protests that he was both chemically clean and mentally stable during the Grand Slam days, and that for that reason he was good for Philip to have around at the house. He also tended to bring out the paternal instincts in Lynott, and in this respect it could be said that Archer's innocence kept his feet on the ground, periodically at least.

"The main problem was," Doish Nagle avows, "that Philip was like a magnet for a lot of people, and a lot of those people knew what Philip was into. These people would use the drug (heroin) as their passport into the band's circle, and all of a sudden you find you can't control your environment. It wasn't so bad when we were in Scotland or somewhere where the drug wasn't available, we could then concentrate on the gig and the music. But in Dublin or London there would be people crawling all over the band, and a lot of these characters didn't want paying for the stuff they provided, not at first anyway. That was when it got dangerous.

"I couldn't believe how many people were on heroin in London," Nagle exclaims. "It almost seemed to be the norm. I was very young at the time and there was never a stage when I thought it was a problem. I never thought it would kill one of us. Some bands have a problem with alcohol, others have a problem with women, others have a problem with heroin . . . it's really, really sad, because everyone suffers. You're helpless once it gets hold of you. Locking people in rooms doesn't help. The only person who can help you is yourself, but if you let it go too far even you can't do anything.

"All the while there's these people hanging around you, like animals on the prowl waiting for signs of weakness," adds Nagle, who eventually overdosed on heroin in 1986 but has since won his battle to stay 'clean'. "There were literally dozens of people who would hang around Philip or pretend to be associated with him, and I didn't know half of them. Sometimes I'd spend all day talking to people I'd never seen before in my life, because they claimed to be connected with Thin Lizzy, or whatever. It meant that you could never just concentrate on the band, you had to deal with being at the centre of this whole crowd of leeches."

In keeping with this scenario, the Kew Road residence was almost open house to untold hordes of hangers-on, and you never knew who you might bump into there. It was an eerie reflection on the tragedy that was unfolding before everyone's eyes, that while shady strangers came and partied all night Philip was too lenient to refuse them their fun.

"He was basically very lonely and he didn't like the house being empty," Sue Peters explains. "He just had to have people staying there all the time, so you'd go round there and bump into all these strange people that you'd never seen before. There was one girl who slept on his sofa for about six months, because he felt sorry for her. There were these two Swedish girls who hadn't got anywhere to go, so Philip invited them back to his house and they stayed for nearly a year. John Sykes had a permanent bedroom there, Mark and Laurence were always there, so were Robbie and Doish, and Robbo would always turn up drunk in the middle of the night . . . You never knew who you were going to meet on the stairs."

"People would come over to Phil's house and do their partying," sneers Sykes, "but then they would go home to recover, while Phil would continue partying with the next lot of people who arrived. He had a constant flow of people through his front door and most of those people knew what he was into, and would oblige willingly in order to keep in with him. I used to argue and fight with him all the time about it. I used to say, 'Phil, this shit will kill you and these arseholes won't give a damn.'

"Really, Phil wasn't always the confident guy most people knew, he was quite insecure at times and needed people around him. Sometimes I'd go to his house and he'd be scratching around on his bass going, 'Oh I can't play this thing, I can't write songs, I'm fucking hopeless.' I'd just laugh at him, because not only did he write some of the most classic rock songs of all time, but he was probably the tightest bass player I ever worked with. Yet he was worried a lot, and he craved reassurance. I guess that's why he didn't mind having a house full of hangers-on, people to tell him how wonderful he was while he was sorting out the next fix."

"The paradox about Phil's social life," Peter Eustace insists, "was that the people who were closest to him were the most dangerous for him to have around. The more straight you were with Phil, the more he tried to distance himself from you. He respected straight dealing, but somehow he didn't quite understand it. He felt ill at ease with straight people, and the most untrustworthy people, the loonies, those who'd steal from him and rip him off, they were people who got closest to him."

The round-the-clock rave-ups at Kew Road became folklore, and this just made the Crowther family more determined to shield Sarah and Cathleen from the madness. They stopped Lynott from seeing his kids at weekends, and naturally Philip was devastated. "The house was full of the children's belongings," says Peters. "He wouldn't let anyone touch anything. There were paintings that they'd done hanging up, toys on the floor, messages he'd written for them on their bedroom walls, just as if they still lived there. Only you didn't mention his family. Ever. He was so sensitive about his kids that the slightest thing could turn his mood. When he couldn't see the kids he fell apart."

Lynott slumped deeper into the cushion of his chosen poisons, still somehow managing to disguise his most dangerous and selfish indulgence from many people. He told acquaintances in the music business that he'd quit heroin for good, and in August joined the Anti-Heroin Campaign to warn against its use. He was even quoted in London's *Evening Standard* as saying that his dalliance with the drug was the scariest period of his life, and that it certainly wasn't the fun it's sometimes made out to be.

Like many drug addicts he had become unable to face the cold truth. He had convinced himself that he didn't have a problem, so he simply dismissed enquiries about his health with smoke screen platitudes. But at the end of the day he was only cheating himself.

Not that Lynott ever sacrificed his dignity in public. Backstage he indulged in many of the illicit pleasures rock'n'roll has to offer. But he was always articulate rather than merely coherent, always alert rather than merely awake. His capacity for the consumption of drink and drugs was made all the more extraordinary by his ability to maintain his poise, certainly on stage and in front of fans and press. He never came across as a drunk or a 'druggie', an unavoidable consequence of self-abuse for most of the unfortunates involved in that scene.

Grand Slam retained their appeal, too, despite the lingering reluctance of the record companies. The band's Christmas shows at the Marquee were once again reviewed with enthusiasm, and the fact that the set now included another four new songs proved that Slam were slowly emerging from the shadows of Lizzy.

'Yellow Pearl' still opened the set, with 'Nineteen' and 'Sisters Of Mercy' still tucked in behind. But then came 'Can't Get Away', an emotive Archer composition featuring one of his best solos, and a dead ringer for a massive hit single. It should have suggested to those with the power of the cheque book that if the band could come up with tracks of this quality after just a few months, then given a bit more time and money they could well prove a lucrative investment.

'Military Man' and 'Cold Sweat' came next in the pre-Christmas show, and then a second new one called 'Gay Boys' was given its début; another slice of Soho life with a groove not too far removed from 'Dancing In The Moonlight'. 'Dedication' and the sing-along silliness of 'Dear Miss Lonely Heart' closed the set, before the first encore unveiled two more new songs: the moody, bluesy 'Crime Rate' and the more typical, uptempo 'Breakdown'. Then came 'Sarah' and the 'Whiter Shade Of Rolling Stone' hybrid, both as relaxed as the festive spirit would allow, and that had to be it if the Marquee weren't to breach any local council rules.

It was a great show made even more remarkable when you consider the condition that at least three members of the band were in at the time. Listening to tapes of the gig nine years later it is difficult to ignore just how good Grand Slam were. It is also difficult to believe that it was one of the band's last ever shows. "I reckon Chris Morrison spent between £80,000–100,000 keeping Grand Slam together during that year," says Mark Stanway, "but there was no light at the end of the tunnel."

"In the end," says Sue Peters, "the money just ran out and Philip just had to put it down to experience. All the other members of the band had families to support, and they couldn't hang on any longer without the financial security of a record deal. Philip was so disappointed that it didn't work out."

"On the whole it was a very bad year for him," Doish Nagle attests. "There were moments when he shone brilliantly, but then he'd quickly burn himself out. I remember manic bursts of energy, but I also remember that Philip wasn't as fiercely motivated as he was when he was in Lizzy and I was in The Bogey Boys. In those days he'd be possessed by his work, always jamming, writing with different people, helping out bands with production, organising stuff and so on. In Grand Slam there would be periods when you weren't sure if the band was going to exist the next day.

"He was," Nagle adds, "still carrying a lot of luggage from Lizzy, and I don't think many people realised just what kind of pressure he was under. He'd tried to break the Lizzy mould, and in fact I thought Slam were softer and more musical than Lizzy, and not so heavily guitar-orientated. But a lot of people resented the fact that he'd started a new band so soon after Lizzy, and that went against him.

"Also, I don't think Grand Slam were as strong a unit as Thin Lizzy. We weren't together long enough to be really, really good friends, and on some levels maybe there was even a bit of a division between the Irish contingent and the English contingent. I don't know really, it was a strange time."

The year ended with Lynott back in Ireland, guesting on stage with Gary Moore in Belfast and Dublin – the guitarist's first visit to his homeland in ten years, which was captured for posterity on the 'Emerald Aisles' video. It was confirmation that the estranged pair had buried the hatchet after years of bad feeling.

"There was a period when we would bump into each other at clubs," laughs Moore, "and we'd just sort of growl at each other. I'd spent a year in America, but when I came to live in London again I'd bump into him at various night-spots and we'd do our best to ignore each other. It was stupid really.

"One night I was at Dingwalls (in Camden Town) with Jeff Beck and a couple of girls and we were having a great laugh. Phil was sitting in the corner sulking, and you could tell he really wanted to come over and join in the crowd, but he wouldn't because I was there. It was really sad, but quite funny as well.

"We first started talking again at the airport, when by pure coincidence we both arrived at the same time. Someone said to me, 'Hey, Lynott's over there!', and I think at the same time one of his guys said to him, 'Hey, Moore's over there!' For a while no-one knew what was going to happen. I think some people thought there was going to be a big fight! But as it turned out I was really chuffed that we could speak again."

In the New Year Lynott and Moore met up again in London, where Moore was working on a single to precede his next album. Moore, moved by his experiences in trouble-torn Northern Ireland, had written a song called 'Out In The Fields' and had invited Philip to do the track with him as a duet under the auspices of producer Peter Collins. The two also recorded 'Military Man' at Eel Pie Studios, an updated version of 'Still In Love With You' with engineer Tony Platt ("That was always Gary's song anyway," Philip argued), and Philip helped out on backing vocals on another new Moore song, 'Nothing To Lose'.

The result of these collaborations wouldn't be heard until the summer. In the meantime, Lynott and Archer flew out to San Francisco in late January to work on some material with Huey Lewis, who by now had broken big in the States with the Top Ten album *Sports*. Never having been slow to associate himself with rising stars, Lynott had recalled the favour he'd done in supporting Clover in the mid-Seventies, and got in on the act pretty sharpish.

"When Chris Morrison asked me to get involved with a couple of tracks I said, 'Yes, but under certain conditions'," Lewis confirms. "I told Philip I was going to pick the keys, I told him I wanted him to sing in a certain way, and I told him I wanted him to show up 'clean'. Philip did manage to find the party in the end – and that's pretty hard to do in Mill Valley! – but generally he was quite together.

"The main thing I wanted was to hear Philip sing up in his range, like he used to. I thought he'd been a bit lazy with his songs of late, and I wanted to work him back up into that hard, aggressive kind of guy that he was before. He ribbed me about the way I was pushing him, but I thought it was right for him."

They spent about a week working on three songs at the Record Plant studios: 'Still Alive' (written by Clover), 'Can't Get Away' (Archer's gem) and 'Just Another Lie'. Lewis's backing band The News had helped Archer lay the basic tracks down, and Lynott came in and overdubbed his vocals later. All involved were reasonably pleased with the outcome.

Archer was less impressed when Chris Morrison managed to secure Lynott a solo deal with Polydor, principally on the strength of 'Can't Get Away'. After San Francisco Archer and Lynott had drifted apart professionally and this coincided with a cooling of Morrison's attitude towards the guitarist. Feeling he was being neglected Archer had a showdown with Morrison, and that was the end of their relationship.

"Morrison then began to shit himself because he was sitting there with all these songs ready to be presented to the record companies, and they were all my songs!" Archer claims. "When Phil got the deal I had to step in and say, 'Hang on a second, that's not your song!' If no-one believes me they should check out some of the recordings that were made of Grand Slam live. The first three nights we played that song Phil introduced it as 'a Laurence Archer song'. It was an awkward situation and I was very disappointed with the way I was treated by Morrison."

Lynott's new deal coincided with the success of 'Out In The Fields', which reached No.5 in the UK during May. After 18 months or so of being given a wide berth by the record companies, Lynott suddenly found himself the flavour of the month again. To some people's embarrassment, he'd proved he still had a great deal to offer. "John Sykes said to me, 'Oh, it's really nice of you to work with Phil,' " says Moore, "but I didn't see it as me doing Phil a favour. Even though the song was written long before Phil got involved, it was his packaging of the whole thing which helped to make it such a big hit. The military uniforms we wore during the promotion were his idea. He had a gift for marketing, a great sense of how to sell something to an audience."

The 'Out In The Fields' single came in a number of formats, all of them with 'Military Man' (which tied in with the concept of the single, and the 'uniforms' image) showing up on the B-side. Some formats included the new 'Still In Love With You' and a bonus live recording of the standard 'Stop Messin' Around', taken from the Belfast show the previous December.

While the song was riding high in May, Lynott and Moore milked the promotional opportunities, appearing on the BBC's *Whistle Test*, the Saturday *Picture Show*, *Razzmatazz* and the Channel 4 rock programme *ECT* ("We did one of our best versions of 'Still In Love With You' that day," says Moore, who is still furious the broadcast was faded out before the end), as well as a couple of German TV programmes. Lynott also made an appearance at Moore's wedding in Lincolnshire in July, where he and Gary got up and did a few numbers for the guests with drummer Gary Ferguson and keyboard player Don Airey. And later in September he joined Moore on stage at Manchester Apollo (23rd) and Hammersmith Odeon two nights running (27th/28th), to share the load of 'Out In The Fields' and 'Parisienne Walkways'.

"That was another of Phil's grand ideas," laughs Moore, whose album, *Run For Cover* (featuring the single, 'Military Man' and 'Nothing To Lose'), was released in August). "He wanted to do the whole tour with me and just get up and do two or three songs a night. No pressure, no hard work, no hassle, but plenty of limelight and a great excuse to get wasted every night. I knew what he was up to . . ."

Philip was secretly upset, though, when his old friends Bob Geldof and Midge Ure, the brains and motivators behind Band Aid, didn't invite him to reactivate Lizzy for the Live Aid spectacular in July. The Who were asked to reform, so were Led Zeppelin, so were Black Sabbath. The nearest Lynott got to the action was auctioning one of his famous mirrored bass guitars (it fetched £900) at a TV studio in Dublin.

"I honestly don't know why Lizzy weren't considered for Live Aid," Ure confesses, "I've never even thought about it before. In hindsight it seems ridiculous, because we were looking for more black artists to play, so Phil would've been ideal. I guess, to be hideously cruel, we were also more interested in going for the most popular contemporary artists. As far as reunions were concerned, we already had The Who and I suppose we thought we weren't going to get anyone with a much bigger name than that. But . . . I don't really know why we didn't get in touch with Phil. You'd have to ask Geldof . . ."

"To be perfectly honest I've never thought about it before," admits Geldof. "It's a very good question. I think perhaps the only two reasons I can suggest are that, one, he wasn't in the best of health, and two, he wasn't really big enough. We were putting on a global jukebox and we had to be ruthless. We were talking about bands that could sell six, eight, ten million albums without even blinking – the biggest acts on the planet! Lizzy were never that big, to be brutal.

"A measure of how far Philip had fallen by then was the fact that not only did Midge and I completely overlook him, but his own manager did too. Chris Morrison was part of the Band Aid Trust, which had existed for six months by the time of Live Aid, and we used to have two or three meetings a week during that period. Not once did Morrison mention Philip's name. Sadly it was over for Philip by then, and the tragedy was he didn't know it."

Lynott swallowed his pride and threw himself into his new solo career, his commitments putting paid to the plan to tour extensively with Gary Moore. After a two-week holiday in Marbella with his mother, his two daughters and John Sykes, he recorded the Grand Slam song 'Nineteen' as a single with a small-time session guitarist called Robin George, and managed to rope in dance DJ Paul Hardcastle (who previously had a No.1 hit with a song called 'Nineteen') to handle the production. It was an audacious move, but easier to understand when the fact that Hardcastle was being managed by Chris Morrison is taken into consideration.

"A friend of mine (Simon Fuller, who worked for Chrysalis) asked me if I wanted to go into partnership with him to manage Hardcastle," says Morrison. "I agreed, and then the following Tuesday 'Nineteen' went straight in the charts at No.4, going on to No.1 the following Tuesday! I went to *Top Of*

The Pops to see Paul do 'Nineteen', and on the same show I had Dead Or Alive, Philip (with Gary Moore) and I was also involved with Band Aid through Midge. I was standing there talking to Philip when Paul Hardcastle walked past. I hadn't even met him at this point so I said, 'Hi Paul, I'm Chris Morrison and I co-manage you.' Philip couldn't believe it. He said, 'You haven't even met the guy and he's No.1!' "

The link up with Hardcastle was more than a case of 'keep it in the family' though, and nothing to do with the coincidental song title, according to Lynott. Philip had grown to appreciate Hardcastle's production work during what he called "my dance phase", and in any case he had for some time been keen to explore and possibly exploit a gap which he saw between dance music and heavy rock.

"I mean," he reasoned with me in October, "if ZZ Top can do dance mixes and Michael Jackson can use Eddie Van Halen, then I don't see why you can't use, say, scratch mixes with heavy sounds."

When the 'Nineteen' single was released in November the results of Philip's experiments could be heard on the B-side of the various formats (along with a rare recording of 'A Night In The Life Of A Blues Singer' from 1979). Hardcastle had produced a dub mix to satisfy Lynott's curiosity with the cross-over concept, and the Philip I met around the time of its release seemed quite content.

Eerily, Lynott's idea of a dance/rock fusion was several years ahead of its time. In the late Eighties, and particularly in the wake of Run DMC's highly successful version of Aerosmith's 'Walk This Way' in 1986, mixing heavy rock with funk and rap became the new craze. Bands like Living Colour, Fishbone, The Beastie Boys, Anthrax, Red Hot Chili Peppers and Faith No More shot to prominence bridging that very gap. If things had been different perhaps Lynott would have found a lucrative niche in that market – which might have buried rumours of a Thin Lizzy reunion once and for all.

Philip flew to San Francisco to shoot a video for 'Nineteen' (its theme was typical Lynott: a gang of bikers cruising the town), but then thoughts turned to the new album, which he was hoping to have produced by Lynyrd Skynyrd producer

Tom Dowd, with guest appearances from John Sykes, Gary Moore, Brian Downey, Gus Isodore, Noddy Holder and Junior amongst others. One working title mischievously suggested by Lynott, effectively a confession of his own chemically induced schizophrenia, was *Dr. Jekyll And Mr. Hyde*.

It seemed certain that 'Harlem' would appear on the record under its new title of 'If I Had A Wish', as well as 'Nineteen' and maybe even 'Sisters Of Mercy' and 'Breakdown' from Slam's set. There was also a brand new track called 'What's The Matter' being knocked into shape at Lynott's home studio. And there was a possibility that Philip might include a song he'd written with Sykes called 'Samantha'.

On paper it all looked quite positive in the winter of '85. Sitting in the lounge of Tony Brainsby's office in Edith Grove, Chelsea, Philip seemed relaxed enough to be able to reflect honestly on the recent past and peer confidently into the future. Not only that, but he was particularly confident that Ron Atkinson's Manchester United were going to walk away with the First Division Championship in the New Year. "There have been times over the past two years when I've been really bored," he admitted, "but then again I've had a lot of time to do other things which I enjoy – like be with my kids, experiment in my studio, practise on the bass and get to know new friends.

"It's also put me back on the street again and given me the chance to check out who's coming up, what new things are happening and discover what I actually like about the new trends. It was nice to be free from the situation where, whenever you talk, the room goes silent – like it does when you've got a record in the charts – and it was great to have an opinion which people disagreed with for a change. I think I learnt a lot from being back down at that level.

"For a while," he added, "with my marriage breaking down and Grand Slam not working out, I was really messed up. But look – the luck of the Irish! – I've landed on my feet and I'm coming out fighting again!"

The tragic irony of Philip's last words to me was acute. He had in fact been coughing and blowing his nose throughout that last interview, and his usual excuse that it was simply asthma didn't convince. He also looked quite bloated around the jowls, and his black jeans were that much tighter. He seemed more like a defeated heavyweight boxer the morning after the big fight, rather than the lithe, athletic figure of the past.

Tony Brainsby remembers that last interview well enough for it to still send a chill down his spine. He didn't say anything to Philip, but he knew there was something seriously wrong. "When you had left that day," he tells me, "I went into the lounge for a quick word with Phil, and then I went and told the girls in the office that I thought I'd just been talking to a dead man. He looked so ill – bent over like an old man, coughing and spluttering – and I got quite a shock. He always used to say to me, 'I always know when my body's had enough, don't worry,' but I used to doubt him all the time.

"I found it very disturbing, seeing it happen right in front of me. I should've seen it coming, but then a lot of people should've seen it coming. Then again there was no telling Phil, because he 'always knew when his body was telling him to slow down'. He was 'lucky' like that . . ."

John Sykes last saw Philip around the same time. He'd returned to England from America because he wasn't in the best of health himself, and he'd gone straight to visit Philip at home. "One night I took Phil to see my old man in Reading," Sykes recalls, "and he got really ill. We were just leaving when he threw open the car door and was sick all over the place. It was obvious that this was more than just a stomach bug or something, so I said, 'Phil, you've got to see a doctor.' All he said was, 'Oh, I'm alright.' Then later as we drove back to Richmond he was sick again. I'd had enough, and I tried to talk him into letting me take him to a doctor there and then, that night. But he wouldn't have it."

Normally Lynott would only have to have a mild asthma attack and he'd be on the phone to the office demanding to see a doctor. His reluctance to seek help this time would seem to suggest that either he'd already seen a doctor and knew he was going to die, or he was frightened to see a doctor in case he was told he was going to die. Lynott certainly knew how serious his condition was.

Scott Gorham, who had spent much of his time in the wake

of Lizzy's demise fighting his own heroin addiction, and who now proudly claimed to have been 'clean' for a year, called in to see Lynott during December. Like numerous other friends and associates, he claims he urged Philip to purge the habit from his life before it was too late.

"I knew he'd been doing it," he says, "because he always had these wild asthma attacks when he was on it. For the first time I said to him, 'Man, are you still doing that shit? I'm telling you, you've gotta quit!' He told me that he really wanted to clean up his act, and he pulled out a guitar and played me a few song ideas. He also mentioned the idea of doing something with Lizzy. But of course by that time he'd gone too far, his body was just about ready to shut down."

Lynott's final promotional trip came in December, when he travelled to Tyne Tees TV studios in Newcastle to record a Christmas special of the pop programme *Razzmatazz*. For the one-off performance of 'Nineteen' Philip called upon the services of Robin George and, for the first time in over two years, Brian Downey.

"One day I got a call from John Salter asking me, on Phil's behalf, if I'd like to do a TV show," says Downey. "I was a little hurt that Phil couldn't call me himself, it wasn't like him at all, but I agreed anyway. I got quite a shock. He was completely out of it. He was very vague and he kept reminiscing about the old days, which was unusual for him. I put it down to too much dope."

Ironically, the presenter of the programme which would be Lynott's last public appearance was David Jensen, the DJ who's patronage had set Lizzy on the road to success in the early Seventies. "We had Slade on the show too," Jensen recalls, "and Phil, Noddy Holder and I spent ages talking about the Slade/Suzi Quatro/Lizzy gigs at the Rainbow. Then later at the airport while we were waiting to fly back to London Phil and I talked about Christmas, and he showed me some Christmas cards he'd had done for his daughters. He told me his mother was coming over for Christmas and he was really looking forward to it. He was basically a family man despite the disarray of his domestic life, and Christmas seemed to be so important to him."

In London Lynott told Downey of his plans to reform Lizzy. It came as something of a surprise, particularly as Philip had been widely quoted in the press as saying that he would only reform the band out of desperation. But it later transpired that he'd booked studio time for mid-January and had been discussing the possibility of getting on the festival circuit for the summer of '86 with a four-piece Lizzy including Sykes, Gorham, and Downey.

Moreover, Robbo claims Philip had told him he wanted to reform the *Live And Dangerous* line-up, and other friends were also confided in. "He said he'd already written new words for all the old songs, like 'The Old Men Are Back In Town'," says Sue Peters. So one way or another a reformation was on the cards.

After *Razzmatazz* Downey was invited to Kew Road to discuss the idea further. He wasn't totally against a reunion, but the scene he encountered at Philip's house set the alarm bells ringing in his head. "It was very bad news," he sighs. "Jimmy Bain was there, totally smashed on heroin. There were all these other sleazy people there, doing the same thing. I was quite disgusted by it. I suggested to Phil that it might be better to leave the meeting until after Christmas, and I went back to my hotel, The Cunard, in Hammersmith. I was supposed to stay at Phil's, but I couldn't face it. I went back to Dublin the next day and I never saw Phil again."

Other visitors to Kew Road in the final weeks of Lynott's life were also shocked by the sight that confronted them. For days Philip would lie in bed, surrounded by empty vodka bottles, take-away food cartons, trays of half-eaten meals, old clothes, odd socks and all manner of junk. It was, someone mentioned, as if he was waiting to die.

"The last time I saw him was around December 15, with Christine and another girl called Angelique," says Sue Peters. "A guy called Steve Johnson who was doing some guitar work with him at the time opened the door and told us that Philip was in bed. We said we'd come back later, but he said, 'No, he wants to see you now, but only one at a time.'

"We all thought that was very strange, but I went up to his room first and found him wheezing something terrible. He said, 'I've got something for you, go and get me case.' I couldn't understand it because usually if you touched his case it was a hanging offence. But this time he asked me to open the case and take out all these possessions of his, which he then said I could keep. I sat on the bed and talked to him for a while, and then as I got up to leave he said suddenly, 'I love you, y'know.' I stopped in my tracks and said, 'I beg your pardon?' He repeated, 'I love you, all of you.' I was speechless.

"I went downstairs and told Christine that I thought something was wrong with Philip, that he was in a really weird mood. She went up to see him next and he was the same with her. It was as if he knew he wasn't going to be seeing us again."

Lynott recovered sufficiently to attend his management's Christmas party, but while there it is believed he was given 'a package' by a friend as a Christmas present, and on arriving home decided to open it early. The contents of the small parcel are unlikely to have been a pair of socks.

Chapter IX

The Sun Goes Down

Philip was found unconscious in the Kew Road house on Christmas Day. His mother Phyllis, who'd left Dennis in Dublin to look after the house and five dogs and had flown over to London to spend the holiday with her son and two granddaughters (the plan was that they'd all return to Dublin on New Year's Eve, where piles of unopened presents would be waiting for them beneath their Christmas tree), completely freaked when it became clear that her son wasn't merely asleep.

An immediate call was made to a Harley Street doctor who, in the words of one member of Lynott's entourage, "was renowned for supplying pop stars with whatever drugs they wanted – allegedly". The doctor, who must remain nameless, suggested that Philip had been experimenting with a drug cocktail, and that he should be left to sleep it off. But Phyllis wasn't happy, and when Caroline phoned later that day she told her that Philip was seriously ill.

Caroline knew immediately what the problem was. She was well aware of her estranged husband's addiction to heroin, and sensed that it had finally beaten him. She told Phyllis she knew of a discreet drug clinic in Wiltshire which could treat Philip, and that she could take him there within an hour and a half. Phyllis urged her to step on it.

With Philip in the back of a car, Caroline set off down the M4, leaving Phyllis at the house with the girls. The rehab centre Caroline had in mind was called Clouds, and was situated in a large Georgian house in the small village of East Knoyle, about 12 miles from Salisbury. But valuable time was lost during the long drive, and after Lynott failed to respond to initial treatment the resident medical director at Clouds, Dr. Margaret McCann, suggested the semi-comatose patient ought to be taken to the intensive care unit of Salisbury Infirmary (now part of Salisbury General Hospital).

Phyllis got a call from the hospital later that night, and she made her way to Salisbury without delay. As it was Christmas the hospital was short-staffed, so Phyllis helped the nurses tend to her son, "kicking up a stink whenever I thought they weren't doing enough for him".

Over the next few days Philip regained consciousness for long periods, and was lucid enough to hold conversations with his mother. For 11 days Phyllis remained at her son's bedside, sleeping in an armchair. She'd mop his brow, wash him and generally fuss over him like any mother would. The only other people to share the vigil were Big Charlie and Graham Cohen, a family friend. Caroline visited the hospital, bringing Sarah and Cathleen on one occasion. Philip cried when he saw his girls.

New Year's Day came and went but there were few signs of improvement. Treatment on a dialysis machine had helped his kidneys function again, but then he developed pneumonia and was put on a respirator. All the time the strain on his already weakened heart was considerable. But Phyllis still refused to believe he was going to die.

As Philip slept Phyllis had many long hours to reflect on her son's predicament, and her mind was awash with agonising questions about how and why things had gone this far. She had understood how easy it was to fall into drugs in rock'n'roll ever since she'd had a glimpse of life on the road in America – a non-stop, sleepless roller-coaster ride of flights, photo sessions, interviews, promo appearances, gigs and parties. She witnessed at first hand the intense demands on her son, as the spokesman and star of the group, and understood why he might occasionally be envious of Brian Downey, who could slip away from the mayhem at will. In her thoughts she reluctantly accepted that over a few years such a lifestyle could turn a few drinks into a few joints, a few pills into coke, and ultimately a coke habit into experimenting with heroin.

Despite deep suspicions Phyllis never knew her son was

using heroin. She'd heard the whispers and had even confronted Philip with the issue the summer before he died. He simply rolled up his sleeves and grinned, 'Look ma, no needle marks, OK?' Like many intravenous users he'd been injecting himself in the foot.

Phyllis still believes she could've prevented her son's fatal addiction had she known about it earlier. The questions continued to churn in her mind. Why didn't anyone tell her? Why didn't anyone try to straighten him out? Why . . .?

As the mental torture peaked, Philip slipped away, finally giving up the struggle on Saturday, January 4, 1986. Two days later a post-mortem by the hospital's chief pathologist Dr. Angela Scott revealed that Philip had developed multiple internal abscesses and staphylococcal and streptococcal septicaemia (blood poisoning), and as a result had suffered kidney, liver and heart failure.

Philip Lynott, The Rocker, was dead at 36.

All the medical jargon simply meant that prolonged drug abuse had killed him. He hadn't died the traditional rock star way, of a sudden overdose, but he'd been overdosing for years and finally his body had succumbed to overwhelming infection. It was a cruel and torturously drawn-out death, not even the sudden snap that claimed Hendrix, Joplin, Morrison, Bolin, Moon, Bonham, Bon Scott and far too many others.

"Philip often said all his heroes had gone to the edge," reflects Chris Morrison, "and he was well aware that a few had gone right over the edge. I knew he was balancing rather precariously himself, but I always thought he'd just manage to stop himself toppling over. He did try to fight his problem, but then someone would send him a package of something, and he'd fall straight off the wagon. When I heard he was in hospital I thought it would do him good, give him a scare, shake some sense into him and maybe change his ways."

"Philip didn't die of a heart attack," says Jim Fitzpatrick. "He died of a lifestyle. He thought he had it sussed, thought he was immortal and that nothing could touch him. I used to watch the way he lived and think, 'Wow – how is he getting away with it?' But in the end, of course, no-one can get away with it."

Fitzpatrick was in the Bailey bar with his ex-wife and two

children when he heard the news. At first he thought the story was a false alarm.

"I didn't believe for a minute he was dead," he admits. "Even when he went into hospital I didn't believe it was serious. I thought it might be a scam, for publicity purposes, because Philip was a great one for jokes like that. But I rang Frank Murray and he told me it was no joke, that he had kidney failure. I couldn't believe it. I'd sent him a telegram saying, 'Don't worry, we'll soon have you on the beach, going for long walks . . .', because we were determined to nurse him back to health. Then he was dead. It was too late."

"I'd heard the 'Phil's in a bad way' story umpteen times before," says Midge Ure, "but he always pulled through. I guess he just couldn't do it anymore, or simply wouldn't. He lied to everyone about what he was and wasn't doing. He became a different person. In days gone by I used to wonder if his debauched lifestyle was all hype, as he would never let anyone bring drugs into the studio while we were working, or even allow people to do drugs near me. He was very protective of me, like a big brother, and I thought that was quite something in the rock'n'roll business. Then he slid away very quickly. When Chris Morrison told me he'd died I freaked. Losing a hero is hard enough. Losing a friend is much worse."

"Everyone will tell you that they tried to talk to Philip about his problem," says Smiley Bolger, "and I did too. He even threw me out of the house once. Of course, the next day he'd ring up and apologise and I'd be only too happy to accept the apology. But I tried hard to stop him damaging himself.

"Philip could eat and drink and do everything more than everyone else. He liked it like that. I used to go to his house for a drink and end up getting absolutely wrecked. Philip would drink far more than me, and still be up at the crack of dawn cooking a great big fried breakfast. He had the constitution of an ox, that's why I never dreamed he'd go the way he did."

"I always thought of him as the Mike Tyson of rock'n'roll," states Gorham. "He'd knock the shit out of anybody while he was in the ring, but sooner or later he was going to get his comeuppance, just as Tyson did from Buster Douglas. No one is unbeatable, but you couldn't tell him. Phil was his own man and you just didn't say shit like that to him, because he didn't want to know."

"I actually thought he had a death wish," says Mark Stanway. "He had this thing about Elvis Presley, and I'm sure he had an idea he was going to go the same way. I've seen some films about Elvis and I've thought, 'Jesus, that's Phil. He thought he was Elvis!' "

"When I heard Philip had died it was fucking awful," says Bob Geldof. "It was a sickening tragedy. But then I heard a story, and not an apocryphal one, about his last days in hospital, which made me laugh so much because it totally summed Philip up. Apparently, Philip woke up and called one of the nurses over. The nurse asked him if he wanted anything and he said, 'Yeah, gissa wank!' I think they should've put that on his gravestone, because it was so Philip. He was right there on his death-bed and yet he was still having a laugh."

Brian Robertson found out from Big Charlie. He instantly blacked out, fell onto the kitchen floor and split his head open, ending up in Kingston Hospital having stitches in a nasty gash. Blinking away tears, Robbo still manages to force a smile when he says, "Fucking typical, eh?

"If the truth be known," he swallows hard, "I knew he was going to die. I saw him shortly before he was taken ill and he looked terrible, a horrible sight, with no control over his body. He pulled me over to him and said a few things that were really personal, and I think he knew he was on the way out.

"It was hard for me because he was like family. He taught me everything I know and I copied him like a kid. If I saw something he was wearing I'd go out and buy the same thing, and he'd hate it. But then they say 'imitation is the highest form of flattery', and that's what it was.

"Phil was a true star. He was an original. We were brothers. Even today I still have vivid dreams about him. I still can't believe he's dead. Sometimes I feel that he's still alive, still around somewhere. I almost expect him to phone me sometimes. It's still refusing to sink in."

Chris O'Donnell picked up a Sunday newspaper at 1.20am on Hammersmith Broadway, on his way home from a night out. It told him 'The Wild Man Of Rock' had died. "I felt angry and bitter," he declares. "Heroin had taken Phil's soul. I'd been a friend of his for ten years but he'd become alien to me. It had changed him as a person, destroyed his soul, and now destroyed his body.

"It hit me during the service, when I actually saw the coffin. I actually cried. I didn't cry for Phil, but I cried for all the opportunities that had been lost. Phil lost himself, because he was a drug addict, and I didn't feel sorry for him for that reason. But I did feel a tremendous sense of loss."

Lynott's body was taken to London where, on Thursday January 9, a service was held at St. Elizabeth's church in Richmond. It was the same church where he had been married almost six years earlier, and where in happier days he attended mass with his children. On this bitter day the two bewildered girls were reduced to laying a wreath of remembrance with a card that read: 'We love you always'.

The hymns chosen were 'Praise My Soul The King Of Heaven', 'Peace Perfect Peace' and 'Lord Of The Dance', which was also chosen for the Lynotts' wedding. Father Raymond Brennan, who had married Philip and Caroline, spoke of the deceased as a multi-talented but shy man who cared deeply for others. He said prayers for all those fighting drug addiction.

There were two readings from the Bible, one by Chris Morrison, and finally a mass. Other mourners included Scott Gorham, Brian Robertson, Eric Bell, Darren Wharton (who would christen his first son, born on Philip's birthday of August 20, 1990, Daniel Parris), John Sykes and his parents (Sykes also named his sons – James Parris and Sean Philip – after Lynott), Laurence Archer, Lemmy, John Coghlan, Neil Murray, Bob Geldof and Paula Yates, plus a swarm of ex-roadies, record and management company people and friends.

After the service there was a wake at the nearby Richmond Hill Hotel, a huge party which moved Robbo to comment, "It's a shame Phil's not here, he would've loved it!" Afterwards Phyllis and a small entourage accompanied the body to Heathrow, where they were ushered through the VIP lounge and taken aboard an Aer Lingus flight to Dublin. When they arrived the press were waiting in force at the airport.

On Saturday, January 11, a second service was held for Philip, at the Howth Parish Church. The church is situated at the top of a steady incline near the bay, and Lynott's coffin was removed from the hearse at the bottom of the hill and passed over the heads of all the men in the village to the church door.

Phyllis never saw her son's coffin, she was too devastated to even lift her head out of her hands. But as in London Caroline and the two children each placed a red rose on the coffin during the service. Those who held a grudge against the Crowther family for their increasing alienation of Philip bitterly dismissed the gesture as Caroline's attempt to 'do a Jackie Kennedy'.

Also in attendance on a cold, windy winter's day in Howth were several ex-Lizzys, including Brian Downey, plus representatives from U2 and former Irish premier Charles Haughey. Irish band Clann Eadair, with whom Lynott had recorded 'A Tribute To Sandy Denny', played two songs in the church.

After the requiem mass Lynott was taken to St. Fintan's Cemetery and buried in plot 13 of the St. Polans section. A small white cross surrounded by an arrangement of white stones marked the spot in much the same way as a cowboy's grave. Once the earth had settled this was replaced by a flat memorial stone, in keeping with the rules of the cemetery. The Gaelic inscription on the grey slab, designed by Jim Fitzpatrick, read: *Go dtuga Dia suaimhneas da anam* (May God give peace to his soul).

Adrian Hopkins flew in for the ceremony from Vancouver, where he was on tour with ice skaters Torvill and Dean, and he wept openly at the graveside. Bob Geldof and his wife flew over from London to pay their last respects, as did Scott Gorham and John Sykes. But there were a few raised eyebrows when Gary Moore failed to attend.

"I was on holiday with my wife in Tenerife at the time," Moore explains. "You get the newspapers a day late over there, so I didn't get to hear the news until the Monday. And it was strange, because the night before I'd had a weird dream about a black cat being strangled. I didn't know what it meant. Then my wife picked up the newspaper and just froze. I knew what had happened straight away.

"That day we went down to the beach, and the awful realisation kept coming over me in waves. It hit me so hard I didn't know what to do. Then that night we went to this bar and 'Out In The Fields' came on the video jukebox . . . all these people were coming up to me saying, 'Oh God, we're so sorry.' I was like a zombie. I just stood there in a daze. It took me ages to get my head together, and I couldn't face coming back for the service."

Another surprising absentee from the funeral was Smiley Bolger, who was in Stockholm at the time of his friend's passing. Lynott was a god in Sweden and Bolger observed the reverence with which most of the Scandinavian obituaries treated the subject. It proved a stark contrast to the way the press in Britain handled the grisly affair.

"The Swedish press preferred to remember him as the artist he was," says Bolger, "and I thought the Irish press was fair to Philip too. But the British press treated him appallingly. When Jimi Hendrix died drugs were cool. When Philip died drugs were bad. Philip caught the drugs backlash in a big way, and his memory was trashed. It left a sour taste in the mouth, and the wounds are only just healing now."

The most distasteful and disrespectful example of tabloid journalism could be found in the *Daily Mirror*, whose rabid lust for sensationalism couldn't even be delayed until the graveside flowers had begun to wither. Just two days after Philip died, the *Mirror* ran a two-part story (continuing the next day) which was gleaned from the imagination of a Phonogram employee who claimed to have been Lynott's girlfriend for the past 18 months. The article was appallingly timed, astonishingly insensitive and littered with inaccuracies.

The informer was one Heather Mitson (also known by her married name, Heather Harold), although in the music paper gossip columns she was known as Heavy Metal Heather. She was a bored housewife from the Midlands who'd moved to London with the express intention of 'meeting' rock stars. To those who mixed in rock's social circles she openly admitted that her ultimate goal was to sleep with American guitarist Ted Nugent. Her attempts to secure this dubious achievement were so outrageous she quickly became a legend in her own lunchtime.

In reality she merely had an affair with a member of US joke band Manowar and flashed her suspenders whenever press photographers were in her vicinity, usually while she was draped over a member of Motorhead. She had 'scored' with Lynott, but then so had dozens of other women on the London rock scene.

Mitson spoke of eating fish and chips in bed, washed down by champagne and brandy. She claimed Lynott was drinking a bottle of brandy a day, and that he tried to get her to take heroin with him. In a particularly graphic passage she insisted that once during lovemaking Lynott had reached under the bed, pulled out a syringe and began injecting himself in the arm with heroin.

She described one visit to the Kew Road house with all the usual clichés: 'About 30 guests – all beautiful people – were casually sipping champagne and mixing cocktails. Other guests were smoking pot and its sickly scent hung in the air. Some were crouched over lines of white powder, sniffing cocaine through their nostrils with £50 notes. In the kitchen a couple of blokes were fiddling around over the flames of the gas cooker. They were heating tiny bits of silver paper containing piles of heroin ...' She also claimed that the house was adorned with chandeliers and expensive rugs.

"As soon as I read that I knew she'd never been to Kew Road," says Sue Peters. "There were no chandeliers in the house at all. Nor expensive rugs. There might have been a load of empty beer cans and piles of washing up in the sink. But Philip did not live in a palace.

"The day the story broke I rang John Salter and asked him who the hell this woman was. I'd worked with Philip quite closely almost throughout the 18-month period that she was supposed to have been his girlfriend, and I'd never ever seen her with him. I didn't recognise her picture in the paper at all. John Salter just said, 'Oh, it's only that stupid Heavy Metal Heather, just ignore her.' But it was infuriating to think that she could claim to be Philip's girlfriend, make up a load of rubbish and get paid for it."

The outrage at the story was universal. In one cheap manoeuvre Mitson lost all her friends in the music business and swiftly retreated back to the Midlands in shame. She has not been seen in London since.

In complete contrast, moving tributes to Lynott poured in from all over the world. Days after his death Radio One presented a *Friday Rock Show Special*, with quotes from many of the musicians with whom he'd worked. Magazines and music papers seized on the tragedy with glowing acknowledgements of their own. And Gary Moore dedicated his forthcoming album, *Wild Frontier*, to his former sparring partner, giving it a distinctly Irish flavour to enhance the effect.

In February at the BPI (British Phonographic Industry) Awards in London Huey Lewis accepted his award for the Best International Group in Lynott's name and honour. He staunchly reiterates the dedication today. "I was sitting there watching Bob Geldof get an award, and Midge Ure get an award, and all these other guys that owed so much to Philip," Lewis storms, "and I was outraged that there was no mention of Philip. So when I got my award I just stood up and said, 'This is for Philip Lynott!', and the whole place cheered. I felt I owed Philip everything.

"To me he was the greatest hard rock artist ever. When he played music, no matter how hard it was, it had soul, and everyone can relate to that. It harkened back to Bing Crosby for me, because it was so charming – charming, yet aggressive. Philip could be all things to all people all at once, and that's why he was the greatest."

At the recording of USA For Africa's 'We Are The World' in January 1985 Bob Dylan had sidled up to Lewis and told him he thought Lynott was a genius. It was one of the greatest compliments ever paid to Philip, and he had been enormously flattered. Lewis recounted the story to Phyllis when he played in Dublin several years after Philip's death and it remains a favourite anecdote. In return, Phyllis gave Lewis a cane that her son would take on his beach walks, specially designed with a glass tube inside that would be filled with brandy for the occasional snifter. For a number of years afterwards Lewis also wore a pair of Lynott's boots on stage.

Back in May '86, 30,000 fans gathered at the RDS in Dublin for the Self Aid concert, the highlight of which was a 'surprise'

Thin Lizzy reunion of sorts, featuring Brian Downey, Scott Gorham, Darren Wharton, Gary Moore and bassist Bob Daisley from Moore's band. The idea for the show came from Bob Geldof, while the event was organised by Eire's TV station RTE (Radio Telefis Eireann), with 27 bands in all helping to raise money for Ireland's unemployed. Names such as Rory Gallagher, Van Morrison and U2 shared much of the glory, but the biggest cheer of the day came when the 'secret guests' took to the stage after headliners U2 to pay tribute to Philip.

With Moore taking lead vocals on the likes of 'Don't Believe A Word' and 'Whiskey In The Jar', Geldof stepping up to sing 'Cowboy Song' and, with U2's Bono joining in the parade at the end, the unique Lizzy line-up muddled through the unrehearsed set as best they could. The Dublin crowd appreciated the effort and stayed well into the early hours to celebrate.

"We didn't have a lot to celebrate in 1986," recalls Bolger, "and it was a particularly devastating year for the Irish in London. Philip was the most famous person to die, but there were at least ten other deaths that year involving characters from the Irish scene who'd moved to London, mainly around the Camden Town area. In Dublin we could not believe what was going on. It was like part of our community was being torn from us."

"It was a tough time," admits Jim Fitzpatrick. "The hardest thing for me to accept was that in my mind it wasn't meant to be like this. I had cosy expectations of the future. I once took a picture of Philip sitting on his porch with a banjo – sort of an old Mississippi scene – and that's how I imagined he'd end up, Blind Lemon Lynott or something. We had that vision of ourselves: the old musician singing the blues on his porch, and the old crotchety artist stumbling up and down the beach outside. It fucking annoys me that that isn't going to happen now."

Brush Shiels' perspective of his former friendly rival paints a slightly different picture, emphasising the changes of character that took place as his career unfolded. "I knew a number of different Philips," he claims. "The first guy I knew was a little bit lonely and a little bit lost. The second guy I knew was on top of the world with Thin Lizzy, but even so he was keen to get my approval for what he was doing, because he was still a bit annoyed at me for kicking him out of Skid Row. And then the third Philip I knew was a very frustrated man, because he was trying to get something going after Lizzy and it wasn't quite working out. He was a sad guy then."

Sadder still is the way Lynott's death has left a bitter legacy of angry confusion, hostility and litigation for his family. Phyllis had, and still has, seething vendettas against all those who'd been known to supply her son with drugs, and nearly a year after his death she instigated the arrest and conviction of ex-Lizzy roadie Liam Kelly for supplying cocaine to Philip right up to the fateful Christmas of '85. In court he admitted the charge but claimed he'd only given Lynott cocaine to prevent him taking heroin. Acton Crown Court rewarded him with a two-year sentence.

Relations between the Lynotts and Crowthers also deteriorated rapidly over the ensuing years. Caroline remarried in 1989 – her new husband, David Taraskevics, worked at Peter Gabriel's studio near Bath – and the couple immediately added another daughter, Natasha, to the ready-made family that Caroline had. But while Phyllis claims she has made continual attempts to get on with Caroline, purely for the sake of Sarah and Cathleen, it seems her former daughter-in-law has made a conscious effort to cold-shoulder her.

The feud hit new depths in the summer of 1993 when Caroline began action in the Irish courts to have Phyllis evicted from Glen Corr, claiming that despite the fact that Philip hadn't left a will, the property was intended for Sarah and Cathleen, and that as their guardian it was therefore rightfully hers until the children reached adulthood. Friends of the Lynotts believe that Caroline simply wants to sell the house to continue a purge against her children's Irish roots, roots that Philip was determined to have ingrained in his kids.

That would seem outrageous enough, but it was only when Caroline eventually won the battle for Glen Corr that the shocking unfairness of the ruling hit home. Caroline, who had only been married to Philip for six years, and had been separated for the last two of those, stood to gain everything.

Phyllis, a penniless pensioner who, unlike Caroline, doesn't benefit from her son's royalties which still roll in, stood to lose everything.

Caroline was offered the chance to comment on the situation for this book, but she refused.

More arguments and wrangling were stirred up even when Phonogram released a Thin Lizzy compilation album, *Dedication*, in early 1991. Chris Morrison had the idea of dusting down the old demo tapes of Grand Slam's song 'Dedication' and having various ex-Lizzy musicians overdub some contributions, thereby creating a 'new' Thin Lizzy song. Gorham and Downey obliged (Gary Moore was also approached: "I agreed to do it so Morrison sent me a tape, I learnt the song, formulated a few ideas and got ready to record it, then a few days later I heard it on the radio – it was already out! I guess the efficiency of Lizzy's organisation never changed!"), and the track was duly included on the album. The trouble was, it was credited as a Philip Lynott song, when it was in fact written by Laurence Archer.

"I wrote the song when I was in Stampede around 1982, and I registered it with the PRS (Performing Rights Society) in 1985," says Archer. "Naturally I was furious with Morrison when I saw what he'd done with 'Dedication', and there was a lot of nasty feeling. In the end I had to sign away the rights to six other songs I'd been involved with in order to get the money for 'Dedication'."

More charitable tributes to Lynott have come regularly in the shape of Smiley Bolger's annual remembrance concerts in Dublin. Each January 4 Bolger has put together a bill of well known musicians and local bands to commemorate Lynott and his music, under the banner of A Vibe For Philo. The first event, subtitled Ode To A Black Man, was held at McGonagles in 1988, and included videos, poetry and acoustic numbers from various guests. Since then the Vibe has grown from an informal get-together to a major event in the Irish rock calendar, attracting stars like Sinéad O'Connor, Elvis Costello and various members of U2, Def Leppard and The Pogues amongst others.

Spin-offs from the anniversary concert have included tribute cassettes and CDs, once again inspired by Smiley Bolger. And in the spring of 1991 the Vibe concept was taken a step further when a plan was hatched to take a band on a tour around Ireland for a series of Evening Of Thin Lizzy concerts. The line-up for the shows was Brian Robertson, Brian Downey, Doish Nagle (bass), Doug Brockie (guitar) and Bobby Tench (vocals).

The idea to launch a Trust in Lynott's name came to fruition during late 1993. A company, The Roisin Dubh Trust Limited, was formed by members of the Lynott family and close friends, the main objective being 'to commemorate the artistic life of Philip P. Lynott with dignity and style'. The first meeting of the Board of Directors established a number of specific goals, including a resolution to provide scholarships for worthy young musicians in his memory, to present awards and record tributes to his memory, and to make donations to other charities and organisations in his memory.

As sure as the shade of Eire is green, people will go on Remembering.

CODA: Are You Out There?

Tuesday January 4th 1994, a bitterly cold day in Dublin. Fibber Magee's on Parnell Street is a rabbit warren of a place, a last-minute replacement venue for the latest Vibe For Philo concert, but nevertheless some 2,000 people are gathered within its shadowy confines to pay their continuing respects on the eighth anniversary of Lynott's passing.

Earlier in the evening the Roisin Dubh Trust was launched at a reception attended by many of those who have made it their business to protect and project Lynott's memory. Sponsored by Smithwick's brewery and covered by RTE, the launch also featured the showing of rare Thin Lizzy footage rescued from Lynott's own personal collection, and made the pages of all the local and national newspapers the following morning.

The fans came from places as far flung as Japan, America and Sweden, while plenty made the pilgrimage across the Irish Sea from Britain. Not even the grisly reminder of political problems served by a bomb in Parnell Square during the afternoon could dampen the emotions of those who stood crammed shoulder-to-shoulder well into the early hours while an assortment of bands and artists paid their tributes.

Philip The Rocker would've glowed in the spotlight of adulation, Philip The Man would've been thoroughly embarrassed by all the fuss. Either way it was tempting to imagine him standing at the bar, a curvaceous blonde on each arm, surveying the scene with a knowing grin and a throaty giggle.

At least that's the way he would've loved to have been remembered, perpetuating the mythological existence of the rock star in much the same way as his songs celebrated the mythology of Ireland, of Hollywood and of the Wild West.

The reality of Philip Lynott is that, whatever he was, Dublin hasn't been the same since he left. But then as long as January 4th is commemorated in the same way, some comfort can be drawn from the fact that should the clouds ever part and a deep Irish voice enquire if anybody is out there, a fiercely positive response is assured.

Discography

THIN LIZZY SINGLES

Whiskey In The Jar / Black Boys On The Corner
Decca F 13355
(Released 11/72)

Randolph's Tango / Broken Dreams
Decca F 13402
(Released 5/73)

The Rocker / Here I Go Again
Decca F 13467
(11/73)

Little Darlin' / Buffalo Gal
Decca F 13507
(4/74)

Philomena / Sha La La
Vertigo 6059 111
(10/74)

Rosalie / Half Caste
Vertigo 6059 124
(5/75)

Wild One / For Those Who Love To Die
Vertigo 6059 129
(10/75)

The Boys Are Back In Town / Emerald
Vertigo 6059 139
(4/76)

Jailbreak / Running Back
Vertigo 6059 150
(7/76)

Don't Believe A Word / Old Flame
Vertigo LIZZY 1
(11/76)

Dancing In The Moonlight / Bad Reputation
Vertigo 6059 9177
(7/77)

Whiskey In The Jar / Vagabond Of The Western World /
Sitamoia
Decca F 13748
(1/78)

Rosalie; Cowgirl's Song (Live Medley) / Me And The Boys
Vertigo LIZZY 2
(4/78)

Waiting For An Alibi / With Love
Vertigo LIZZY 3
(2/79)

Do Anything You Want To / Just The Two Of Us
Vertigo LIZZY 4
(6/79)

Things Ain't Working Out Down At The Farm / The Rocker /
Little Darlin'
Decca THIN 1
(8/79)

Sarah / Got To Give It Up
Vertigo LIZZY 5
(9/79)

Killer On The Loose / Don't Play Around
Vertigo LIZZY 6
(9/80)

Killer On The Loose / Don't Play Around / Got To Give It Up
(Live) / Chinatown (Live)
Vertigo LIZZY 7 701
(9/80)

Trouble Boys / Memory Pain
Vertigo LIZZY 9
(8/81)

Hollywood (Down On Your Luck) / Pressure Will Blow
Vertigo LIZZY 10
(2/82)

Cold Sweat / Bad Habits / Angel Of Death (Live) /
Don't Believe A Word (Live)
Vertigo LIZZY 11 22
(2/83)

Cold Sweat / Bad Habits / Angel Of Death (Live) /
Don't Believe A Word (Live) (12")
Vertigo LIZZY 11 12
(2/83)

Thunder And Lightning / Still In Love With You (Live)
Vertigo LIZZY 12
(4/83)

Thunder And Lightning / Still In Love With You (Live) (12")
Vertigo LIZZY 12 12
(4/83)

The Sun Goes Down / Baby Please Don't Go
Vertigo LIZZY 13
(7/83)

The Sun Goes Down (Remix) / The Sun Goes Down/
Baby Please Don't Go (12")
Vertigo LIZZY 13 12
(7/83)

Whiskey In The Jar / The Rocker
Old Gold OG 9330
(10/83)

Dancing In The Moonlight / Don't Believe A Word
Old Gold OG 9484
(1/85)

THIN LIZZY EPs
New Day (Dublin / Remembering Pt. ii / Old Moon Madness /
Things Ain't Working Out Down At The Farm)
Decca F 13208
(8/71)

Live Killers (Are You Ready / Dear Miss Lonely Hearts /
Bad Reputation)
Vertigo LIZZY 8
(4/81)

Live Killers (Extra track: Opium Trail, 12″)
Vertigo LIZZY 8 12
(4/81)

Whiskey In The Jar / The Rocker / Sarah / Black Boys On
The Corner (Ltd. ed. 12″)
Archive 4 TOF 108
(8/86)

THIN LIZZY LPs
Thin Lizzy
Decca SKL 5082
(4/71)

Shades Of A Blue Orphanage
Decca TXS 108
(3/72)

Vagabonds Of The Western World
Decca SKL 5170
(9/73)

Night Life
Vertigo 6360 116
(11/74)

Fighting
Vertigo 6360 121
(9/75)

Jailbreak
Vertigo 9102 008
(3/76)

Remembering – Part One
Decca SKL 5249
(8/76)

Johnny The Fox
Vertigo 9102 012
(10/76)

Bad Reputation
Vertigo 9102 016
(9/77)

Live And Dangerous (double)
Vertigo 6641 807
(6/78)

Black Rose (A Rock Legend)
Vertigo 9102 032
(4/79)

The Continuing Saga Of The Ageing Orphans
Decca SKL 5298
(9/79)

Chinatown
Vertigo 6359 030
(10/80)

The Adventures Of Thin Lizzy
Vertigo LIZ TV1
(3/81)

Renegade
Vertigo 6359 083
(11/81)

Rockers
Decca TAB 28
(12/81)

Thunder And Lightning
Vertigo VERL 3
(3/83)

Life (double)
Vertigo VERD 6
(11/83)

The Boys Are Back In Town
Contour CN 2066
(11/83)

The Collection (double)
Castle Communications CCSL: 117
(11/85)

Whiskey In The Jar
Contour CN 2080
(4/86)

THIN LIZZY CDs

Lizzy Killers
Vertigo 800 060 2
(1983)

The Collection
Castle Communications CCSCD 117
(7/87)

PHIL LYNOTT SOLO SINGLES

Dear Miss Lonely Hearts / Solo In Soho
Vertigo SOLO 1
(3/80)

Dear Miss Lonely Hearts / Solo In Soho (12")
Vertigo SOLO 1 12
(4/80)

King's Call / Ode To A Black Man
Vertigo SOLO 2
(6/80)

Yellow Pearl / Girls (yellow vinyl)
Vertigo SOLO 3
(3/81)

Yellow Pearl / Girls (12")
Vertigo SOLO 3 12
(3/81)

Together / Somebody Else's Dream
Vertigo SOLO 4
(7/82)

Together (dance mix) / Together / Somebody Else's Dream
Vertigo SOLO 4 12
(7/82)

Old Town / Beat Of The Drum
Vertigo SOLO 5
(9/82)

Nineteen / Nineteen (Dub Version)
Polydor POSP 777
(11/85)

Nineteen / Nineteen (Dub Version) / A Day In The Life Of A
Blues Singer (12")
Polydor POSPX 777
(11/85)

Nineteen / Nineteen (Dub Version) / Whiskey In The Jar
(Live) (double pack with one-sided bonus disc by Thin Lizzy)
Polydor POSPD 777
(11/85)

King's Call / Yellow Pearl
Vertigo LYN 1
(1/87)

King's Call / Yellow Pearl / Dear Miss Lonely Hearts (12")
Vertigo LYN 1 12
(1/87)

PHILIP LYNOTT SOLO LPs

Solo In Soho
Vertigo 9102 038
(4/80)

The Philip Lynott Album
Polydor 6359 117
(10/82)

RELATED RELEASES

Parisienne Walkways / Fanatical Fascists
(by Gary Moore; Phil Lynott composed both songs, plays on
both and sings lead vocal on the A-side)
MCA 419

A Merry Jingle / A Merry Jangle
(by the Greedies)
Vertigo GREED 1
(11/80)

Please Don't Leave Me / Please Don't Leave Me (instrumental)
(by John Sykes; Phil Lynott wrote and plays on both)
MCA 792
(9/82)

We Are The Boys / Rockin' On Stage
(by Rockers)
CBS A 3929
(11/83)

We Are The Boys (Extended Version) / Rockin' On Stage (12")
CBS TA 3929
(11/83)

Out In The Fields / Military Man / Still In Love With You /
Stop Messin' Around (Ltd. ed. double pack)
(by Gary Moore and Phil Lynott)
10 TEND 49
(5/85)

Out In The Fields / Military Man / Still In Love With You (12″)
10 TEN 49 12
(5/85)

Acknowledgements

A Book For While I'm Away

Mark Putterford, the author of *Phil Lynott: The Rocker*, died in November 1994, and this edition of his book has been amended only slightly from the original edition. Mark's original acknowledgements, dated January 1994, read as follows:

This book was researched and written between August 5 1993 and January 6 1994. It was compiled from over forty personal interviews with relatives, friends and working associates, and while it is acknowledged that as a matter of respect some parts of the subject's life should remain private, this account is intended to be an open, honest and sincere, if sometimes painful, tribute. Indeed, perhaps the greatest tribute of all is the willingness with which most of those named hereafter gave their kind support and invaluable co-operation to the project.

For overwhelming trust and extraordinary hospitality, I would like to express enormous gratitude to Philomena (Phyllis) Lynott and Dennis (The Menace) Keeley.

Also in Dublin a million thanks and the odd pint of Guinness to: Peter Lynott, Timothy Lynott, Brian Downey, Jim Fitzpatrick, Smiley Bolger, Brush Shiels and Doish Nagle.

In London, a massive thank you to: Gary Moore, Brian Robertson, Scott Gorham, Eric Bell, Midge Ure, Snowy White, Bob Geldof KBE, Chris O'Donnell, Peter Eustace, Sue Peters, Ted Carroll, Lawrence Archer, John Burnham, Frank Murray, Adrian Hopkins, Tony Brainsby, David Jensen, Alan Phillips and Chris Morrison.

In Manchester: Percy Gibbons and Darren Wharton.

In Wolverhampton: Mark Stanway.

In Belfast: Adam Winstanley and Black Rose.

In America: John Sykes and Huey Lewis.

Thanks also to: Phil Scott, Phil Easton, Denis O'Regan, John Salter, Colin Hesketh, Malcolm Dome, Dave Ling, Deirdre Moran, Jodie Holman, Colin Steadman, Mel Galley and Caroline Greenwood.

Very special thanks to: Terrie Doherty, whose inspiration and enthusiasm made this book possible.

With love: Mum, Joanne, Rocky and Rosie, and finally my incredible wife, Lynn. I will never forget the love and support you have given me.

In memory of Bill Cayley.

MARK PUTTERFORD